FACES OF
CONTEMPORARY
MANAGEMENT

FACES OF
CONTEMPORARY
MANAGEMENT

Editors: Barbara Kożuch, Katarzyna Sienkiewicz-Małyjurek

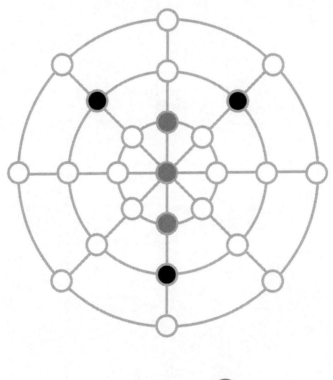

VOLUME 1

JAGIELLONIAN UNIVERSITY PRESS

The publication of this volume was financed by the Jagiellonian University in Krakow – Faculty of Management and Social Communication and Institute of Public Affairs

REVIEWER
Dr hab. Bogusław Plawgo, prof. UwB

COVER DESIGN
Małgorzata Flis

ISBN 968-83-233-4093-5
ISBN 978-83-233-9418-1 (e-book)

www.wuj.pl

Jagiellonian University Press
Editorial Offices: Michałowskiego St. 9/2, 31-126 Cracow
Phone: +48 12 663 23 82, Fax: +48 12 663 23 83
Distribution: Phone: +48 12 631 01 97, Fax: +48 12 631 01 98
Cell Phone: +48 506 006 674, e-mail: sprzedaz@wuj.pl
Bank: PEKAO SA, IBAN PL 80 1240 4722 1111 0000 4856 3325

TABLE OF CONTENTS

INTRODUCTION

In modern management, that is mainly focused on organisational innovations and effective managing of people, the importance of uncertainty, dynamics of changes, and risk in the right functioning of organisations are emphasised. These conditions relate to the private sector as well as public and non-governmental organisations. Together with the scarcity of resources they generate the need for using contemporary management concepts. Essential importance is attached to the human factor operating in the network of relationships. Moreover, the holistic orientation alongside the ability to analyse the functioning of organisation specific areas, as well as using appropriate management methods become necessary. However it is difficult to analyse specific areas of an organisation without taking into account the dynamics of political, organisational, and social factors. Therefore, the faces of contemporary management relate to a vast range of methods directed at ensuring effectiveness in functioning of organisations.

In this book, attempts were made to reflect the current research trends in management sciences. For this purpose, the publications focused on three main research fields. The first of these refers to the Human Resource Management, the second to Corporate Social Responsibility, and the third takes into account contemporary management methods. Articles included in this study concern both the theory and practice of contemporary management.

The first chapter by **Barbara Mazur** refers to the Green Human Resource Management with emphasis on the Green Work Life Balance. The author presents in it the sustainability in Human Resources Management, sociological, psychological, strategic, and "green" approach to the analysed subject and interactions between life and work domains. She focuses on green work-life-balance policies. As a result, she finds that Sustainable HRM is conditioned by the relations between individual model approaches.

In the second article **Algirdas Giedraitis** and **Rimantas Stašys** explore working group's value orientations within a construction company. They show the value orientation, value of group working, the most important professional values, and the hierarchical structure of value formation. In the article, a model of forming value orientation within the working group is developed. The authors also conduct a quantitative analysis of factors of the developed model. In the conclusions they state that presently factors related to value orientations are a basis of work in a group.

In the next article by **Monika Konieczny** she presents the Gamified Agile as an innovative tool to improve communication between the product owner and the development team. Based on the proposed four-dimensional model she conducted an experiment using 12 different teams in 10 companies. She finds that simulation games and gamification can be used in such research areas as communication, stimulating innovation, and collaboration. The positive results of experimental verification lead her to the conclusion that the Gamified Agile can be used in contemporary management as an effective instrument that can support the Product Owner.

Erika Župerkienė, **Aurimas Župerka**, and **Julius Paulikas** in the article entitled "The role of training while helping organisations to overcome resistance to innovations" focus on reasons and obstacles for resistance to innovation. They research correlations between employees' education and their positive attitude with regard to innovation and look for the basic and additional actions in this area. Their analyses identify three-stages of the precautionary model of overcoming staff resistance to innovation.

Examining the role of the state in providing a framework ensuring responsible business, **Joanna Szymonek** uses the OECD Guidelines for Multinational Enterprises and effectiveness of functioning of the OECD National Contact Points (NCP). She explores the role of the state in fostering responsible business. She conducts a detailed analysis of possibilities and barriers in this area and identifies such type of circumstances as political, strategic, social, economic, and operational factors.

Andrea Benedek and **Katalin Takács-György** examine the corporate social responsibility (CSR) to internal factors of the corporate managers. They analyse individual values of general managers, their attitudes to CSR, and relation between this value and the practice of actions. Moreover, the authors thoroughly examine the correlation of CSR attitude of the company leader and the CSR practice, the mediative effect of the CSR attitude factors on self-enhancement, and CSR practice. The article ends with very interesting conclusions relating to the up-to-date responsible corporate management.

In the next article **Kristupas Žegunis** and **Rimantas Stašys** examine the Lithuanian healthcare system. They start with developing performance assessment methodology and identifying challenges and problems in this area. In the analysis, they focus on the healthcare services from the perspective of service providers, users, and policy makers. As a result, the authors try to find actions, which could help effectively improve the performance results of the healthcare system.

In the article entitled "The impact of organisational culture on the performance of a Lithuanian CLINICAL LAB" **Julius Ramanauskas**, **Rimantas Stašys**, and **Ilona Osminina** analyse internal and external information sources of the Lab by a questionnaire survey and a structurised interview. They investigate which quantitative parameters can be used to assess the organisational culture of the divisions of a clinical lab. In the article they assume that successful Lab divisions boast a strong organisational culture which makes a really positive impact both on individual performance elements and on the overall performance.

Organisational trust is a research area of the article by **Barbara Kożuch**, **Regina Lenart-Gansiniec**, and **Katarzyna Sienkiewicz-Małyjurek**. They try to assess the impact of trust in schools on the enrolment results and to identify the level of trust in upper-secondary schools. Their findings show the degree to which the primary trust factors are harnessed in managing upper-secondary education institutions.

The paper by **Paulina Kubera** examines the specificity of the innovation process and the rationale behind public intervention in this field and identifies crucial areas in this area. In the process of analysis, she presents the specificity of the innovation process and rationale for public innovation support. She found that there are various approaches for impact assessment of the innovation policy and their common use creates valuable opportunity to proper assessment.

The strategy of organisational development is examined by **Justyna Bugaj**. Her paper identifies good practices of European universities in the area of strategic human resources management (SHRM). She conducted research on the base of a case study of the Utrecht University. In her conclusions the author emphasises that, in the Polish circumstances, such a strategy would require considerable modifications.

Knowledge management is a main research area of **Andrzej Pawluczuk**. By comparing approaches to knowledge management among employees at different management levels and in different companies, he tries to find the major differences in knowledge management and how they extend. He analyses the sources of knowledge, IT tools supporting knowledge management in organisation, level of sharing own knowledge and obtained experience with co-workers, the influence of leadership in the organisation on knowledge management, the level of trustiness and co-operation among employees, and barriers in implementing knowledge management in the organisation. He concluded that public sector workers acknowledge significantly great barriers in the implementation of knowledge management.

As a whole this publication aims at presenting chosen contemporary trends of research in management and organisation connected with innovations and managing people. We hope that its contents will be an incentive to reflection and used as a basis for further discussion about contemporary management.

Barbara Mazur
Bialystok University of Technology
e-mail: b.mazur@pb.edu.pl

GREEN HUMAN RESOURCE MANAGEMENT

Abstract

Background. The paper focuses on Green Human Resource Management and places emphasis on Green Work Life Balance. Green Work Life Balance focuses on the integration of private and professional life of the employee with reference to environmental attitudes, practices, and behaviours. According to this concept, green attitudes, practices, and behaviours must be enforced in both life domains of the employees in order to ensure that the green goals of the organisation are achieved.

Research aims. The aim of the article is to show the links between the presented as separate approaches from De Prins' model of Sustainable Human Resources Management – the sociological, psychological, strategic, and green. This paper focuses on the link between the psychological approach – namelyWork Life Balance – and the green one. It presents a new paradigm in the understanding of the issue. It also stresses the relation between the private and organisational roles of the employees.

Methodology. The paper adopts a theoretical approach. It consists of a review and synthesis of varied sources of literature on Sustainable HRM, which is a relatively new approach to HRM in management sciences.

Findings. The article concludes that Sustainable HRM is conditioned by the relations between individual De Prins' model elements. Therefore, the effect of sustainability in HRM can be fully tapped only if the individual model approaches–sociological, psychological, strategic, and green – remain in close relationship, and interweaving each other.

Keywords: sustainability, HRM, green work-life balance.

INTRODUCTION

Many firms are beginning to shift from reliance on processes which exploit the environment toward those environmentally sustainable. Changes in corporate perspectives on the environment are evident in written policy statements, "environmental" job titles, attention devoted to managing relations with environmental groups, marketing strategies, decisions about capital investments, auditing practices, new product design and development, and production processes.[1] The number of studies which seek to illuminate the role of HRM activities in supporting and perhaps even driving environmental management initiatives is increasing. This research might be helpful for organisations willing to reduce environmental degradation and tap the benefits of environmental protection and renewal, thus substantially contributing to the future benefit of all organisational stakeholders.

The assumption in this paper is that Green HRM can meet its full potential only by sustaining work-life balance. Employees learn different kinds of behaviour: not only in the workplace, but also in their private life. Since alternating interactions between professional and private life occur, a "green work-life balance concept" is suggested to promote and encourage environmentally friendly behaviour in both life domains. The concept offers potential benefits – not only to the environment, but also to the company and its employees – by increasing work motivation and job retention. However, challenges such as employees' reluctance to allow corporate influence on private life need to be addressed.

It has long been recognised that interactions between private life and working life can occur[2] and many researchers have dealt with this topic in general. It can be therefore assumed that environmental attitudes and behaviour at work and in private life also influence each other. Consequently, it can be argued that the impact of Green HRM on "greening employees" will always be influenced by the employees' personal environmental experiences. As a result, Green HRM might fail in realising its full potential if its focus is purely on the employees in their working role. Therefore, a new perspective for Green HRM is proposed: considering *employees as human beings* who learn and develop environmental attitudes and behaviour in working life as well as in private life. In order to successfully promote an environmentally friendly and responsible use of resources at the workplace, Green HRM needs to set up activities supporting environmentally friendly behaviour at the workplace and in private life.

Sustainability in Human Resources Management

Research connecting sustainability and problems relevant to HRM can be traced in the literature on Strategic HRM, Corporate Social Responsibility, Sustainable Work Systems as well as Sustainable HRM[3]. The approaches identified in this literature

---

[1] J.F. Molina-Azorín, E. Claver-Cortés, M.D. López-Gamero, J.J. Tarí (2009). *Green Management and Financial Performance: A Literature Review.* "Management Decision", vol. 47, no. 7, pp. 1080–1100; M.P. Sharfman, C.S. Fernando (2008). *Environmental Risk Management and the Cost of Capital.* "Management Journal", vol. 29, no. 6, pp. 569–592.

[2] R.M. Kanter (1977). *Work and Family in the United States: A Critical Review and Agenda for Research and Policy.* Russell Sage Foundation, New York.

[3] I. Ehnert, W. Harry (2012). *Recent Developments and Future Prospects an Sustainable Human Resource Management: Introduction to the Special Issue,* "Management Review", vol. 23, no. 3, p. 221–238; B. Mazur (2013). *Linking Diversity Management and Corporate Social Responsibility,* "Journal of Intercultural Management", vol. 5, no. 3, pp. 39–47.

review differ with regard to the origin of their understanding of sustainability, their objectives, focus, and theoretical foundations.[4] The concept of Sustainable Human Resource Management (SHRM) is realized in De Prins' holistic model consisting of four approaches to Sustainable HRM.

De Prins[5] distinguishes four approaches to the concept. The first, second, and fourth of them are exhibited in specific policies: sociological, psychological, strategic human resource management and green approaches. Sustainable Human Resource Management framework including all of those approaches is depicted in figure 1 and then developed.

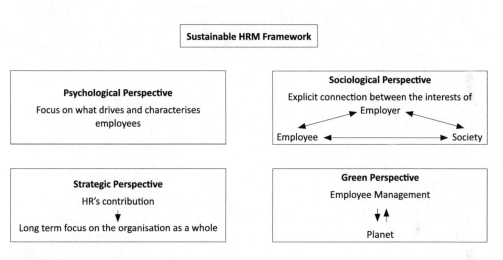

Figure 1. Sustainable HRM Framework

Source: author's own elaboration on the basis of P. De Prins (2011). *Duurzaam HRM: Synthetische academische introductie*, cit. by I. Rompa, *Explorative Research on Sustainable Human Resource Management*. http://www.innovatiefinwerk. nl/sites/.../sustainable_hrm.pdf (access: 2.09.2015).

The sociological approach aims at "socialising" HRM practices. This form of personnel management is long-term focused and aims at continuity, whereby the interests of the employer, the employee, and society are explicitly connected. Most important notions of this approach are engagement policies, health policies, and societal themes like diversity, age-conscious and family-friendly personnel policies.

The psychological approach relies on the topics employees themselves find important. According to De Prins, if people are the focal point of a sustainable competitive

[4] I. Ehnert (2006). *Sustainability Issues in Human Resource Management: Linkages, Theoretical, Approaches, and Outlines for an Emerging Field*. Paper prepared for 21st EIASM SHRM Workshop, Aston, Birmingham, March 28th–29th. http://www.sfb637.uni-bremen.de/.../SFB637-A2-06-004-I (access: 2.09.2015); Z. Stankeviciute, A. Savaneviciene (2013). *Sustainability as a Concept for Human Resource Management*. "Economics and Management", vol. 18, no. 4, pp. 838–846.

[5] P. De Prins (2011). *Duurzaam HRM: Synthetische Academische Introductie*, Retrieved J., cit. by I. Rompa, *Explorative Research on Sustainable Human Resource Management*. http://www.innovatiefinwerk.nl/sites/.../ sustainable_hrm.pdf (access: 2.09.2015).

advantage, the knowledge and fostering of what drives and characterizes them is of utmost importance. In this understanding, human capital differs substantially from financial or technological capital. Essential themes within this approach are work-life balance, autonomy, self-development, and employability.

The third approach examines how Sustainable HRM is related to **strategic HRM**, and focuses on how Sustainable HRM impacts typical HR domains such as recruitment and selection, employee turnover, appraisal- and employability-aspects of an organisation. The HR attempts to achieve organisational goals, which entail more than just profits. Typical themes are the belief that people can constitute sustainable competitive advantage, social achievements, and sustainable management of HR sources. However, the specifications of the related policies are still under review.

The fourth approach is **green HRM** – the ways in which employees and employee management relate to the planet-component of the triple bottom line. It focuses on those HRM aspects which can help "green" the organisation, and on the impact of a green character on employer's attractiveness and branding. Relevant themes in this approach are mentioning green behaviour as a competence, training in sustainability awareness, stimulating environmentally conscious behaviours, and green employer branding.

The next section of this article is dedicated to the analysis of the interference of psychological and green approaches and their policies.

The organisation is one of the two major domains of an employee's life. The managers, particularly HR managers, use their skills to convey eco-friendly values to the employees. Employees also learn environmental attitudes and behaviour in private life. Employees' private environmental performance is closely related to their individual ways of living and their everyday behaviour.[6] Environmentally relevant behaviour in everyday life is vividly expressed in consumption patterns. Since it is the very nature of consumption to use resources, all consumption behaviour is likewise environmentally relevant behaviour. The concept of Green Work Life Balance lies in two Green HRM approaches: the psychological one, with its WLB policies, and the green one – as depicted in figure 2 below.

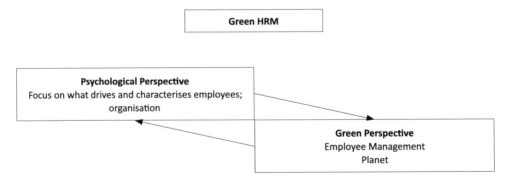

Figure 2. Green HRM: Psychological Perspective and Green Perspectives
Source: author's own elaboration.

---

[6] P. Söderholm (2010). *Environmental Policy and Household Behaviour: Sustainability and Everyday Life.* Earthscan, London.

Since environmentally relevant behaviour is practiced in working life and private life, it is likely that employees' environmental attitudes and activities are generated from experience in both life spheres. While Green HRM focuses on promoting employees' environmental behaviour in the company, employees carry on with their private life consumption patterns.

Interactions between life and work domains

Both: the recognition of possible interactions between working life and private life, and the resulting conclusion that HRM should consider these interactions are generally not new. On the one hand, multiple studies of the interference of working life and private life have been conducted. On the other hand, the implementation and prevalence of work-life balance policies in companies have considerably increased.[7] However, neither developments have yet been connected to Green HRM. Thus, table 1 presents a short overview of mechanisms explaining the possible linkages between working life and private life. The basic principles of work-life-balance-policies are demonstrated.

While early conceptualisations described working life and private life as "naturally" independent and segmented domains, nowadays it is assumed that people make efforts to actively separate their life domains.[8] Apart from these segmentation models, both life domains are usually conceptualised as reciprocally influenced by each other.[9] The established approaches that draw on these reciprocal influences include the conflict model, the enrichment model, the spillover model, and the compensation model.[10]

Employees themselves determine how much segmentation or integration of both life domains they need. They actively decide whether to use domain-specific resources or experiences from a different domain. Nevertheless, their freedom of choice and action, but also their chances to negotiate different demands, are very much shaped by a company's infrastructure, its policies, and employees' personal resources (e.g. time, information, money, etc.).[11] Other domain members and border keepers are also considered important, since, for instance, communicating with superiors about family demands can help to improve their understanding of employees' problems. Previously conducted research on Work-life balance has focused mainly on negative interaction effects between working life and private life. However, positive effects can also be

[7] E.E. Kossek, S. Lambert (2005). *Work and Life Integration: Organizational, Cultural, and Individual Perspectives.* Lawrence Erlbaum Associates, Mahawa – New Jersey; A.M. Ryan, E.E. Kossek (2008). *Work-life Policy Implementation: Breaking Down or Creating Barriers to Inclusiveness?* "Human Resource Management Journal", vol. 47, no. 2, pp. 295–310.

[8] N. Rothbard, K. Phillips, T. Dumas (2005). *Managing Multiple Roles: Work-family Policies and Individuals' Desires for Segmentation.* "Organization Science", vol. 16, no. 3, pp. 243–258.

[9] J. Edwards, N. Rothbard (2000). *Mechanisms Linking Work and Family: Clarifying the Relationship between Work and Family Constructs.* "Academy of Management Review", vol. 25, no. 1, pp. 178–199.

[10] *Ibidem*; D.E. Guest (2002). *Perspectives on the Study of Work-life Balance.* "Social Science Information", vol. 41, no. 2, pp. 255–279.

[11] N. Rothbard, K. Phillips, T. Dumas, *op.cit.*

Table 1. Relevant models on private life-work life interactions

The Conflict Model	It focuses on the difficulties bringing together the needs of two life domains. The problems of balancing life and work domains often appearwhen everyday life resources(energy, time, and attention) are dividedunevenly. The conflicts are caused by stress, time, behaviour, etc. Because of the resources limitations, they cannot be equally distributed. This in turn creates role conflicts and imbalances, which have a negative effect on private or work life.
The Enrichment Model	In this model the experiences, value additions, or achievements deriving from one life domain create a positive impact on the other, thus improving both those domains. According to Rothbard (2001), in this model, employees compilediverseresources arising from many roles fulfilled by them.
The Spillover Model	This model can be understood as a part of the enrichment as well as the conflict model (Lambert, 1990). Many times transfers of specific experiences, traits, or resources between the work and life domains (Edwards and Rothbard, 2000) occur. The spillovercan have a positive or negative impact depending on the experience of the individual in either of the life domains. For instance,achievements at the work place can be transmitted to positive behaviour and more satisfaction in personal life. On the other hand, negative experiences in private life may lead to low self-esteem and decreased performance level in the work place.
The Compensation Model	This model assumes that experiences gained in one life domain contribute to a contradictory behaviour in the other (Lambert, 1990). Employees cantry to compensate the negative experiences in one domain by making an extra effort in the other. This often results in decreased morale, self-esteem, involvement, time devotion, and attention in the dissatisfying domain and greater involvement in the satisfying one. It eventually allows to create an imbalance between the life domains. Dissatisfaction in one domain encourages more positive involvement in the other in order to compensate the negativity.

Source: author's own elaboration based on: M.A. Datta (2015). *Green work-life balance: A new concept in green HRM.* "International Journal of Multidisciplinary Approach and Studies", vol. 02, no. 2, pp. 85–86.

assumed. Depending on peoples' personal competences and the specific conditions of their life domains (e.g. human resource policies), employees might either benefit or suffer from work-life interactions.

Regarding the presented linkages between working life and private life, the following assumptions can be made. Firstly, the enrichment model and the positive spillover model prove that interactions between working life and private life can bring about *positive effects*. It can be assumed that learning and practicing environmentally friendly behaviour in one domain can stimulate or strengthen similar activities in the other domain. Positive spillovers from working life to private life have already been demonstrated. Berger and Kanetkar[12] have shown that employees' participation in successful waste management programs can have positive effects on their perception of environmental issues in private life and their individual effectiveness in dealing with these issues. Rashid, Wahid, and Saad[13] have documented that employees' participation

[12] I.E. Berger, V. Kanetkar (1995). *Increasing Environmental Sensitivity via Workplace Experiences.* "Journal of Public Policy and Marketing", vol. 14, no. 2, pp. 205–215.

[13] N.R. Rashid, N.A. Wahid, N.M. Saad (2006). *Employees Involvement in EMS, ISO 14001 and its Spillover Effects in Consumer Environmentally Responsible Behaviour.* International Conference on Environment Proceedings (ICENV 2006), 13th–15th November, Penang, Malaysia.

in environmental management systems can spill over and influence environmentally responsible attitudes and behaviour in the employees' private life. Research on positive life-to-work effects with regard to environmental behaviour is still scarce.

Secondly, the conflict model and the negative spillover model assume that *negative effects* between working life and private life can occur. Behaviour with problematic effects on the environment in one domain can bring about or strengthen similar behaviour in the other domain. Life-to-work interferences might occur when employees routinely practice non-environmentally friendly behaviour at home, for instance wasting water and energy. Work-to-life interferences might occur, for instance, when a company and its environmental management fails in setting up successful environmental activities or in providing an infrastructure for environmentally friendly behaviour. Research on negative effects between environmental behaviour at work and in private life is still scarce.[14]

Thirdly, the compensation model outlines that (non)environmentally friendly activities in one domain can bring about the very *opposite behaviour* in the other domain. Employees who are obliged to behave in an environmentally friendly way in the workplace, for instance, could tend to neglect environmental concerns in private life. In contrast, employees who – although they would like to – do not have the chance to act in an environmentally friendly way at the workplace (e.g. the cafeteria only provides plastic dishes and fast food), could be motivated to behave in a more environmentally friendly manner at home (e.g. cooking fresh and organic food). Here again, research on compensation effects between working life and private life with regards to environmental behaviour (from life-to-work and work-to-life) is scarce.[15]

Finally, border theory shows that employees need to be considered as active managers of their life domains, whose scope of action is influenced by their employer, other domain members and their personal resources. It can be assumed that employees' scope of action for environmentally friendly behaviour at work and in private life is also shaped by the company, domain members, and the employees' personal resources. Moreover, the border theory illustrates that other domain members, such as colleagues and superiors, play an important role in facilitating or constraining employees' environmental performance in both life domains. Therefore, it is possible that the exchange of experience regarding environmental issues at home and at work influences their environmental performance. Green HRM is aimed at handling these interaction effects and employees' chances to manage their life domains. On the one hand, positive interaction effects need to be facilitated. On the other hand, negative interaction effects need to be prevented. Additionally, employees' subjective chances for environmentally friendly behaviour at work and in private life need to be considered. It is argued in the following section that the green work-life balance concept is designed to meet these challenges.

---

[14] V. Muster, U. Schrader (2011). *Green Work-life Balance: A New Perspective for Green HRM*, "German Journal of Research in Human Resource Management", vol. 25, no. 2, pp. 140–156.
[15] *Ibidem.*

Green work-life-balance policies

Nowadays, it is a routine practice in HRM to consider employees' work-life interrelation and to support them in managing both demands of working life and private life. Work-life balance policies are designed to create mutually beneficial situations for employees and the company. Employees' mental and physical wellbeing should be improved. Companies expect the results to improve their attraction, productivity, and the retention of employees.[16] Nevertheless, there are both positive and negative findings concerning the effectiveness of work-life balance policies for both the company and employees. Work-life balance policies are perceived as gender-neutral assistance for all private demands with regards to leisure, education, and family activities. However, employees' demands as mothers and fathers are offered special attention and work-life balance policies often focus mostly on work-family balance. Work-life balance policies are dominated by time based instruments (like flexible work schedules and part time arrangements), since the limitation of time and its unequal distribution is seen to be the starting point of many inter-role conflicts. Aside from time-based policies, other services which can be information-based (like parental counselling), service-based (like corporate nurseries) or finance-based (like family allowances) are discussed.

Work-life balance policies' goal is not to even out or establish employees' use of resources, since employees might have individual perceptions of "balances" and personal wellbeing. Likewise, work-life balance policies are not designed to cut off or change specific demands and requirements of life domains. These policies are meant to facilitate the reconciliation of working life and private life.[17] However, up to now, these policies have mostly neglected large parts of private life, including consumption activities and other environmental issues.

Green work-life balance is understood as the reconciliation of working life and private life with regards to environmental values, attitudes, and behaviour. It comprises mutual enforcement and harmonisation of environmentally friendly orientations in private life and working life. It is believed that negative effects deriving from the interaction between twolife domains can be reduced by balancing out environmentally friendly behaviour, since no environmentally friendly behaviour will be downgraded. Moreover, balance can bring about positive interaction effects, as diverse environmentally friendly experiences can enrich each other. Green work-life balance policies focus on employees' twofold role as consumers and producers, due to employees learning and practicing environmentally relevant behaviour in these two roles.[18]

---

[16] I. Ehnert (2009). *Sustainable HRM*. Physica Verlag, Heidelberg.

[17] E.g. A.M. Ryan, E.E. Kossek, *op.cit.*

[18] V. Muster (2011). *Companies Promoting Sustainable Consumption of Employees.* "Journal of Consumer Policy", vol. 34, no. 1, pp. 161–174.

CONCLUSIONS

Many companies are struggling to effectively improve employees' environmental behaviour. A discrepancy between environmental policies and actual behavioural patterns in organisational everyday life has been identified as a challenge.[19] Sustainable HRM is conditioned by the relations between individual De Prins' model's elements. Therefore, the effect of sustainability in HRM can be fully tapped only if the individual model approaches (sociological, psychological, strategic, and green) remain in close relationship, and interweaving each other.

It can be assumed that the full potential of Green HRM in theory and practice has not yet been realised. In order to strengthen green organisational behaviour, it is important to acknowledge that environmentally relevant attitudes and behaviour are not learned exclusively at the workplace, but also in private life. People have diverse modes of living. In everyday life, they practice specific consumption patterns, which have different effects on the environment.[20] Therefore, employees' private role as consumers is considered crucial for learning and practicing environmental attitudes and behaviour. As work-life studies have verified that there are complex interactions between peoples' roles in professional and private life, both spheres should be considered interdependent.[21] Thus, it is a natural assumption that private experiences also influence peoples' environmental behaviour in working life. In this respect, Green HR policies that only focus on peoples' role as employees and their work-related behaviour are insufficient. As Elloy and Smith illustrate, consideration of the complex array of work-roles and private roles requires "a holistic approach to HRM".[22] This perspective is also suggested for Green HRM: considering *employees as human beings* with multiple roles in different life spheres.

References

Berger I.E., Kanetkar V. (1995). *Increasing environmental sensitivity via workplace experiences.* "Journal of Public Policy and Marketing", vol. 14, no. 2, pp. 205–215.
Berrone P., Gomez-Mejia L. (2009). *Environmental performance and executive compensation: An integrated agency-institutional perspective.* "Academy of Management Journal", vol. 52, no. 1, pp. 103–126.
Brio J.A., Fernandez E., Junquera B. (2007). *Management and employee involvement in achieving an environmental action-based competitive advantage: An empirical study.* "The International Journal of HRM", vol. 18, no. 4, pp. 491–522.

---

[19] B. Daily, J.W. Bishop, N. Govindarajulu (2008). *A Conceptual Model for Organizational Citizenship Behavior. Directed toward the Environment.* "Business & Society", vol. 48, no. 2, pp. 243–256; E. Fernandez, B. Junquera, M. Ordiz (2003). *Organizational Culture and Human Resources in the Environmental Issue: A Review of the Literature.* "The International Journal of HRM", vol. 14, no. 4, pp. 634–656; C.A. Ramus (2002). *Encouraging Innovative Environmental Actions: What Companies and Managers Must Do.* "Journal of World Business", vol. 37, pp. 151–164.

[20] P. Söderholm, *op.cit.*

[21] J. Edwards, N. Rothbard, *op.cit.*

[22] D.F. Elloy, C.R. Smith (2003). *Patterns of Stress, Work-family Conflict, Role Conflict, Role Ambiguity and Overload among Dual Career Couples: An Australian Study.* "Cross Cultural Management", vol. 10, no. 1, p. 63.

Datta M.A. (2015). *Green work-life balance: A new concept in green HRM*, "International Journal of Multidisciplinary Approach and Studies", vol. 02, no. 2, pp. 85–86.

Daily B., Bishop J.W., Govindarajulu N. (2008). *A conceptual model for organizational citizenship behavior. Directed toward the environment.* "Business & Society", vol. 48, no. 2, pp. 243–256.

Daily B.F., Huang S.C. (2001). *Achieving Sustainability through attention to human resource factors in environmental management.* "International Journal of Operations and Production Management", vol. 21, pp. 1539–1552.

De Prins P. (2011). *Duurzaam HRM: Synthetische Academische Introductie*, Retrieved J., cit. by I. Rompa, *Explorative Research on Sustainable Human Resource Management.* http://www.innovatiefinwerk.nl/sites/.../sustainable_hrm.pdf (access: 2.09.2015).

Edwards J., Rothbard N. (2000). *Mechanisms linking work and family: Clarifying the relationship between work and family constructs.* "Academy of Management Review", vol. 25, no. 1, pp. 178–199.

Elloy D.F., Smith C.R. (2003). *Patterns of stress, work-family conflict, role conflict, role ambiguity and overload among dual career couples: An Australian study.* "Cross Cultural Management", vol. 10, no. 1, pp. 55–66.

Ehnert I. (2006). *Sustainability issues in human resource management: Linkages, theoretical, approaches, and outlines for an emerging field.* Paper prepared for 21st EIASM SHRM Workshop, Aston, Birmingham, March 28th–29th. http://www.sfb637.uni-bremen.de/.../SFB637-A2-06-004-I (access: 2.09.2015).

Ehnert I. (2009). *Sustainable HRM.* Physica Verlag, Heidelberg.

Ehnert I., Harry W. (2012). *Recent developments and future prospects an sustainable human resource management: Introduction to the special issue*, "Management Review", vol. 23, no. 3, pp. 221–238.

Fernandez E., Junquera B., Ordiz M. (2003). *Organizational culture and human resources in the environmental issue: A review of the literature.* "The International Journal of HRM", vol. 14, no. 4, pp. 634–656.

Govindarajulu N., Daily B.F. (2004). *Motivating employees for environmental improvement.* "Industrial Management & Data Systems", vol. 104, no. 4, pp. 364–372.

Guest D.E. (2002). *Perspectives on the Study of work-life balance.* "Social Science Information", vol. 41, no. 2, pp. 255–279.

Jabbour C.J., Santos F.C.A. (2008). *The central role of HRM in the search for sustainable organizations.* "The International Journal of HRM", vol. 19, no. 12, pp. 2133–2154.

Kanter R.M. (1977). *Work and Family in the United States: A Critical Review and Agenda for Research and Policy.* Russell Sage Foundation, New York.

Kossek E.E., Lambert S. (2005). *Work and Life Integration: Organizational, Cultural, and Individual Perspectives.* Lawrence Erlbaum Associates, Mahawa – New Jersey.

Lambert S.J. (1990). *Processes linking work and family: A critical review and research agenda.* "Human Relations", vol. 43, pp. 239–257.

Madsen H., Ulhoi J.P. (2001). *Greening of human resources: Environmental awareness and training interests within the workforce.* "Industrial Management & Data Systems", vol. 101, no. 2, pp. 57–63.

Massoud J.A., Daily B.F., Bishop J.W. (2008). *Reward for environmental performance: Using the scanlonplan as catalyst to green organisations.* "International Journal of Environment, Workplace and Employment", vol. 4, no. 1, pp. 15–31.

Mazur B. (2013). *Linking diversity management and corporate social responsibility*, "Journal of Intercultural Management", vol. 5, no. 3, pp. 39–47.

Molina-Azorín J.F., Claver-Cortés E., López-Gamero M.D., Tarí J.J. (2009). *Green management and financial performance: A literature review.* "Management Decision", vol. 47, no. 7, pp. 1080–1100.

Muster V. (2011). *Companies promoting sustainable consumption of employees.* "Journal of Consumer Policy", vol. 34, no. 1, pp. 161–174.

Muster V., Schrader U. (2011). *Green work-life balance: A new perspective for green HRM*, "German Journal of Research in Human Resource Management", vol. 25, no. 2, pp. 140–156.

Ramus C.A. (2002). *Encouraging innovative environmental actions: What companies and managers must do.* "Journal of World Business", vol. 37, pp. 151–164.

Rashid N.R., Wahid N.A., Saad N.M. (2006). *Employees Involvement in EMS, ISO 14001 and its Spillover Effects in Consumer Environmentally Responsible Behaviour.* International Conference on Environment Proceedings (ICENV 2006), 13th–15th November, Penang, Malaysia.

Renwick D. (2008). *Green HRM: A Review, Process Model, and Research Agenda. Discussion Paper Series*. The University of Sheffield. http://www.shef.ac.uk/content/1/c6/08/70/89/2008-01.pdf (access: 02.09.2015).

Rothbard N., Phillips K., Dumas T. (2005). *Managing multiple roles: Work-family policies and individuals' desires for segmentation*. "Organization Science", vol. 16, no. 3, pp. 243–258.

Ryan A.M., Kossek E.E. (2008). *Work-life policy implementation: Breaking down or creating barriers to inclusiveness?* "Human Resource Management Journal", vol. 47, no. 2, pp. 295–310.

Sharfman M.P., Fernando C.S. (2008). *Environmental risk management and the cost of capital*. "Management Journal", vol. 29, no. 6, pp. 569–592.

Söderholm P. (2010). *Environmental Policy and Household Behaviour: Sustainability and Everyday Life*. Earthscan, London.

Stankeviciute Z., Savaneviciene A. (2013). *Sustainability as a concept for human resource management*. "Economics and Management", vol. 18, no. 4, pp. 838–846.

Stringer L. (2009). *The Green Workplace. Sustainable Strategies that Benefit Employees, the Environment, and the Bottom Line*. Palgrave Macmillan, New York.

Algirdas Giedraitis
Klaipėda University
e-mail: giedraitis.algirdas@gmail.com
Rimantas Stašys
Klaipėda University
e-mail: rimantas.stasys@ku.lt

WORKING GROUP'S VALUE ORIENTATION WITHIN A CONSTRUCTION COMPANY

Abstract

Background. Unsuccessful search of suitable employees for working groups is the largest obstacle in development of a construction business. Knowing, that employees are the most important resource, managers (owners) of business organisations are confronted with a serious problem to retain high quality specialists. A model of forming universal working group's value orientation is offered in this article. By applying it, goals of the organisation may be reached through consciously created orientation of values of the working group. During the process of adaptation and training, it is recommended to involve new employees into the process of values contamination and assimilation. The manager of the group must form (and retain) such orientation of values, which would provide members of the group with satisfaction of the performed task and would not disturb each personal goals.

Research aims. Research aim is to make a model of the working group's value orientation within a construction company and inspect it using research.

Methodology. Method analysis of scientific literature; quantitative research – written quiz (questionnaire). Questionnaire, processing of results and analysis were used.

Findings. After assessment of the working group's value orientations within a construction company it is possible to state, that employees like to work in a group, where regularity and honesty of the employee is appreciated, possibilities of constant development exist, the group is distinguished by oneness, the group's value orientation is understandable and acceptable to all of its members, and all members seek for a general goal.

Keywords: value orientation, working group, construction company.

INTRODUCTION

In case of a lack of qualified construction employees, competition of such resources between construction organisations shall increase. Since builders are the most important factor in organisations of such nature, managers (owners) of business organisations are confronted with a serious problem of searching for highly qualified employees and their integration into the working group. Qualified, educated employees, or those possessing great work experience do not always entrench in working groups for various reasons. Companies try to attract employees, who often work at their competitor's company. Higher wages, education of personnel, and search of suitable employees are necessary to this aim.

The results of employees' variation at the business organisation were analysed by many researchers. Žukauskaitė states, that it is very difficult to determine the real damage that the company incurs after resigning of an employee.[1] Damage can be not only financial, but of other nature as well. Variety may have a negative influence on the culture and morale of the company, as well as on the employees' loyalty. According to Vveinhardt, if there is a dysfunction of interpersonal relations, the mobbing phenomenon often occurs.[2] Pacevičius and Jaunulytė distinguished the main consequences of mobbing[3]: absenteeism; incapacity for work; reduction of productivity; variety of employees. It is very important to select members of the group when forming working groups or because of the variety of employees, when their composition changes.

As Zakarevičius states, only those organisations will successfully exist under complicated activity globalisation, internationalism, and competitive conditions, which will constantly increase their internal human potential.[4] Companies must coordinate their activity through a system of values, but not with rules or instructions.[5] Many of these authors state, that individual value orientation is created for solving such problems, which would help to seek for common goals of the group or members of the group using non-violent methods.

---

[1] I. Žukauskaitė (2008). *Naujų darbuotojų kaita: ryšys su organizacine socializacija.* "Organizacijų vadyba: sisteminiai tyrimai", vol. 48, p. 154.

[2] J. Vveinhardt (2009). *Mobingo kaip diskriminacijos darbuotojų santykiuose poveikis organizacijos klimatui.* "Verslas: teorija ir praktika-Business: Theory and Practice", vol. 10, no. 4, p. 288.

[3] J. Pacevičius, E. Janulytė, E. (2009). *Mobingas kaip organizacinio gyvenimo problema: priežasčių, raiškos ir pasekmių įvertinimas ir analizė.* "Ekonomika ir vadyba: aktualijos ir perspektyvos", vol. 1, no. 14, p. 189.

[4] P. Zakarevičius (2003). *Pokyčiai organizacijose: priežastys, valdymas, pasekmės. Monografija.* VDU, Kaunas.

[5] A. Seilius (2004). *Aplinkos poveikio ir sėkmingo vadovavimo organizacijoms prielaidos. Iš Valdymo problemos: teorija ir tendencija. Kolektyvinė monografija.* KU leidykla, Klaipėda; M. Siegall, T. McDonald (2004). *Person-organisation value congruence, burnout and diversion of resources,* "Personnel Review", vol. 33, no. 3, pp. 291–301; J. Strautmanis (2008). *Employees' values orientation in the context of corporate social responsibility.* "Baltic Journal of Management", vol. 3, no. 3, pp. 346–358; L. Šimanskienė, A. Seilius (2009). *Komandos: Samprata, Kūrimas, Vadovavimas. Team: Concept, Development, Leadership.* KU leidykla, Klaipėda; J.R. Edwards, D.A. Cable (2009). *The value of value congruence.* "Journal of Applied Psychology", vol. 94, no. 3, pp. 654–677.

Work in groups dominates in modern business. A working group may seek a common goal and improve only when having effective orientation of values, which helps the members of the group to work better, acknowledge the right of other members of the group to have their own values and acceptable methods of work performance. Therefore, if the discrepancies between values are great then it is hard to form a group, seek for harmony of the group's actions and common goals of the group.

As Zakarevičius et al. state, it is not easy to combine interests of employees.[6] When seeking strength and wholeness of the culture of an organisation, it is necessary to take appropriate planned actions so that the organisation could successfully solve problems of adapting to the constantly variable environment. Employees should be involved into finding solutions to such problems as well as the company's orientation of values should be adopted.

There is not much empirical research about the group's value orientation influence when forming efficient working groups, consequently managers of organisations need help when seeking for better financial results, involving new members of working groups into activity of organisations, so that they would feel dependence to that group and organisation, in which they work, and could be proud of the reached working results together with managers and owners. The problem under solution is complex.

Problem – how to appropriately orient values of the working group.

Research subject – orientation of the working group's values within a construction company.

Research aim – to make a model of the working group's value orientation within a construction company and inspect it using researches.

Research methods – method analysis of scientific literature; quantitative research – written quiz (questionnaire). A group of 19 respondents participated in the research, which assessed their own group's value orientation within a construction company.

WORKING GROUP'S VALUE ORIENTATION

Companies are not a simple union of individuals, as people work in groups there and have dependence to the company.[7] The concept of a group is understood as two and more people, working in an organisation, in a certain division or separate structure, taking position, which corresponds to professional readiness, who can perform tasks assigned by the organisation and under management of a formal manager.[8] A group can only exist when persons attract each other.[9] Interdependence in a group is de-

---

[6] P. Zakarevičius, J. Kvedaravičius, T. Augustauskas (2004). *Organizacijų vystymosi paradigma*. VDU, Kaunas.

[7] A. Seilius, *op.cit.*

[8] L. Šimanskienė, A. Seilius, *op.cit.*

[9] D. Abrams, M.A. Hogg, S. Hinkle, S. Otten (2004). *The Social Identity Perspective on Small Groups. Theories of Small Groups – Interdisciplinary Perspectives.* Sage Publications Inc. October Sage Publications, Inc., Thousand Oaks, CA, p. 99–137.

scribed as the ability of professionals to explicitly understand different own and other specialists' role, common goals, success of collaborating people, and personal benefit. Work in a group requires agreement of group members, thorough involvement into activities, by relying on each other, as well as interdependence.[10] Therefore, when selecting employees for companies, ability to work in groups is appreciated the most. One of the ways to appropriately form working groups is to relate group activity with values.

Savanevičienė and Šilingienė define values as the features of a particular group educated by experience and individual attitude of its members into solution of tasks and existing phenomena.[11] Values are long-term goals, which are presented as the main principles of human life.[12] The most difficult is to define what group work really considers as values. First of all they must be well considered, survived values, giving a sense to that work, which is performed by people. But irrespective of it, they were created consciously or incidentally, they always are ideals of a company's and its group's activity, that determine formation of groups, condition nature and content of the activity assessment process. Thus value orientation is analysed at group and individual levels (see table 1).

Table 1. Classification of values in respect of the subject

Subject	Values
Individual	Family, friendship, responsibility, loyalty, integrity, goodwill, honesty, honour, wisdom, mercy, love, self-sacrifice, freedom, innovation, creativity, growth, independence, maintenance of goodwill, loyalty, maturity, close personal relations, and indulgence.
Group	Collaboration, goodwill, team spirit, loyalty, learning, discipline, accuracy, dutifulness, regularity, accuracy, creativity, honesty, wisdom, peace, democracy, competiveness, self-sacrifice, control, seeking for results, profit, social power, social acknowledgement, stability, invisibility, strict rules, national safety and order.

Source: concluded by the author according to J. Vveinhardt (2009). *Mobingo kaip diskriminacijos darbuotojų santykiuose poveikis organizacijos klimatui.* "Verslas: teorija ir praktika-Business: Theory and Practice", vol. 10, no. 4, pp. 285–297, and A. Stankuvienė (2013). *Autoritarizmo veiksniai ir diagnostiniai instrumentai.* "Socialinių mokslų studijos", vol. 5, no 1, pp. 57–73.

When values of an individual, group and the company itself coincide, then great energy is concentrated.[13] Thus in order to create a work group, it is necessary to give to the members of the group a long-term goal, give a sense to their everyday work and behaviour. Values of the manager of the group and employees of the group must coincide, as if the values do not coincide, then an employee may lose his/her job.

Vasiliauskas, Aramavičiūtė and Jokūbaitis state that values are an index, revealing the essence of human life and priorities of life (for professional activity as well).[14]

---

[10] J.M. Kouzes, B.Z. Posner (2003). *Iššūkis vadybai.* Smaltija, Kaunas; A. Seilius, *op.cit.*

[11] A. Savanevičienė, V. Šilingienė (2005). *Darbas grupėse.* Technologija, Kaunas.

[12] Y. Berson, S. Oreg, T. Dvir (2005). *Organisational Culture as A Mediator of Ceo Values And Organisational Performance.* Academy of Management Proceedings, New York.

[13] L. Šimanskienė, A. Seilius (2009). *Komandos: Samprata, Kūrimas, Vadovavimas. Team: Concept, Development, Leadership.* KU leidykla, Klaipėda.

[14] R. Vasiliauskas (2005). *Vertybių ugdymo teoriniai ir praktiniai aspektai.* "Acta Paedagogica Vilnensia", vol. 14, pp. 8–17; V. Aramavičiūtė (2005). *Auklėjimas ir dvasinė asmenybės branda.* Gimtasis žodis Vilnius; A. Jokubaitis (2012). *Vertybių tironija ir politika.* Vilniaus universiteto leidykla, Vilnius.

Values arise from essential individual and group needs and accent stability, order and invisibility inside the company.[15] Interdependence, informal communication, respect, and understanding are especially important for development of collaboration.[16] Values make assumptions for effective group work and it is reflected in activity results.[17] Loretto defines 10 important professional values, which the employees of every company must have (see figure 1).

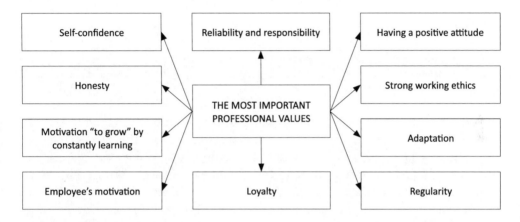

Figure 1. Most important professional values

Source: own description based on P. Lorreto, (2008). *Top 10 Values Employers look for in employees about COM. Internship*, unpublished.

The appropriateness of values is one of the most important features when selecting employees into working groups.[18] *First of all*, human orientation in the environment improves and a sense of uncertainty is reduced. *Secondly*, common endeavours of group members allow to better satisfy the needs of each separate member. Those individuals unite into groups and their participation in a group for becomes a measure to reach common goals. Coordination of resources and division of labour enables the group to perform more than the separate members would. In such way resources, that not only ensure survival, but also a stronger sense of safety, are created.

As Uzdila states, value is a trinomial and hierarchical structure[19]: value orientation (lower level), value attitude (more significant – middle level), and value (highest level).

[15] A. Stankuvienė (2013). *Autoritarizmo veiksniai ir diagnostiniai instrumentai*. "Socialinių mokslų studijos", vol. 5, no. 1, pp. 57–73.

[16] Bronstein L.R. (2003). *Model for Interdisciplinary Collaboration*. "Social Work", vol. 48, no. 3, pp. 297–306.

[17] A. Patapas, G. Labenskytė (2011). *Organizacinės kultūros ir vertybių tyrimas N apskrities valstybinėje mokesčių inspekcijoje*. "Viešoji politika ir administravimas", vol. 4, pp. 589–603.

[18] Verplanken B. (2004). *Value Congruence and Job Satisfaction Among Nurses: A Human Relations Perspective*, "International Journal of Nursing Studies", vol. 41, no. 6, pp. 599–605; J. Kvedaravičius (2006). *Organizacijų vystimosi vadyba*. Vytauto Didžiojo Universitetas, Kaunas.

[19] J.V. Uzdila (2008). *Šeimotyros kaip dalyko poveikis studentų matrimonialinėms nuostatoms*. "Pedagogika", vol. 89, pp. 151–160.

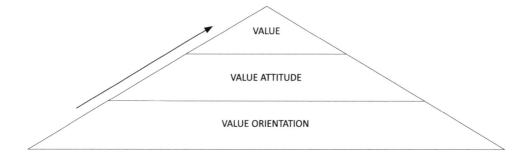

Figure 2. Hierarchical structure of value formation
Source: own description based on J.V. Uzdila (2008). *Šeimotyros kaip dalyko poveikis studentų matrimonialinėms nuostatoms.* "Pedagogika", vol. 89, pp. 151–160.

Value orientation is a developed ability of the conscious to regulate activity and behaviour according to convictions, moral norms, and life perspectives, to distinguish what is valuable in personal and public life.[20] Value orientation – the principles of right and wrong that are accepted by an individual or a social group. Work group value orientation is formed according to value orientations of every individual, which reflect the ideology and culture of the whole group. Value orientation forms by taking over social experience and evidences when implementing goals, forming ideals, pouring convictions, presenting interests, etc.

Value orientation is typical both to the individual and the group, according to essential characteristics and may be directly and purposefully compared. Value orientation of each person depends on the group, where it acts. Each member of the group is affected by his/her own inner world (personal value orientations), as well as the working group's orientation. A person's *value orientation* forms through interaction of its sociogenic (persons forming depending on relations with other people) needs with values of social environment, during the process of ontogenesis. Therefore, development of value orientation is no less significant result than knowledge, abilities of practical and intellectual activity.[21]

One of the main tasks of value orientation is to provide group members with understanding of its identity. The more members of the group acknowledge values and observe them, the stronger the sense of group unity and identity is. According to Gronskienė, if values of particular individuals are incongruent, different, even converse, there is a great possibility for arising of conflicts within the group.[22] Incongruenity of values may be aroused not only by a different position of employees, but also

---

[20] L. Jovaiša (2007). *Enciklopedinis edukologijos žodynas.* Gimtasis žodis, Vilnius.

[21] V. Aramavičiūtė (2005b). *Vertybės kaip gyvenimo prasmės pamatas.* "Acta Paedagogica Vilnensia", vol. 14, pp. 18–26; V. Aramavičiūtė (2005). *Auklėjimas ir dvasinė asmenybės branda.* Gimtasis žodis, Vilnius; G. Čiuladienė (2006). *Paauglių vertybinis aspektas ir raiškos tendencijos.* "Acta paedagogica Vilnensia", vol. 16, pp. 106–117.

[22] I. Gronskienė (2008). *Žemės ūkio organizacijų deklaruojamų vertybių modelis.* "Management Theory and Studies for Rural Business and Infrastructure Development", vol. 13, no. 2, pp. 54–61.

different values of individuals that formed on the background of historical conditions, traditions, and a distinctive culture.[23]

Supposedly, there are many problems inside each group. Such problems determine the fluctuation of employees and are not solved. The employees' fluctuation problem demotivates employers to invest into employees.[24] Shareholders are subject to select a manger, who will reflect their attitude and organisation management methods. In turn, managers of the companies select their subordinates with similar features and in such way create a homogenous organisation.[25]

According to Vanagas, the manager must inspire the belief of employees, that they can improve their working environment and change things, that prevent good performance of work.[26] The manager herself/ himself is also influenced by the expectations of organisation members, as employees in each company have their own wishes and needs.[27] Only by following his/her own vision and values, the manager disseminates positive emotions within the company and is able to adopt to the emotional environment of the group, then relations management skills help him/her create harmony in the company.

Together with improvement of the human resources management process, defects of management are more clearly visible in companies. It is publicly acknowledged that a company experiences economic loss because of a significant fluctuation of employees. After an employee retires, an employer has to employ another person. It is related to the employee's search, selection, and training costs. In accordance with the research performed by the Institute for Labour and Social Research[28], the search for some employees may take some time, even several months or more. Companies try to attract employees, who most often work at the competitors' company, by providing more attractive work offers and better work conditions.

While the search for a new employee is taking place, then work of the retired employee is divided between several employees. It hinders the work of other employees, extends time of the work performed, and creates a possibility of mistakes and misunderstandings. A newly employed person will not be able to start work for the full day, as she/he will lack specific knowledge and skills. Irrespective of the fact that an employee has the necessary experience, the new order of the company obliges them to learn anew. The company must give both material and non-material investment, so

---

[23] P. Jucevičienė, A. Poškienė, L. Kudirkaitė, N. Damanskas (2000). *Universiteto kultūra ir jos tyrimas.* Technologija, Kaunas.

[24] I. Žukauskaitė, I., *op.cit.*; E. Nazelskis (2010). *Profesinio orientavimo ir konsultavimo priemonių taikymas darbuotojų kaitai mažinti.* "Profesinis rengimas. Tyrimai ir realijos", vol. 19, p. 121.

[25] H. Haugh, L. McKee (2004). *The cultural paradigm of the smaller firm.* "Journal of Small Business Management", vol. 42, no. 4, pp. 377–394.

[26] P. Vanagas (2004). *Visuotinės kokybės vadyba.* Technologija, Kaunas.

[27] L. Šimanskienė (2008). *Organizacinės kultūros diagnozavimo metodika.* KU leidykla, Klaipėda.

[28] V. Rosinaitė, D. Bernotas, S. Biveinytė, I. Blažienė, V. Česnuitytė, V. Gražulis, B. Gruževskis, A. Misiūnas, A. Pocius, E. Stancikas, A. Šileika, K. Šlekienė, R. Zabarauskaitė (2007). *Magistrantų integracijos į darbo rinką monitoringo sistemos sukūrimas.* Darbo ir socialinių tyrimų institutas. http:// www.dsti.lt/tyrimai. html (access: 22.11.2013).

that the employee would adapt to the new environment and would start to work for the full day. Special methods of searching for employees and selection are invoked, training for various levels of employees are organised, modern systems for staff assessment and payment for work are implemented, and individual plans for employees' activity, training, and career are prepared.

Socialisation of the new employee is a long-term process, which impedes not only work efficiency, but also the activity of other working employees as well as of the whole company.[29] Thus, the new employee may be more efficient and bring a lot of positive changes, new information, experience, and ideas. Such contribution of the new person may help the company not only to adapt to a variable environment more rapidly, but also improve the microclimate and reduce possibility of conflicts.[30]

The scientific literature indicates that studying (examining) staff attitudes towards values enables one to reveal their individual values and show what is important for them.[31] So first of all, values of employees should be ascertained and later combined with the working group's values. The process of the working group's value contamination is very important in the company. When an employee realises herself/himself as a member of the group, she/he is inclined to highlight and give prominence to similarities and differences of values between group members.

Thus, in order to form successful orientation of group's values by accepting new employees to work, it should be started from the process of value contamination (figure 3).

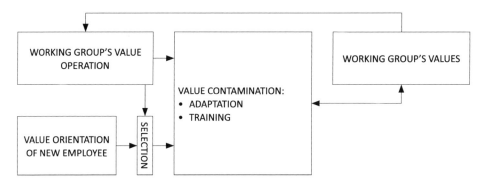

Figure 3. Model of forming value orientation within working group
Source: own.

The purpose of value orientation in the working group is forming and implementing base values of the group, by conveying value orientation to each new member of the group during the contamination process through adaptation and training.

---

[29] A. Stankevičienė, A. Liučvaitienė, A. Šimelytė (2010). *Personalo kaitos stabilizavimo galimybės Lietuvos statybos sektoriuje.* "Verslas: teorija ir praktika", vol. 11, no. 2, pp. 151–158.

[30] W.S. Siebert, N. Zubanov (2009). *Searching for the optimal level of employee turnover: A study of a large U.K. retail organization.* "Academy of Management Journal", no. 52, pp. 294–313.

[31] E. Martišauskienė (2004). *Paaugliu dvasingumas, kaip pedagoginis reiškinys: monografija.* VPU, Vilnius.

Adaptation is understood as application of professional skills to work in a particular company (group).[32] The new employee is familiarised with the work place, its rules, as well as with her/his direct supervisor and a person who is responsible for her/his adaptation and is introduced to the team. Thus, the first three months are the most important at the adaptation stage and they coincide with the trial period.[33] According to Maniukaitė, the adaptation process requires from a person a thorough revision of values and value orientation.[34] Therefore, the new employee must be provided with information about the tasks assigned to the group, used work methods and perform all other actions, which shall help assimilate in the group more rapidly. Whether the new employee makes a tandem with the old employees and if their interrelation encourages development of the socialisation process will depend on the sincerity of the community.

Training is a process oriented at work, the purpose of which is to provide employees with knowledge and skills, necessary for the effective implementation of a particular function.[35] Training is used with the aim to train the new employee according to the requirements to perform her/his work and to reclaim innovations. The training result manifests by occurrence and use of new possibilities. It is very important for the employee to learn together with members of the group by performing certain tasks. Only in such way the employee and the group will improve and get knowledge.

Only those values are important in the created model, which are shared with the work group. Value orientation in the work group becomes values, when attitudes of such values occur. Feedback performs the control function, when results of the working group are compared to the long-term plans of the company. Thus, it is very important that new employees of the group would be purposefully involved in the value orientation creation process, would better understand values and accept them. The working group's value orientation must be acknowledged by all members of the group.

In summarising theoretical and empirical works it could be stated, that newly formed (or supplemented with new members of the group) working group's value orientation must be directed at reaching of priority goals of the organisation. Such values may express relation with the employees of the working group. They may also be the criteria and measures for reaching the goal. However, values must be related to the goals of the group's employees. The role of the group's manager and the influence of her/his managing solutions when forming orientation of the company's values are very important. New members of the group bring to the group new convictions, values, and assumptions. Employees seek to be members of such groups, where they

---

[32] G. Rancova (2004). *Dėmesio – kolektyve naujokas. Naujų darbuotojų adaptacijos organizacijoje sistema.* "Biuro administravimas", vol. 11, pp. 3–6.

[33] R. Šukytė, L. Rudnickienė (2010). *Viešosios organizacijos darbuotojų atranka ir adaptacija.* "Vadyba. Socialiniai mokslai", vol. 1, no. 17, p. 168.

[34] G. Maniukaitė (2003). *Akademinio jaunimo vertybinės orientacijos: autoritetų ir idealų krizė. Jaunimo vertybinės orientacijos,* ed. A. Vosyliūtė. Socialinių tyrimų institutas, Vilnius, pp. 22–28.

[35] A. Garalis (2004). *Besimokanti organizacija: mokymo (si) metodai ir jų taikymo galimybės // Ekonomika ir vadyba: aktualijos ir perspektyvos.* Ernesto Galvanausko mokslinė konferencija. Šiauliai: Šiaulių universiteto leidykla, no. 4, pp. 81–87.

can differ positively, where possibilities of seeking self-expression are made. And employees, who did not adapt and retire, bring out knowledge, ideas, and commercial secrets.

METHOD

The research method is an anonymous questionnaire. This questionnaire consists of six parts: demographic and five groups of statements (from 8 to 10 statements), where the respondents are asked to assess their own and the group's value orientations at a construction company according to a three level scale (yes; no; don't know).

Questionnaire's reliability assessment. For processing of data received during the research, SPSS 15.0 version of statistical analysis and the data processing program were used.

The reliability of the questionnaire was determined by calculating Cronbach's alpha coefficient, the result of which is –0.93. This scale is sufficiently reliable, when Cronbach's alpha is >0.7 and very reliable, when Cronbach's alpha is >0.8. Since the obtained result of Cronbach's alpha is significantly larger than 0.8, the questionnaire may be considered as very reliable.[36]

Research scope. Considering the research goal and raised tasks, *non-probabilistic* method of selection of exploratory groups is provided – *purposeful conclusion of groups.*[37] Here the researcher involves in the group persons, who, according to him, are typical in respect of the exploratory feature, who are easy to find and who are near.[38] In researches of a small scope as often as not exploratory groups are formed by not fully keeping to the principle of coincidence. Undoubtedly, groups formed in such way shall not reflect the population completely. Results of any researches may be sufficiently reliable, if the researcher does not intend to extrapolate them to the whole population, i.e. transform outside the exploratory group. Groups are often selected using this method and performing exploratory (preliminary) research.[39]

19 respondents participated in this research: 91% men and 9% women. Other demographic data of the respondents are provided in table 2.

Most of the respondents had vocational education (43.5%), according to age from 30 to 40 years (34.5%), according to seniority from 16 to 35 years (58.6%)

---

[36] R. Vaitkevičius, A. Saudargienė, *op.cit.*

[37] K. Kardelis (2007). *Mokslinių Tyrimų Metodologija Ir Metodai.* Lucilijus, Šiauliai.

[38] R. Tidikis (2003). *Socialinių Mokslų Tyrimų Metodologija.* Lietuvos teisės universiteto Leidybos centras, Vilnius.

[39] K. Kardelis, *op.cit.*

Table 2. Frequency Distribution of the participants

		%
1. Education of the respondents	secondary	11.3
	vocational	43.5
	post secondary	22.7
	incomplete higher	1.4
	higher non-university	7.0
	higher university	14.1
2. Age of the respondents	up to 20 years	8.0
	21–30 years	28.8
	30–40 years	34.5
	40–50 years	28.2
	50–60 years	21.1
	60 and more	6.0
3. Seniority of the respondents	0–10 yeas	7.0
	11–15 years	17,5
	16–25 years	32.4
	26–35 years	26.2
	36–45 years	11.3
	45 and more	5.6
4. Position of the respondents in the group	Manager of the group (and 2 foremen)	11.3
	Woodworkers-carpenters	15.4
	Finishers	17.4
	Bricklayers	29.3
	Painters	9.9
	Helpers	11.3
	Other	25.1

Source: own elaboration.

RESULTS AND DISCUSSION

The purpose of the questionnaire was to find out what place in the system of values takes the importance of work in a group (table 3). The purpose of this is to provide members of the group with understanding of identity with the group.

Reasons why employees work in this group is work according to specialty (91.2%), possibilities of constant improvement (91.8%), and the main source of subsistence (90.8%). What is undoubtedly less important for the respondents is work monotony (10.3%). It shows, that this group takes care of safety of the working place, wellness of employees, and qualification refreshers. Sincere endeavours of each employee to seek perfect quality determine the reliability of the company, strengthen its reputation, and increase demand for the offered services.

Table 3. Importance of work in a group

Statements	Answers (%)		
	Yes	No	Don't know
Guaranteed constant wage	75.6	23.6	0.8
Work according to specialty	**91.2**	4.8	4.0
Self-realisation	72.5	24.8	2.7
Work is the main value of life	82.3	14.5	3.2
Possibilities of constant improvement	**91.8**	5.4	2.8
Main source of subsistence	**90.8**	7.8	1.4
Personal liability for welfare of the group	75.6	15.2	9.2
Proud of own work	65.3	21.6	13.1
Monotony	10.3	79.1	10.6
Dissatisfaction with the working conditions	11.6	85.3	3.1

Source: own elaboration.

According to theories of management science, good relationship in a group is an important factor. Respondents believe that the group's values (table 4) are understandable and acceptable to all members of the group (92.6%), all formed groups are exclusive (94.8%), and that the group's follow convictions when making various decisions (87.5%).

Table 4. Orientation of group's values

Statements	Answers (%)		
	Yes	No	Don't know
Standards of behaviour exist	**85.2**	12.3	2.5
A personally and socially desirable method of behaviour is determined	78.2	16.3	5.5
The system of values is understandable and acceptable for all its members	**92.6**	5.5	1.9
Groups follow convictions when making various decisions	**87.5**	9.8	2.7
Convictions and moral principles reside in the culture of the group	**85.6**	2.5	11.9
The employee's relation with the group is assessed	65.8	22.5	11.7
The culture of the group is the main component	86.1	9.2	4.7
Groups have an individual character	79.4	12.5	8.1
The group is exclusive	**94.8**	1.2	4.0

Source: own elaboration.

Table 4 shows that the manager of the group tries to create such environment where employees would feel comfortable and together would be productive as well as useful for the working group. Usually, job descriptions are created not for a particular work position, but for a common group of works. Thus, in order to implement this, it is necessary to know, how employees value the group, their work place and conditions, what motivates them, what is lacking for more effective work, what they expect from the manager of the group, and what are their expectations and future plans? And the most important, what is the importance of the employee's values for the group? (table 5).

Table 5. Employees' value orientation

Statements	Answers (%)		
	Yes	No	Don't know
Self-confidence	78.9	14.5	6.6
Reliability and responsibility	82.6	12.6	5.1
Positive attitude	81.4	12.3	6.3
Strong working ethics	87.2	9.7	3.1
Adaptation	59.6	34.5	5.9
Regularity	94.2	3.2	2.6
Loyalty	79.8	15.6	4.5
Employee's motivation	89.7	7.8	2.5
Motivation while constantly learning	90.4	7.2	2.4
Honesty	92.3	6.2	1.5

Source: own elaboration.

These results showed (table 5), that regularity (94.2%) and honesty (92.3%) of the employee in the working group are appreciated. The employees' motivation (89.7%) and seeking knowledge (90.4%) are very important in the working group. Activeness of members in this group is greater because of the fact that every person exactly conceives her/his role and place in the activity of the group. An employee working in such a company feels appreciated and important. She/he sees her/his future with this company and the company is not ready to lose such an employee.

Since the company is competitive and objectives of the group are combined considering the construction business and human resources, values of adaptation in the group are analysed (table 6).

Table 6. Values of the adaptation process

Statements	Answers (%)		
	Yes	No	Don't know
Important profit	65.8	31.1	3.1
Collaboration	78.4	15.4	6.2
Discipline	71.5	24.1	4.4
Competence	87.6	10.3	2.1
Regularity	97.5	2.5	0.0
Loyalty	90.2	6.3	3.5
Creativity	79.8	14.2	6.0
Seeking a common goal	94.5	3.6	1.9

Source: own elaboration.

Regularity (97.5%), seeking a common goal (94.5%), loyalty (90.2%), and profit (only 65.8%) show (Table 6), that group employees do not seek day-to-day success, but long-term goals. These main values of the group will help during the formation of a successful working group.

United work of the group is important when seeking good work results, so it is very important that all employees would recognise values, which are important during the training process (table 7).

Table 7. Values of the training process group

Statements	Answers (%)		
	Yes	No	Don't know
New employees are encouraged to risk and be innovative	68.9	18.9	12.2
New employees are encouraged to seek new knowledge	36.8	59.8	3.4
New employees are encouraged to take over good experience	39.8	28.3	1.9
A consultant is assigned for new employees	48.5	49.7	1.8
Stability and steady rules are emphasised in group activity	**89.7**	8.1	2.2
Decisions are made in the group considering the opinions of the employees	50.4	47.1	2.5
New employees are encouraged to learn in the group	86.1	10.6	3.3
Work in the group is organised on a team basis	**90.1**	7.8	2.1

Source: own elaboration.

As the data from table 7 shows, the following values of work in groups are mostly developed during the training process: work is organised on a team basis (90.1%); stability and steady rules are felt at work (89.7%). However, it is necessary to pay additional attention to the stimulation of employees to seek knowledge (36.8%) and skills (39.8%). Each member of the group must be explained how she/he should raise her/his qualifications. An employee is motivated to perform her/his assigned tasks, knowing what she/he is expected to do and what she/he must do in order to reach own goals. Consultants for new employees are connected with the lack of competences (48.5%). It is simple enough to be educated during training. It is also necessary to ascertain what prevents from making successful collective decisions (50.4%), – because of incompatibility of attitudes or differences in thinking. Here group employees should be familiarised with the methods of making decisions of work in groups.

Employees in the working group are different individuals. Therefore, the performed training of employees is related to standardised processes. It is important to mention that difficulties or mistakes arising at construction companies cannot repeat. Having experience, the manager of the group should provide for arising dangers and make decisions how to prevent them in advance. Less disagreement arises in such way. Thus disagreements shall help to find a correct method for solving problems. Employees must be the initiators of changes, ready for dialogue in a group, being able to observe interactions and to risk.

The questionnaire showed that work in groups is important for employees and that not everything is determined by wage or favourite job. Freedom of making decisions and implementation as well as assumed personal liability for group results not only encourage, but also educate employees, allow them to actively participate during formation of the group. Real success of the group is ensured only when all members of the group can enjoy their results. Group values must be integrated into processes, policies, and principles of activity. Value orientation, acceptable to all, reveals additional possibilities and talents of employees, confidence in management occurs, employees' interrelation improves, increases the will to participate in the life of the organisation, environmental protection, and economical and social development.

CONCLUSIONS

Unsuccessful search for suitable employees for working groups is the largest obstacle in development of a construction business. Knowing that employees are the most important resource, managers (owners) of business organisations are confronted with a serious problem to retain high quality specialists. A model of forming universal working group's value orientation is offered. By applying it, goals of the organisation may be reached through consciously created orientation of values of the working group. The newly selected staff, during adaptation and learning process, should be included in the values of contamination and assimilation process. Thus it is necessary to provide obligation of the manager of the group to form (and retain) such orientation of values, which would provide members of the group with satisfaction during performance of their tasks by not forgetting the goals of the employee herself/himself.

Results of the research showed, that employees like to work in a group, where the employee's regularity and honesty are appreciated, there are possibilities of constant improvement, the group distinguishes by its oneness, all members seek a common goal, and the value system is understandable and acceptable for all members of the group. The totality of the working group's values corresponds to the values of the employees, their behaviour and creed. Group members are not satisfied only with monotony (10.3%). The reason may be work specifics at construction companies. Thus managers of the working group should consider it when allocating work tasks, as it has great significance for activity results of the construction company. The research results show that there is no frequent fluctuation of employees at the analysed construction company. Professional employees work there and this construction company is competitive.

It should be stated that the created "model of forming value orientation in the working group" is used when forming working groups at construction companies. By applying it, goals of the organisation may be reached through consciously created working group's value orientation.

References

Abrams D., Hogg M.A., Hinkle S., Otten S. (2004). *The Social Identity Perspective on Small Groups. Theories of Small Groups – Interdisciplinary Perspectives.* Sage Publications Inc., Thousand Oaks, CA, pp. 99–137.

Aramavičiūtė V. (2005a). *Auklėjimas ir dvasinė asmenybės branda.* Gimtasis žodis, Vilnius.

Aramavičiūtė V. (2005b). *Vertybės kaip gyvenimo prasmės pamatas.* "Acta Paedagogica Vilnensia", vol. 14, pp. 18–26.

Barkema H., Baum J., Mannix E. (2002). *Management challenges in a new time.* "Academy of Management Journal", October, vol. 45, no. 5, pp. 916–930.

Berson Y., Oreg S., Dvir T. (2005). *Organizational Culture as A Mediator of Ceo Values And Organizational Performance.* Academy of Management Proceedings, New York.

Bronstein L.R. (2003). *Model for interdisciplinary collaboration.* "Social Work", vol. 48, no. 3. pp. 297–306.

Čiuladienė G. (2006). *Paauglių vertybinis aspektas ir raiškos tendencijos.* "Acta paedagogica Vilnensia", vol. 16, pp. 106–117.

Edwards J.R., Cable D.A. (2009). *The value of value congruence.* "Journal of Applied Psychology", vol. 94, no. 3, pp. 654–677.

Garalis A. (2004). *Besimokanti organizacija: mokymo (si) metodai ir jų taikymo galimybės // Ekonomika ir vadyba: aktualijos ir perspektyvos.* Ernesto Galvanausko mokslinė konferencija. Šiauliai, Šiaulių universiteto leidykla, no. 4, pp. 81–87.

Gronskienė I. (2008). *Žemės ūkio organizacijų deklaruojamų vertybių modelis.* "Management Theory and Studies for Rural Business and Infrastructure Development", vol. 13, no. 2, pp. 54–61.

Haugh H., McKee L. (2004). *The cultural paradigm of the smaller firm.* "Journal of Small Business Management", vol. 42, no. 4, pp. 377–394.

Jokubaitis A. (2012). *Vertybių tironija ir politika.* Vilniaus universiteto leidykla, Vilnius.

Jovaiša L. (2007). *Enciklopedinis edukologijos žodynas.* Gimtasis žodis, Vilnius.

Jucevičienė P., Poškienė A., Kudirkaitė L., Damanskas N. (2000). *Universiteto kultūra ir jos tyrimas.* Technologija, Kaunas.

Kardelis K. (2007). *Mokslinių Tyrimų Metodologija Ir Metodai.* "Research Methodology and Techniques". Lucilijus, Šiauliai.

Kouzes J.M., Posner B.Z. (2003). *Iššūkis vadybai.* Smaltija, Kaunas.

Kvedaravičius J. (2006). *Organizacijų vystimosi vadyba.* Vytauto Didžiojo Universitetas, Kaunas.

Lorreto P. (2008). *Top 10 Values Employers Look for in Employees about COM.* Intership, unpublished.

Martišauskienė E. (2004). *Paauglių dvasingumas, kaip pedagoginis reiškinys: monografija.* VPU, Vilnius.

Maniukaitė G. (2003). *Akademinio jaunimo vertybinės orientacijos: autoritetų ir idealų krizė. Jaunimo vertybinės orientacijos: straipsnių rinkinys,* Socialinių tyrimų institutas, Vilnius, pp. 22–28.

Nazelskis E. (2010). *Profesinio orientavimo ir konsultavimo priemonių taikymas darbuotojų kaitai mažinti.* "Profesinis rengimas: tyrimai ir realijos", vol. 19, p. 121.

Pacevičius J., Janulytė E. (2009). *Mobingas kaip organizacinio gyvenimo problema: priežasčių, raiškos ir pasekmių įvertinimas ir analizė.* "Ekonomika ir vadyba: aktualijos ir perspektyvos", vol. 1, no. 14, pp. 187–196.

Patapas A., Labenskytė G. (2011). *Organizacinės kultūros ir vertybių tyrimas N apskrities valstybinėje mokesčių inspekcijoje.* "Viešoji politika ir administravimas", vol. 4, pp. 589–603.

Rancova G. (2004). *Dėmesio – kolektyve naujokas. Naujų darbuotojų adaptacijos organizacijoje sistema.* "Biuro administravimas", vol. 11, pp. 3–6.

Rosinaitė V., Bernotas D., Biveinytė S., Blažienė I., Česnuitytė V., Gražulis V., Gruževskis B., Misiūnas A., Pocius A., Stancikas E., Šileika A., Šlekienė K., Zabarauskaitė R. (2007). *Magistrantų integracijos į darbo rinką monitoringo sistemos sukūrimas.* Darbo ir socialinių tyrimų institutas. http:// www.dsti. lt/tyrimai.html (access: 22.11.2013).

Savanevičienė A., Šilingienė V. (2005). *Darbas grupėse.* Technologija, Kaunas.

Seilius A. (2004). *Aplinkos poveikio ir sėkmingo vadovavimo organizacijoms prielaidos. Iš Valdymo problemos: teorija ir tendencija. Kolektyvinė monografija.* KU leidykla, Klaipėda.

Siebert W.S., Zubanov N. (2009). *Searching for the optimal level of employee turnover: A study of a large U.K. retail organization.* "Academy of Management Journal", vol. 52, pp. 294–313.

Siegall M., McDonald T. (2004). *Person-organization value congruence, burnout and diversion of resources.* "Personnel Review", vol. 33, no. 3, pp. 291–301.

Stankevičienė A., Liučvaitienė A., Šimelytė A. (2010). *Personalo kaitos stabilizavimo galimybės Lietuvos statybos sektoriuje. Possibilities of personnel turnover stabilization in Lithuanian construction sector.* "Verslas: teorija ir praktika", vol. 11, no. 2, pp. 151–158.

Stankuvienė A. (2013). *Autoritarizmo veiksniai ir diagnostiniai instrumentai.* "Socialinių mokslų studijos", vol. 5, no. 1, pp. 57–73.

Strautmanis J. (2008). *Employees' values orientation in the context of corporate social responsibility.* "Baltic Journal of Management", vol. 3, no. 3, pp. 346–358.

Šimanskienė L., Seilius A. (2009). *Komandos: Samprata, Kūrimas, Vadovavimas. Team: Concept, Development, Leadership.* KU leidykla, Klaipėda.

Šimanskienė L. (2008). *Organizacinės kultūros diagnozavimo metodika.* KU leidykla, Klaipėda.

Šukytė R., Rudnickienė L. (2010). *Viešosios organizacijos darbuotojų atranka ir adaptacija. Vadyba.* "Socialiniai mokslai", vol. 1, no. 17, pp. 167–180.

Tidikis R. (2003). *Socialinių Mokslų Tyrimų Metodologija.* Lietuvos teisės universiteto Leidybos centras, Vilnius.

Uzdila J.V. (2008). *Šeimotyros kaip dalyko poveikis studentų matrimonialinėms nuostatoms.* "Pedagogika", vol. 89, pp. 151–160.

Vveinhardt J. (2009). *Mobingo kaip diskriminacijos darbuotojų santykiuose poveikis organizacijos klimatui.* "Verslas: teorija ir praktika-Business: Theory and Practice", vol. 10, no. 4, pp. 285–297.

Vaitkevičius R., Saudargienė A. (2006). *Statistika Su Spss Psichologiniuose Tyrimuose. SPSS Statistics psychological research.* VDU, Kaunas.

Vanagas P. (2004). *Visuotinės kokybės vadyba.* Technologija, Kaunas.

Vasiliauskas R. (2005). *Vertybių ugdymo teoriniai ir praktiniai aspektai.* "Acta Paedagogica Vilnensia", vol. 14, pp. 8–17.

Verplanken B. (2004). *Value congruence and job satisfaction among nurses: A human relations perspective,* "International Journal of Nursing Studies", vol. 41, no. 6, p. 599–605.

Zakarevičius P. (2003). *Pokyčiai organizacijose: priežastys, valdymas, pasekmės. Monografija.* VDU, Kaunas.

Zakarevičius P., Kvedaravičius J., Augustauskas T. (2004). *Organizacijų vystymosi paradigma.* VDU, Kaunas.

Žukauskaitė I. (2008). *Naujų darbuotojų kaita: ryšys su organizacine socializacija.* "Organizacijų vadyba: sisteminiai tyrimai", vol. 48, pp. 153–169.

Monika Konieczny
Akamai Technologies Poland
e-mail: monika@konieczny.be

GAMIFIED AGILE – INNOVATIVE TOOL TO IMPROVE COMMUNICATION BETWEEN THE PRODUCT OWNER AND THE DEVELOPMENT TEAM

Abstract

Background. Technology growth observed in the last decades has a huge impact on the IT sector. Many public and private organisations decide to introduce various high-tech improvements based on the latest IT solutions to increase efficiency, optimize processes, lower the costs, etc. The success of those actions strongly depends on a deep understanding of the project goal, identification of all the crucial stakeholders and their needs, limitations, organisation context and culture, and many more. To increase the success of the project it is important to make the communication between the principal and the performer as efficient as possible. Unfortunately based on various research studies and observations inefficient collaboration is one of the frequent reasons of the IT solutions implementation failures.

Research aims. The aim of this paper is to identify dysfunctions in the collaboration between the Product Owner and the development team and verify whether Gamified Agile – a set of tools based on Agile methodologies, simulation games, and gamification – could be a potential solution to it.

Methodology. In the first phase – identification of the main problems occurring in the collaboration between the Product Owner and the development team – literature analysis, interview, and participating and non-participating observations are used. In the second phase - verification whether Gamified Agile could be used as a tool to improve it – experiment, interview, participating and non-participating observations are used.

Findings. The experiment during which the Gamified Agile tool was used by 12 different teams in 10 companies during the retrospective, lead to conclusions that the set of tools can be used as an instrument to improve communication and understanding between the Product Owner and the development team in the daily work on the project in all of its phases. The positive results of experimental verification of the tool lead to the conclusion that the Gamified Agile can be used as an effective instrument that can support the Product Owner and the development team in improving collaboration between them.

Keywords: agile, collaboration, gamification, simulation game.

INTRODUCTION

Rapid technological growth observed in the past two decades has a significant impact on various economic and social changes happening in the contemporary world. The turbulent environment requires public and private organisations to respond quickly and effectively to the constantly occurring changes in order to meet the demands of competitiveness and productivity.[1] One of the ways to achieve it is to introduce IT solutions. Consequently, the size and growth rate of the IT sector, both worldwide and in Poland, indicates its importance in modern economy.[2] Unfortunately, the number of IT projects completed with full success (on time, within budget, fulfilling all the requirements) is still not rewarding enough.[3] That motivated the author to conduct a research to identify the main causes of the observed issues and then based on further investigation propose a set of supporting tools to help teams and customers in the project development process.

The most important asset of the project are people engaged within it with their knowledge and experience.[4] Therefore, the main area of the research were the methods of managing teams, especially teams of programmers and internal as well as external communication processes. The chosen direction of the research were instruments of influence on teams based on simulation games and gamification that are focused on the humanistic side of project management processes. The positive outcomes of using simulation games and gamification in education, marketing, and healthcare[5] were an inspiration to verify the possibilities of using this kind of tools in helping teams of developers and Product Owners in improving their communication processes.

BACKGROUND

The game is an entirely voluntary activity, having induce pleasure as well as the course and meaning.[6] The game can also be seen as a system in which players are engaged in an artificial conflict, described by the applicable rules and the result are measurable actions.[7]

---

[1] K. Perechuda (2008). *Scenariusze, dialogi i procesy zarządzania wiedzą*. Difin, Warszawa.

[2] http://idc.com; http://www.gartner.com; http://www.computerworld.pl (access: 3.06.2015).

[3] http://standishgroup.com; http://www.versionone.com (access: 3.06.2015).

[4] C. Bartlett, S. Ghoshal (2002). *Building Competitive Advantage Through People Magazine: Winter 2002.* "Research Feature", January 15; A. Bounfour (2013), *The Management of Intangibles: The Organisation's Most Valuable Assets*. Routledge, Abingdon-on-Thames.

[5] M. Kostera (2003). *Antropologia organizacji. Metodologia badań terenowych*, Wydawnictwo Naukowe PWN, Warszawa; J. McGonigal (2011). *Reality is Broken: Why Games Make Us Better and How They Can Change The World*. Penguin Press HC, London; K. Werbach, D. Hunter (2012). *For the Win: How Game Thinking Can Revolutionize Your Business*. Wharton Digital Press, Boston; G. Zichermann, J. Linder (2013). *The Gamification Revolution: How Leaders Leverage Game Mechanics to Crush the Competition*. McGraw-Hill, New York.

[6] J. Huizinga (1985). *Homo ludens. Zabawa jako źródło kultury*. Wydawnictwo „Czytelnik", Warszawa.

[7] K. Salen, E. Zimmerman (2003). *Rules of Play: Game Design Fundamentals*. The MIT Press, Boston.

It is also active consisting in solving problems in a positive and creative atmosphere.[8] In this case the game becomes an object consisting of components, principles, and a set of criteria, such as a rule, aim, variable mileage, freedom, or common experience.

The simulation game is played enriched with the element of competition, which rules are fixed and approved by the participants. Those types of games let carrying out numerous experiments together with a team. The main goal can be getting a better understanding of the mechanisms that occur in everyday work on the project in order to analyse possible improvements. It can be also used to build the knowledge and experience necessary to make better decisions in various areas during the work on the project.[9]

Gamification are the activities involving the use of gaming mechanisms in areas not related to games. It is an enrichment of the work environment to make it as intriguing as the gaming world in order to enhance the participants' involvement and influence changes in their behaviour to address specific issues.[10] Gamification effectiveness relies on meeting the needs of the participant and the mechanisms of his/her motivation, both external and internal. The existing research achievements in literature, discussions with experts, as well as practical verification of the use of such solutions in their daily work with the selected team executing IT projects have shown promising results. The introduction of the simulation game and gamification to the agile methodology used made it possible to increase the team efficiency communication and overall collaboration with the Product Owner. The results obtained inspired further literature studies and field research. Based on the gained information a Gamified Agile model was built. In the next phase experimental verification of the model was conducted.

METHOD

The goal of the study was to investigate the impact of using the simulation game and gamification in everyday cooperation between the team and the Product Owner in order to solve problems in communication areas.

The study was conducted in the interpretative-symbolic trend.[11] The study was divided into four phases. During the first one problems affecting the development teams and the Product Owner were analysed. In this phase, the following methods

[8] J. Schell (2008). *The Art of Games Design a Book of Lenses*. Morgan Kaufmann, Burlington.

[9] E. Miłosz, M. Miłosz (1995). *Symulatory systemów gospodarczych w kształceniu menedżerów*. "Komputer w Edukacji", vol. 3–4, Wydawnictwo Leopoldinum Fundacji dla Uniwersytetu Wrocławskiego.

[10] G. Zichermann, C. Cunningham (2011). *Gamification by Design: Implementing Game Mechanics in Web and Mobile Apps*, 1st edition. O'Reilly Media, Sebastopol, California; P. Tkaczyk (2012). *Grywalizacja*. One Press, Helion, Gliwice.

[11] M. Kostera (1996). *Postmodernizm w zarządzaniu*. Polskie Wydawnictwo Ekonomiczne, Warszawa; M.J. Hatch (2002). *Teoria organizacji*. Wydawnictwo Naukowe PWN, Warszawa; G. Morgan (2008). *Obrazy organizacji*. Wydawnictwo Naukowe PWN, Warszawa; Ł. Sułkowski (2012). *Metodologie emic i etic w badaniach kultury w zarządzaniu*. "Management and Business Administration. Central Europe", vol. 1, no. 114, pp. 64–71.

were used: analysis and synthesis of the literature, interview, participating and non-participating observations. The goal of the second phase was to analyse the current state of simulation games and gamification knowledge on the use of tools in improving collaboration between the Product Owner and the development team through analysis and synthesis of selected literature. Multi-faceted preliminary studies allowed to collect data, which detailed analysis and synthesis led to the formulation of functional and non-functional requirements, on which the Gamified Agile model was built.

The Gamified Agile model consists of two parts. The base part – a set of values that constituted within the humanistic management manifesto combined the Agile Manifesto.. They define the priorities and the way the people engaged in the project see themselves, the individual members and the relationships between them, the customer/Product Owner, and the product. The second part is the Scrum methodology enriched with the elements of simulation games and gamification.

In the next phase the model verification in the form of an experiment carried out in four companies diversified in terms of maturity (companies, employees, team), culture and size was conducted. Each team was characterised by different maturity, dynamism, and complexity of projects. The study was conducted within six months. The aim of the experiment was to verify whether the Gamified Agile can help Product Owners and the development teams in improving efficiency of their communication. The experiment, during which participant observation and ethnographic research was conducted was done in a form of a pilot implementation of the Gamified Agile. This exercise was done as a retrospective during which the model was used as the main tool. Teams had a chance to work in a secure environment to test try to enrich their existing processes with Gamified Agile elements. Then a meeting summary, after the first full iteration carried out after the experiment, was done. After a brief introduction to the workshop, the team ran a self-diagnosis during which strengths, the positive elements of the process and the working environment, as well as those aspects that require improvement or change were identified. Then the Tigerish Tiger game was played. Its main objective was to analyse communication processes, both internal and external, as well as a desire to implement innovative and customised solutions to solve the encountered problems. The team's task was to paint a tiger on a chosen participant's face according to imprecise customer requirements. The game began with a brief introduction in the form of a story about a company dealing with the implementation of custom projects, such as painting wild animals on people's faces. Over the years of working together solid processes had been developed, under which customer orders were executed. The team then received crayons to paint the tiger and a head scarf to cover the eyes of the person responsible for painting the tiger and started the work. After summing up the exercise, the team participated in the Crazy Cake simulation during which they looked at a process of project implementation to seek for its advantages and disadvantages as well as opportunities for improvements. The main objective was to prepare a cake that would meet the client's expectations, according to the currently used process of project implementation. During the cake preparation the team members were to analyse whether it was possible to introduce improvements or innovations. The workshops were completed with a detailed summary during which the team and the product owner diagnosed the cause of existing problems and proposed solutions. Then decisions which changes, improvements to introduce were made and an implementation plan was prepared. After the end of the next full sprint during which the team had the opportunity to implement improvements, the researcher met again with the team and the product owner. The participants shared their insights on modification, implementation of elements of games and gamification into the process, encountered problems and ways of solving them, thoughts, and plans to implement further innovative tools. In the last phase the data collected during the experiment was analysed and conclusions were drawn.

RESULTS AND DISCUSSION

Verification of the suitability of the Gamified Agile model is made in the form of a comparison of the main manifestations of organisational effectiveness of teams before the experiment and after its implementation, and analysis of data collected during the observations and conclusions. Due to the characteristics of the examined issues, to assess the Gamified Agile a combination of coherent organisational efficiency models proposed by M. Bielski, B. Ziębicki, and T. Kafel was used. The created model consisted of four dimensions described by metrics: human relationships: equality, rip personnel, initiative, employee satisfaction, internal consistency, openness, productivity as a result of employee involvement; behavioural: labour integration degree, decision-making autonomy scope, sense of security; internal processes: the authority and discipline, information processing efficiency, openness in communication, internal cohesion, structure complexity, and rules' simplicity. The dimensions are strongly correlated, so it is necessary to study them as a whole, bearing in mind the existing interference and dependence. Due to the nature of the studied phenomenon and defined objectives, testing was performed using the method of an experiment in natural environment. The choice was dictated by the need to verify and assess the application of the model in the target environment, know the opinions and reactions of future Gamified Agile users, offering the participants to obtain real benefits from the use of the proposed tools already at the stage of the pilot implementation and popularisation of the idea in the IT environment. The natural experiment method is burdened with risks associated with the inability to fully control the environmental conditions, some of which may have a direct or indirect impact on the outcome of the experiment. This risk can be used as an opportunity to examine a number of factors present in the natural environment, both single and assemblies, which would be extremely difficult to simulate in the laboratory.[12] The main research technique that was used during the experiment was participant observation, allowing collecting material indicating the existence or lack of existence of benefits of the model use. Casual interviews with the participants, both during the workshops and after their completion, were used as a supporting technique. The researcher's professional experience gained in the daily work with teams of programmers allowed to minimise disturbance of the natural environment as well as a full understanding of the causes and consequences of the observed phenomena.[13] The first assessment was made by the investigator based on interviews with developers, scrum the masters, product owners, participant observation, including an evaluation of the team members made during the initial self-diagnosis in the form of a retrospective; the second one of the conclusions of the discussions that took place after the first iteration of the experiment, when the participants had the opportunity to implement and use the newly recognised tools and solutions. In most cases the participants highly evaluated both equality and openness prevailing in teams, allowing them to share critical remarks on the process, methods, and tools used. They pointed out that despite the rip teams at a satisfactory level, they had always been able to effectively provide each other with feedback. Many of them perceived that either they, or the rest of the members had ideas for introducing innovative tools and solutions, but often lacked motivation or support of a team or manager, to make them happen or were not sure whether the introduction of the ideas would have a positive effect on the atmosphere and work efficiency. These remarks coincided with the results of interviews and observations made before the experiment.

During the workshop, team members had the opportunity to improve the existing relationships and build new ones. They were also able to try various innovative ideas in a safe environment and observe the reaction of the other team members and Product Owners. According to the opinions shared by the team members of the group which noted the greatest improvement, a significant increase in efficiency was related to the introduction of numerous improvements to the daily process developed based on observations made during the workshop, and addition of gamification elements that really appealed to the developers.

Internal processes are a very important dimension because of their direct impact on the success or failure of the project. Developers and product owners analysed how efficient processing of information and openness in communication were, because, according to their experience, proficiency in these areas was essential to delivering appropriate software and to minimise the potential risks. One of the most problematic areas was effective communication. Receiving incomplete data, delays in communication,

---

[12] L.R. Gay (1992). *Educational Research*, 4th edition. Merrill, New York; D. Moore, D. McCabe (1993). *Introduction to the Practice of Statistics*. New York, Freeman; T. Dunning (2012). *Natural Experiments in the Social Sciences: A Design-Based Approach (Strategies for Social Inquiry)*. Cambridge University Press, Cambridge.

[13] M. Kostera (1996). *Postmodernizm…*; K. Charmaz (2009). *Shifting the grounds: Constructivist grounded theory methods for the twenty-first century* [in:] J.M. Morse, P.N. Stern, J.M. Corbin, B. Bowers, K. Charmaz, A.E. Clarke (eds.), *Developing Grounded Theory: The Second Generation*. University of Arizona Press – Left Coast Press, Walnut Creek, CA; Ł. Sułkowski, *op.cit.*

the use of less efficient channels such as e-mail as the main way of communicating of the product owner with the team, were the most frequently mentioned problems in everyday work by the participants. Communication between the team and the product owner, in most cases was characterised by much less openness than inside the team. By analysing the structure and processes occurring in the studied organisations the correlation between the occurrence of a complex hierarchical structure and complex procedures with lower assessment of internal processes was observed. Both Tiger Tiger and Crazy Cake turned out to be an opportunity to analyse the causes of communication problems and make an attempt to implement corrective actions. During the game, participants were encouraged to play the role different from theirs to get a better understanding of the difficulties faced by other persons involved in the project. In addition, because of the different knowledge and experience – to be able to propose innovative improvements. Knowledge and experience gained during the workshops have helped teams in improving the efficiency of internal processes, as well as inspired to seek alternative methods of diagnosing and implementing innovative techniques. The improvement was particularly well seen in the case of parameters such as efficient information processing, openness in communication, and internal cohesion. The most noticeable improvement by a team was successfully implemented in the groups with lower initial evaluation.

CONCLUSIONS

The main objective of the study was to perform a detailed analysis of the applicability of simulation games and gamification as tools supporting Product Owners and the development team in increasing efficiency of communication among them. The results of the analysis of the gathered research material allowed forming of the following conclusions:

1. Simulation games and gamification can be successfully used as innovative tools to help in areas such as: communication, stimulating innovation, and collaboration for development teams and Product Owners existing in different working cultures, which are part of both organisations with a formal, hierarchical character, as well as those of the matrix or free structures.
2. The key factor for success in applying the Agile Gamified model is to conduct a thorough initial analysis of the Product Owners and the team needs in the form of participant observation, unstructured interviews with team members and key stakeholders.
3. Adjusting the model to the team's needs allows for achieving better outcomes. The participants repeatedly positively assessed the experienced individual approach. Participation in the experiment resulted in benefits such as possibility of immediate application of jointly developed solutions.

4. Involving as many members of the team in the process of new tool introduction and encouraging them to jointly develop, adjust the tool to their needs allows achieving first successes even in the initial phases.

Positive results obtained in the conducted experimental verification lead to the conclusion that the Gamified Agile is an effective instrument for supporting the development team and the Product Owner in increasing efficiency of their daily collaboration and as a result increasing the chances of accomplishing a fully successful project.

References

Bartlett C., Ghoshal S. (2002). *Building competitive advantage through People Magazine: Winter 2002.* "Research Feature", January 15.

Bounfour A. (2013). *The Management of Intangibles: The Organisation's Most Valuable Assets*, Routledge, Abingdon-on-Thames.

Charmaz K. (2009). *Shifting the grounds: Constructivist grounded theory methods for the twenty-first century* [in:] J.M. Morse, P.N. Stern, J.M. Corbin, B. Bowers, K. Charmaz, A.E. Clarke (eds.), *Developing Grounded Theory: The Second Generation*, University of Arizona Press – Left Coast Press, Walnut Creek, CA.

Chrapko M. (2012). *Scrum. O zwinnym zarządzaniu projektami.* Wydawnictwo Helion, Gliwice.

Cockburn A. (2006). *Agile Software Development: The Cooperative Game*, 2nd edition, Addison-Wesley Professional, Boston.

Cohn M. (2009). *Succeeding with Agile: Software Development using Scrum.* Addison-Wesley Professional, Boston.

Dunning T. (2012). *Natural Experiments in the Social Sciences: A Design-Based Approach (Strategies for Social Inquiry).* Cambridge University Press, Cambridge.

Gay L.R. (1992). *Educational Research*, 4th edition. Merrill, New York.

Hatch M.J. (2002). *Teoria organizacji.* Wydawnictwo Naukowe PWN, Warszawa.

Huizinga J. (1985). *Homo ludens. Zabawa jako źródło kultury.* Wydawnictwo „Czytelnik", Warszawa.

Kostera M. (1996). *Postmodernizm w zarządzaniu.* Polskie Wydawnictwo Ekonomiczne, Warszawa.

Kostera M. (2003). *Antropologia organizacji. Metodologia badań terenowych.* Wydawnictwo Naukowe PWN, Warszawa.

McGonigal J. (2011). *Reality is Broken: Why Games Make Us Better and How They Can Change The World.* Penguin Press HC, London.

Miłosz E., Miłosz M. (1995), *Symulatory systemów gospodarczych w kształceniu menedżerów.* „Komputer w Edukacji", vol. 3–4, Wydawnictwo Leopoldinum Fundacji dla Uniwersytetu Wrocławskiego.

Moore D., McCabe D. (1993). *Introduction to the Practice of Statistics.* Freeman, New York.

Morgan G. (2008). *Obrazy organizacji.* Wydawnictwo Naukowe PWN, Warszawa.

Perechuda K. (2008). *Scenariusze, dialogi i procesy zarządzania wiedzą.* Difin, Warszawa.

Salen K., Zimmerman E. (2003). *Rules of Play: Game Design Fundamentals.* The MIT Press, Cambridge.

Schell J. (2008). *The Art of Games Design a Book of Lenses.* Morgan Kaufmann, Burlington.

Schwaber K. (2009). *Agile Project Management with Scrum Developer Best Practices.* Microsoft Press, London.

Sułkowski Ł. (2012). *Metodologie emic i etic w badaniach kultury w zarządzaniu.* "Management and Business Administration. Central Europe", vol. 1, no. 114, pp. 64–71.

Tkaczyk P. (2012). *Grywalizacja.* One Press, Helion, Gliwice.

Werbach K., Hunter D. (2012). *For the Win: How Game Thinking Can Revolutionize Your Business.* Wharton Digital Press, Boston.

Zichermann G., Cunningham C. (2011). *Gamification by Design: Implementing Game Mechanics in Web and Mobile Apps*, 1st edition. O'Reilly Media, Sebastopol, California.

Zichermann G., Linder J. (2013). *The Gamification Revolution: How Leaders Leverage Game Mechanics to Crush the Competition.* McGraw-Hill, New York.

Erika Župerkienė
Klaipėda University
e-mail: erika.zuperkiene@ku.lt
Aurimas Župerka
Klaipėda University
e-mail: aurimas_zuperka@hotmail.com
Julius Paulikas
Klaipėda University
e-mail: jpaulikas@gmail.com

THE ROLE OF TRAINING WHILE HELPING ORGANISATIONS TO OVERCOME RESISTANCE TO INNOVATIONS

Abstract

Background. In the article we analysed the issue whether staff training can help business organisations to overcome resistance to innovations. Scientific literature highlights the need to deal with unwanted employee resistance from the beginning of introducing innovations or changes.

Research aims. To find the reason for resistance to innovations of business organisations' employees.

Methodology. In order to examine the identified problem quantitative research was conducted – written survey of employees of a group of enterprises of public passenger transport. The instrument of the survey was a questionnaire. In order to process the data obtained during the research version 19.0 of the program of statistical analysis and data processing SPSS (Statistical Package for the Social Sciences) was used. The credibility of the questionnaire was determined by calculating Cronbach's alfa coefficient (0.842). For the purpose of determining the statistical significance of respondents' answers we applied the procedure of testing a non-parametric hypothesis; there were calculated correlation coefficients; factor analysis was applied as well.

Findings and Results. The research revealed that the higher the employee's education is, the more favourably the employee is inclined to value more organisational, but not personal, measures or actions of managers while reducing resistance to innovations. Meanwhile, those employees who possess lower education fear more to lose their jobs; they associate the introduction of innovations with increased requirements related to qualifications. It has been established that the higher the employees' education, the lower their negative attitude with regard to innovation is.

The results of research partially confirmed the raised hypothesis – resistance to innovation is lower in those organisations, where more attention is paid to staff training.

Conclusions and Recommendations. The analysis of literature and the results of research lead to the conclusion that resistance to innovation can be overcome by the following general methods: education, training, communication, participation and involvement of employees, alleviation and support, negotiation and agreements, and manipulation or direct/indirect force. It is recommended while introducing innovation in enterprises to apply the proposed model of negotiation of staff resistance to innovations.

Keywords: innovation, resistance to innovation, training, organisation.

INTRODUCTION

It is necessary for enterprises, which seek to create high added value and be competitive on the international market, to implement innovations in their daily activities. Business innovations are faced with many challenges, such as: receipt of funds, sufficiency of equipment and infrastructure, existing staff training, hiring of appropriate people, their training and further maintenance, planning of service of employees and providers as well as development and migration of them through new communication channels. Besides these challenges of implantation and development of complicated innovations, companies meet other factors, which can ruin the whole innovation implementation efforts. Many researchers emphasize that staff resistance to change is one of the factors, which is the most common reason of failure of innovation implementation.[1] The particularity of business innovation is that technological innovations in everyday life on the social level are accepted very willingly, however implementation of innovations in the workplace leads to employees' dissatisfaction and is accepted with difficulty.

In the article we analysed the following problem – can training of staff help business organisations to overcome resistance to innovation? Though mastering of technology is very useful and it is recommended for any business, not all participants of

---

[1] J. Berna-Martinez, F. Macia-Perez (2012). *Overcoming resistance to change in business innovation processes.* "International Journal Of Engineering & Technology", vol. 4, no. 3, pp. 148. http://web.ebscohost.com/ehost/pdfviewer/pdfviewer?sid=48edd70a–6590–49d1–a508–17c032fb4497%40sessionmgr12&vid=19&hid=22 (access: 31.10.2013); T. Zwick (2002). *Employee resistance against innovations*, interaktyvus. "International Journal Of Manpower", vol. 23, no. 6, p. 542. http://www.emeraldinsight.com/journals.htm?issn=01437720&volume=23&issue=6&articleid=848353&show=html (access: 31.10.2013); M. Mansor, N. Mat, N. Abu, A. Johari (2013). *Factors influencing intention resistance to change: A study of service organization in Malaysia*, interaktyvus. "Journal Of Applied Sciences Research", vol. 9, no. 4, p. 2620. http://web.ebscohost.com/ehost/detail?vid=13&sid=48edd70a–6590–49d1–a508–17c032fb4497%40sessionmgr12&hid=22&bdata=JnNpdGU9ZWhvc3QtbGl2ZQ%3d%3d#db=aci&AN=89243912 (access: 31.10.2013); J. Kvedaravičius, D. Lodienė (2002). *Pokyčiai ir organizacijų sėkmė.* "Organizacijų vadyba: sisteminai tyrimai", p. 115.

the innovation process treat it equally. This causes resistance to changes, induced by innovations.[2] According to some scholars, approximately 70% of organisations have failed to implement change programmes due their employees' resistance to changes.[3] For this reason, overcoming of employee resistance to innovation is a particularly relevant problem in areas of development of innovation, management of changes, and personnel management. The analysis of this problem and means of its solving would help to improve successful implementation of the innovation process.

REASONS FOR RESISTANCE TO INNOVATION

The most common reaction that produces the most negative consequences for innovation and its implementation in the company is employees' resistance to innovation. Scientists state that most innovation is influenced by the success of the staff, which must be taken into account while preparing the introduction of any innovation.[4] The employees' resistance to innovation is a significant barrier for required innovations and source of antagonisms in labour relations.[5]

In the scientific literature such causes for employees' resistance are accentuated: 1) they associate every change, particularly related to innovation, with a certain risk and uncertainty. According to Aladwani A. M. there are two fundamental sources of resistance to innovation – envisaged risk and habits.[6] Studies performed by J. Berna-Martinez and F. Macia-Perez have shown that reasons for resistance of secondary or higher level staff are concerns about how the hierarchical position, skills, and personal interests would change[7]; 2) staff fear of necessity to learn something new and worry regarding qualifications and so on (according to T. Zwick[8]); managers of enterprises have to take into account the fact that a higher prevalence of inside resistance exists against these innovations for which employees see their jobs threatened or if the planned innovation reduces the payback time of the necessary qualifications; as Berna-Martinez and Macia-Perez state, resistance of lower-level employees is mostly determined by lacunas of technological knowledge, which leads to a lack of confidence of

---

    [2] M. Rashid, M. Sohail, M. Aslam (2011). *Impact of employee adaptability to change towards organizational competitive advantage*, interaktyvus. "Global Journal of Management and Business Research", vol. 11, no. 7, p. 11. http://www.journalofbusiness.org/index.php/GJMBR/article/view/540/481 (access: 5.11.2013).

    [3] M. Mansor, N. Mat, N. Abu, A. Johari, *op.cit.*, p. 2621.

    [4] S. Pogosian, I. Dzemyda (2012). *Inovacijos versle ir jas lemiantys veiksniai teoriniu ir politiniu aspektu.* "Ekonomika ir vadyba: aktualijos ir perspektyvos", vol. 1, no. 25, p. 67.

    [5] T. Zwick, *op.cit.*, p. 542.

    [6] A.M. Aladwani (2001). *Change management strategies for successful ERP implementation*, interaktyvus. "Business Process Management Journal", vol. 7, no. 3, p. 269. http://www.emeraldinsight.com/case_studies. htm/case_studies.htm?articleid=843482&show=html (access: 31.10.2013).

    [7] J. Berna-Martinez, F. Macia–Perez, *op.cit.*, p. 159.

    [8] T. Zwick, *op.cit.*, p. 551.

employees.[9] Employees resist changes because they have to learn something new; there is resistance because people feel excluded, they are afraid of studying new things[10]; 3) ignorance and lack of sufficient information about innovation and changes, caused by it. In S. Mittal's opinion in most cases it is not a contradiction against the favour of a new process, but often fear of the unknown future and the ability to adapt to it[11]; 4) of particular importance is not so much the same change or innovation, but management of its implementation. The studies, carried out by R. Van Dick showed that a significant component of resistance of personalities is namely resistance to change management.[12]

Other reasons are indicated as well: M. Mansor, N. Mat, N. Abu, and A. Johari[13] indicate that instability of provisions has a positive and significant impact on the intention to resist changes; J.P. Kotter and L.A. Schlesinger[14] indicate 4 most frequent reasons why people resist changes, i.e.: desire not to lose something valuable, wrong perception of change and its implication, belief that the change does not make any sense to the organisation, and low tolerance for change.

METHODS

In order to examine the identified problem quantitative research has been conducted – written survey of employees of a group of enterprises of public passenger transport. The instrument of the survey was a questionnaire. As participants of study we chose the enterprises of Klaipėda Public Passenger Transport, which provide passenger services in an unanimously coordinated system. Nine such companies operate in Klaipėda city and they employ approximately 501 employees.

The choice of such sector of enterprises is based on the fact that over the last 5 years in the system of Klaipėda Public Passenger Transport the following innovations have

---

[9] J. Berna-Martinez, F. Macia-Perez, *op.cit.*, p. 159.

[10] P. Jager (2001). *Resistance to change: A new view of an old problem.* "The Futurist", vol. 35, no. 3, p. 27. http://www.gfoa.org/services/documents/dunham3.pdf (access: 14.11.2013).

[11] S. Mittal (2012). *Managing employee resistance to change a comparative study of indianan organizations and MNCSIin Delh–NCR Region.* "Researchers World: Journal Of Arts, Science & Commerce", vol. 3, no. 4, pp. 64–71. http://web.ebscohost.com/ehost/pdfviewer/pdfviewer?sid=48edd70a–6590–49d1–a508–17c032fb4497%40sessionmgr12&vid=13&hid=22 (access: 21.10.2013).

[12] R. Van Dijk, R. Van Dick (2009). *Navigating organizational change: Change leaders, employee resistance and work-based identities.* "Journal of Change Management", vol. 9, no. 2, p. 158. http://www.tandfonline.com/doi/full/10.1080/14697010902879087 (access: 31.10.2013).

[13] M. Mansor, N. Mat, N. Abu, A. Johari (2013). *Factors influencing intention resistance to change: A study of service organization in Malaysia.* "Journal Of Applied Sciences Research", vol. 9, no. 4, pp. 2620–2630. http://web.ebscohost.com/ehost/detail?vid=13&sid=48edd70a–6590–49d1–a508–17c032fb4497%40sessionmgr12&hid=22&bdata=JnNpdGU9ZWhvc3QtbGl2ZQ%3d%3d#db=aci&AN=89243912 (access: 31.10.2013).

[14] J. Kotter, L.A. Schlesinger (1979). *Choosing strategies for change*, interaktyvus. "Harvard Business Review", vol. 57, no. 2, pp. 106–114. http://web.ebscohost.com/ehost/pdfviewer/pdfviewer?sid=cb47c264–0656–4ac3–ad3e–46a5f629d980%40sessionmgr11&vid=15&hid=25 (access: 14.11.2013).

been introduced: e-ticket system, a system of bus travel routes and positioning, a system of passenger information as well as an integrated network of routes. Having introduced these innovations, public transport fares and the net cost of tickets decreased, expenditures of passenger transport were optimised, also the number of passengers and travels increased. In this way, the innovation has led to significant changes in all enterprises of this sector. The need for innovations in this sector is particularly high as it concerns a large part of the society, is concerned with technological processes and is directly related with improvement of environment protection in the city and region. In the future in this sector the following innovations are planned: integration of the e-ticket system with common electronic payment and systems of distribution of other services, a car-sharing system as well as other innovations. The survey was conducted from May till June of 2014.

In order to process the data, obtained during the research, version 19.0 of program of statistical analysis and data processing SPSS (Statistical Package for the Social Sciences) was used.

The credibility of the questionnaire was determined by calculating the Cronbach's alfa coefficient (0.842). For the purpose of determining the statistical significance of respondents' answers we applied the procedure of testing of a non-parametric hypothesis; we counted the correlation coefficients; we applied factor analysis as well.

RESULTS

The study revealed that the statistical average respondent is a working-age man. In terms of their age, most of the respondents were from 45–54 and 55–64 age groups. By education, the majority of the respondents is comprised of holders of secondary (31.6%) and specialised (26.1%) secondary education, and higher education (25.6%). According to their positions the respondents are distributed as follows: almost 80% of respondents (79.4%) consists of drivers, 10.4% – operating personnel, 4.9% – specialists, 3.2% – accountants, while managers constitute 2.4%.

The research revealed that most of the respondents have a positive attitude towards the implemented innovations. Managers, accountants, and specialists, i.e. persons with higher university and non-university higher education have the least negative attitude towards implemented innovations. Also, the tendency was noticed that male workers have much more sceptical attitude than female workers towards any actions of managers while implementing innovation.

The respondents were asked to evaluate which actions of managers would be the most effective for reducing resistance to innovation. Distribution of the respondents' answers is given in table 1 below.

Table 1. Evaluation of actions of managers while reducing resistance to innovation (%)

Statement	I agree completely (5)	I agree (4)	I am not sure (3)	I do not agree (2)	I do not agree completely (1)
1 Creation of a generally favourable environment for promotion of innovation in the organisation	19.4	32.6	33.9	11.2	2.9
2 Involvement of employees as the main actors of change in the process of innovation	21.1	39.3	24.8	12.4	2.5
3 Staff training	23.3	44.2	15.0	12.5	5.0
4 Material incentive of employees	32.8	32.8	10.7	8.2	15.6
5 Coercion and threats against resisting employees	0.8	4,2	12.5	29.6	52.9
6 Rendering of innovation benefits to employees	18.3	41.1	17.0	15.8	7.9
7 Permanent information of employees about the situation	27.2	41.2	15.2	12.8	3.7

Source: formed by authors on the basis of survey data.

On the basis of the data, presented in the table, it could be stated that the respondents valued most favourably those actions of managers, which, in their opinion, would be the most effective while reducing resistance to innovation: material incentive of employees, permanent information of employees about the situation, and staff training. The respondents were most doubtful regarding creation of a generally favourable environment and involvement of the employees. Respondents did not approve the usage of coercion and threats against resisting employees the most.

The calculated Spearman's correlation coefficients demonstrate that there is reliance of evaluations on gender (we counted average correlation coefficients for respectively listed actions: $r_s = 0.056$; $r_s = 0.051$; $r_s = 0.049$; $r_s = 0.051$).

Considering that the majority of employees of transportation companies are men, it can be individually assessed how opinions regarding actions of managers, devoted to reduce the resistance to innovation, are distributed between male respondents. The results are presented below in table 2.

On the basis of the data, presented in table 2, it could be seen that these actions of managers as material incentive of employees (32.3%), permanent information of employees (27.2%, answer "I agree completely"), and staff training (20.7%, answer "I agree completely") could be met by male employees with the most approval. A tendency is noticed that the older the worker, the less influence of material advantages she/he experiences evaluating more favourably those innovations, which are implemented in the company (Spearman's correlation coefficient $r_s = 0.63$).

By education the opinion of the respondents statistically significantly differed only in two cases – creation of a generally favourable environment for promotion of innovation in the organisation and rendering of innovation benefits to employees. In the first case employees, those with a university degree, almost did not hesitate

Table 2. Distribution of male opinion regarding actions of managers, devoted to reduce the resistance to innovation (%)

Statement	I agree completely (5)	I agree (4)	I am not sure (3)	I do not agree (2)	I do not agree completely (1)
1	Creation of a generally favourable environment for promotion of innovation in the organisation	17.5	29.9	36.6	12.9	3.1
2	Involvement of employees as the main actors of change in the process of innovation	17.5	39.2	25.8	14.9	2.6
3	Staff training	20.7	42.5	16.1	15.0	5.7
4	Material incentive of employees	32.3	30.3	10.3	8.7	18.5
5	Coercion and threats against resisting employees	1.0	4.1	13.0	26.9	54.9
6	Rendering of innovation benefits to employees	17.1	37.3	18.1	18.7	8.8
7	Permanent information of employees about the situation	27.2	39.0	15.9	14.9	3.1

Source: formed by authors on the basis of calculation.

regarding this measure's efficiency (creation of a generally favourable environment for promotion of innovation in the organisation and rendering of innovation benefits to employees) (even 90% agreed with the effectiveness of the action). The least approval was expressed by those with secondary education (there were only 33.3% of respondents, which agreed with the effectiveness of this measure). Among these respondents there is the largest number of unsympathetic respondents (22.3%).

In the second case, similar tendencies are noticed: those with a university degree (95%) expressed approval, whereas employees with secondary education had a sceptical attitude (almost 36% expressed their disapproval).

Spearman's correlation coefficients demonstrate sufficiently strong correlation (in both cases $r_s = 0.063$). The conclusion can be drawn – the higher the employee's education, the more favourably the employee is inclined to evaluate organisational (i.e. not personal) measures/actions of managers while reducing resistance to innovations.

The results of the study are partly proved by the raised hypothesis – resistance to innovation is lower in those organisations where more attention is paid to staff training. However, attention must be paid to the fact that staff training was assessed subjectively (i.e. the respondents themselves had to evaluate the staff training situation in their company), an objective evaluation was not performed i.e. it was not evaluated how much and what kind of training really took place in every interviewed company. It should also be noted that more female workers than men from the enterprises expressed favour to training.

Attention should be paid to the objective circumstances, which can lead to limitations of the study results. It should be noted that the research was performed only in one city, Klaipėda (Lithuania); only one specific sector was investigated – companies, operating in the system of public passenger transport. These companies also have their own specifics – most of the workers are men, aged 45 to 64 years, education – secondary, secondary special, or higher. Innovations, which are implemented in these enterprises are particularly specific and they are often determined not by the managers' desire to improve organisational performance, but by the objective of state institutions or their bodies in their goal to improve the system of public transport, to make it as comfortable as possible for its users.

FINAL CONSIDERATIONS

Attention should be paid that those respondents who indicated that learning at work is constantly encouraged and favourable conditions are created for it tend to state that they react positively to processes of implementation of innovation. Those, who have a sceptical attitude towards staff training in their companies, tend to choose neutral positions in processes of implementation of innovation, they tend to wait for what will come. Analysing the responses of the respondents regarding the factors that determine their positive attitude to innovation, it was established that most workers (35.3%) fully accepted that the positive attitude is mostly promoted by material incentive; not less approval (33.6%) was given to participation in training and raising of qualifications.

While organisations are seeking to overcome resistance to innovation, such means as material incentive, permanent information of employees about the situation, and staff training received the most approval of the respondents. The respondents hesitated most whether creation of a favourable environment for innovation and involvement of employees are the appropriate means of overcoming resistance. The respondents did not approve the usage of coercion and threats against resisting employees the most. The research revealed that the higher the employee's education, the more favourably the employee is inclined to evaluate organisational (i.e. not personal) measures/actions of managers reducing resistance to innovation.

On the basis of the performed research it can be stated that staff training can be one of the means to overcome staff resistance to innovation, but it must be used in combination with other means. It is recommended while implementing innovation in companies to apply a precautionary model of overcoming staff resistance to innovation, which consists of 3 stages: 1) there are identified social-demographic characteristics of employees, because they can have an influence on the positive or negative attitude of employees regarding innovation: gender, education, age of employees, position (the research data revealed that men are more sceptical than women, that educated employees meet innovation more favourably and so on); 2) from the beginning of the process of implementation of innovation basic and additional actions regarding all employees are taken. The basic actions are: staff training, material incentive for employees, and permanent information of the employees about the situation. Additional actions are: creation of a generally favourable environment for promotion of innovation; involvement of employees as the main actors of change in the process of innovation; rendering of innovation benefits to employees; usage of pressure (coercion and threats) against resisting employees; 3) having started to implement innovation in the organisation, having performed actions of the first and second stages, it is necessary to use monitoring for observation how staff reacts to the implemented innovation. Having identified and established the attitude of employees, the means, which are applied, are differentiated according to the employee's position. Since by empirical research it was established that for those, who react differently to innovation a greater effect can be made by different means, in the third stage of reducing of staff resistance to innovation the employees are grouped according to their attitude to innovation (Negative/Neutral/Positive) and according to possibilities of the organisation to apply the most effective means to them. It should be noted that "Participation in training and raising of qualifications" are efficient means while overcoming resistance to innovation at both the negative and positive attitudes to the latest innovations.

References

Aladwani A.M. (2001). *Change management strategies for successful ERP implementation*, interaktyvus. "Business Process Management Journal", vol. 7, no. 3, pp. 266–275, http://www.emeraldinsight.com/case_studies.htm/case_studies.htm?articleid=843482&show=html (access: 31.10.2013).

Berna-Martinez J., Macia-Perez F. (2012). *Overcoming resistance to change in business innovation processes*. "International Journal Of Engineering & Technology", vol. 4, no. 3, pp. 148–161. http://web.ebscohost.com/ehost/pdfviewer/pdfviewer?sid=48edd70a–6590–49d1–a508–17c032fb4497%40sessionmgr12&vid=19&hid=22 (access: 31.10.2013).

Jager P. (2001). *Resistance to change: A new view of an old problem*. "The Futurist", vol. 35, no. 3, pp. 24–27. http://www.gfoa.org/services/documents/dunham3.pdf (access: 14.11.2013).

Kotter J., Schlesinger L.A. (1979). *Choosing strategies for change*. "Harvard Business Review", vol. 57, no. 2, pp. 106–114. http://web.ebscohost.com/ehost/pdfviewer/pdfviewer?sid=cb47c264–0656–4ac3–ad3e–46a5f629d980%40sessionmgr11&vid=15&hid=25 (access: 14.11.2013).

Kvedaravičius J., Lodienė D. (2002). *Pokyčiai ir organizacijų sėkmė*. "Organizacijų vadyba: sisteminai tyrimai", pp. 114–124.

Mansor M., Mat N., Abu N., Johari A. (2013). *Factors influencing intention resistance to change: A study of service organization in Malaysia*. "Journal Of Applied Sciences Research", vol. 9, no. 4, pp. 2620–2630. http://web.ebscohost.com/ehost/detail?vid=13&sid=48edd70a–6590–49d1–a508–17c032fb4497%-40sessionmgr12&hid=22&bdata=JnNpdGU9ZWhvc3QtbGl2ZQ%3d%3d#db=aci&AN=89243912 (access: 31.10.2013).

Mittal S. (2012). *Managing employee resistance to change a comparative study of indianan organizations and MNCSIin Delh–NCR Region*. "Researchers World: Journal Of Arts, Science & Commerce", vol. 3, no. 4, pp. 64–71. http://web.ebscohost.com/ehost/pdfviewer/pdfviewer?sid=48edd70a–6590–49d1–a508–17c032fb4497%40sessionmgr12&vid=13&hid=22 (access: 21.10.2013).

Pogosian S., Dzemyda I. (2012). *Inovacijos versle ir jas lemiantys veiksniai teoriniu ir politiniu aspektu*. "Ekonomika ir vadyba: aktualijos ir perspektyvos", vol. 1, no. 25, pp. 63–76.

Rashid M., Sohail M., Aslam M. (2011). *Impact of employee adaptability to change towards organizational competitive advantage*. "Global Journal of Management and Business Research", vol. 11, no. 7, pp. 9–15. http://www.journalofbusiness.org/index.php/GJMBR/article/view/540/481 (access: 5.11.2013).

Svirskienė G. (2005). *Naujosios žinių ekonomikos iššūkiai ir organizacinis pasipriešinimas naujovėms*. "Ekonomika ir vadyba: aktualijos ir perspektyvos", vol. 5, pp. 365–372.

Van Dijk R., Van Dick R. (2009). *Navigating organizational change: Change leaders, employee resistance and work-based identities*. "Journal of Change Management", vol. 9, no. 2, pp. 143–163. http://www.tandfonline.com/doi/full/10.1080/14697010902879087 (access: 31.10.2013).

Zwick T. (2002). *Employee resistance against innovationss*. "International Journal Of Manpower", vol. 23, no. 6, pp. 542–552. http://www.emeraldinsight.com/journals.htm?issn=01437720&volume=23&issue=6&articleid=848353&show=html (access: 31.10.2013).

Joanna Szymonek
Jagiellonian University
e-mail: joanna.szymonek@doctoral.uj.edu.pl

FOSTERING RESPONSIBLE BUSINESS CONDUCT IN FOREIGN DIRECT INVESTMENT IN CEE COUNTRIES. THE ROLE OF THE STATE

Abstract

Background. Multinational companies are seen as the key players of global markets. Despite the growing power of business and multinational corporations, the state has the role to play in the execution of responsible and lawful behaviour of companies through employment of a variety of measures e.g. legal provisions, judicial mechanisms, and internationally recognised soft law standards.

Research aims. The aim of this article is to discuss the role of the state in providing the framework ensuring responsible business conduct through the implementation of the OECD Guidelines for Multinational Enterprises and effectiveness of functioning of the OECD National Contact Points (NCPs) as tools for observance of corporate behaviour.

Methodology. The argumentation presented is based on literature review, conference materials, documentary and internet sources analysis and synthesis, as well as interviews conducted with representatives of the OECD National Contact Points located in selected CEE countries and Western Europe.

Keywords: corporate social responsibility, foreign direct investment, OECD Guidelines for Multinational Enterprises.

INTRODUCTION

Globalization, internationalisation of business ,and the processes of privatisation of the state function, shifted the power from the state to the market, whereas multinational companies (MNC) have been perceived as the primary shapers of contemporary global economy.[1] According to Dylus, the crisis of state structures is caused by unilateral

---

[1] P. Dicken (2003). *Global Shift Reshaping the Global Economic Map in the 21ˢᵗ Century.* Sage Publication, London.

dynamics of economic growth rooted in the lack of proportion between politics, economy, and society.[2] Foreign direct investment (FDI) is considered as a measure of activities of MNC.[3] The state uses various strategies to attract FDI, that plays an important role in development of economies especially in the context of technology transfer, improvement of productivity, creation of workplaces, transfer of managerial skills, and gaining access to global markets.[4] That was also the case of Central and Eastern European (CEE) countries that remain attractive areas to establish business operations.[5] Despite certain benefits associated with MNC's, some shadows also emerge mostly in the area of violations of human rights, tax evasion, environmental pollution, etc. The need for greater transparency and accountability of MNCs seems to be getting high priority in the global debate on socially responsible business, especially in the context of the upcoming legislation on non-financial reporting of enterprises.[6] The concept of corporate social responsibility (CSR) is not new, current definition specifies CSR as the "responsibility of the enterprises for their impact on society".[7] This approach revised the role of enterprises in contemporary economy and society. Some authors claim that corporations use confusing and complex corporate structures in order to separate the parent company from local subsidiaries, thus protecting MNC from legal liability, but retaining the control over subsidiaries through creation of special policies, technological, and financial power.[8] A more radical opinion was expressed by Ireland stating that "corporate legal form was, and is in large political construct developed to accommodate and protect rentier investors, a construct which institutionalizes irresponsibility".[9] As business does not operate in a vacuum, corporate misconduct should be a subject of interest to the state. The aim of this article is to discuss the role of the state in fostering responsible business conduct in the context of implementation of the OECD Guidelines for Multinational Enterprises (OECD Guidelines).

The role of the state – United Nations perspective

The approach to understanding the role of the state is related to the Guiding Principles on Business and Human Rights as a tool for implementation of the United Nations

[2] A. Dylus (2005). *Globalizacja, refleksje etyczne.* Zakład Narodowy im. Ossolińskich, Wrocław.

[3] P. Dicken, *op.cit.*

[4] P. Enderwick (2005). *Attracting "desirable" FDI: Theory and evidence.* "Transnational Corporations", vol. 14, no. 2, pp. 93–119.

[5] EY (2014), *EY's Attractiveness Survey Europe 2014. Back in the Game.* http://www.ey.com/GL/en/Issues/Business-environment/european-attractiveness-survey (access: 10.05.2015).

[6] Ministry of Economy (2015). *Nowe przepisy UE dotyczące ujawniania danych pozafinansowych.* http://www.mg.gov.pl/node/22566 (access: 21.01.2015).

[7] European Commission (2011). *Renewed EU strategy 2011–2014 for Corporate Social Responsibility,* European Commission, Brussels.

[8] R. Meeran (1999). *Liability of Multinational Corporations: A Critical Stage.* http://www.labournet.net/images/cape/campanal.htm (access: 20.02.2015).

[9] P. Ireland (2010). *Limited liability, shareholders rights and problem of corporate irresponsibility.* "Cambridge Journal of Economics", vol. 34, p. 837.

(UN) "Protect, Respect and Remedy Framework".[10] The framework proposed by professor John Ruggy is build on III pillars i.e. "The state duty to protect human rights", followed by "The Corporate responsibility to respect human rights" and the last pillar "Access to remedies". Although all of these pillars are linked and interpenetrating, the article will focus on the first pillar. Understanding of the state's duty to protect is composed from the set of foundational and operational principles guiding the state through the actions that should be taken in order to ensure respecting of human rights. Two approaches can be distinguished i.e. protection of citizens from unlawful behaviour of MNC's through regulatory measures, legislation, punishment, adjudication, and effective policies preventing enterprises from further abuses. The second approach: encouraging enterprises towards greater responsibility, is also embedded in a soft regulatory framework. The state uses a variety of measures e.g. legal framework and soft law i.e. the Guiding Principles on Business and Human Rights or/and the OECD Guidelines. Non-effective policies, weak regulatory framework, less severe penalisation may in some instances cause purposeful irresponsibility of MNCs. Weak legislation, legal loopholes, or lower labour standards are often used by businesses to reduce their operational costs, claiming in the same time their responsibility trough well developed PR strategies. The protective and preventive role of state is therefore important to ensure lawful and responsible behaviour of companies. In case of FDI, the state often faces a particular clash of interests between the expectations of foreign investors and citizens. Multinationals tend to exercise their power and dictate the conditions of doing business by using the threat of delocalisation i.e. moving the investment to another country[11], even though the use of this threat is forbidden under the Guidelines.[12] Despite the growing role of international business, the regulatory function of the state in enforcement of law and international standards should not be forgotten.

Measures and tools in the hands of a responsible state – the OECD Guidelines for Multinational Enterprises

Apart from legal measures, the state can influence business behaviour using non-legally binding standards such as the OECD Guidelines. They represent a set of recommendations on responsible companies' behaviour created by governments adhering to the OECD Declaration on Investment and Multinational Enterprises.[13] Under this declaration, governments are obliged to promote and implement the OECD Guidelines, through the activity of the National Contact Points (NCPs). Poland, Hungary, Czech

---

[10] United Nations (2011). *Guiding Principles on Business and Human Rights*. United Nations, New York – Geneva.

[11] P. Marginson (2006). *Europeanisation and Regime Competition*. "Industrielle Beziehungen", vol. 13, no. 2, pp. 98–113.

[12] OECD (2011). *OECD Guidelines for Multinational Enterprises*, OECD Publishing. http://dx.doi.org/10.1787/9789264115415-en (access: 10.05.2015).

[13] *Ibidem.*

Republic, and Slovakia, as big FDI receivers, adhered to the OECD Declaration. The NCPs started to work on complaint procedures concerning corporate misconduct in the year 2000. The complaints have usually been submitted by representatives of civil society or trade unions, which is related to parties involved in OECD activities i.e. the Business and Industry Advisory Committee to the OECD (BIAC), The Trade Union Advisory Committee to the OECD (TUAC), and representative of civil society i.e. OECD Watch. In 2011, the OECD Guidelines were revised together with the revision of effectiveness of OECD NCPs. The shift of changes resulting from the revision aimed at mediation, conciliation, and extrajudicial dispute resolution that should be offered by NCPs. In the revised version of the Guidelines' compliance with domestic law was explicitly underlined as well as a clear connection with new definition of CSR i.e. companies should assess and identify the risks of negative impact of their business operations and implement strategies that would prevent the occurrence of risks. The document also made clear that compliance with the Guidelines covers all parties i.e. parent companies and local entities.[14] The nexus "state and business" lies in the enforcement by the state of responsible behaviour of business.

Social monitoring of MNC's behaviour

Social monitoring of MNCs' compliance with the OECD Guidelines is conducted by civil society organisations (CSO) and trade unions. Both of them developed monitoring tools revealing corporate misconduct. Those tools deliver information about abusive cases and the mechanisms and actions used by NCPs to resolve the conflicts. The specific website established by TUAC provides comparative information on cases submitted by trade unions worldwide and information on the functioning of particular OECD NCPs in the adhering country. The representatives of civil society also conduct their monitoring although a different model of presenting information is used. The effects of monitoring will be presented further in the text.

DISCUSSION AND RESULTS

In the course of analysis of the collected data, some similarities in OECD NCP operations in CEE countries have emerged. Firstly, Polish, Hungarian, Slovak, and Czech OECD NCPs were established in a single government department i.e. in the Polish Information and Foreign Investment Agency, Hungarian Ministry of National Economy, Slovak Ministry of Economy, and finally Czech Ministry of Industry and Trade. The

---

[14] OECD (2012). *2011 Update of OECD Guidelines for Multinational Enterprises. Comparative Table of Changes to the 2000 Texts.* https://mneguidelines.oecd.org/text/ (access: 10.05.2015).

other similarities arise in the lack of tripartite models (Poland, Hungary, and Slovakia) which means that other parties i.e. CSOs or trade unions are not involved in NCP operations. Other approaches e.g. creating multistakeholder oversight or an advisory body is also lacking. According to the analysis made by TUAC, apart from the Czech Republic, none of mentioned above NCPs has taken steps to ensure its impartiality. In comparison to models established by other OECD countries e.g. France, tripartite structure of NCP is composed of representatives of a variety of ministries, employers, and trade union organisations. Similarly Denmark has created the Independent Expert Body with participation of representatives of a variety of ministries, employer organisations, trade unions, and academic institutions. The lack of engagement of other stakeholders, such as social partners, CSOs, or academics may lead to a lack of impartiality in the course of dispute resolution. This could be the case of the Polish NCPs, established in an Agency servicing foreign investors, what may question the impartiality of procedures of handling complaints, as the Agency tends to represent the interests of investors. According to the available sources, among CEE countries, NCPs in the Czech Republic received 5 complaints submitted by Czech trade unions and the Polish NCPs received 4 complaints, whereas Hungarian and Slovak trade unions did not submit any complaints concerning violations of the OECD Guidelines. Those cases concerned violations of the right to organise and collective bargaining (in the Czech Republic), violations of trade union rights, trade union activists' discrimination, and sexual harassment in case of Poland (TUAC, n.d). In 99% of complaints filed by trade unions worldwide, corporate abuses have occurred in employment and industrial relations i.e. right to organise and collective bargaining, as well as information and consultation procedures e.g. providing information on restructuring with major employment effects i.e. closure of a particular entity followed by collective redundancies. In some countries e.g. Poland, the abuse of trade unions' rights is not only a lack of compliance with the OECD Guidelines, but most of all a breach of domestic law.[15] In case of Hungary the complaint was filed by an independent lawyer representing a worker of a multinational enterprise and concerned a health and safety issue.[16] Despite the fact that NCPs should be impartial in handling the complaints facilitating dialogue between parties, the structure of NCPs and their location may affect the results of handling procedures. The OECD Watch recommends avoiding establishing of the NCPs in a single government department, and advises to set up oversight, or a multistakeholder advisory or steering body that will ensure impartiality of actions taken by OECD NCPs.[17] The mediation role of the NCPs provides the victims with faster and cheaper access to solutions than typical judicial mechanisms. However, this

---

[15] J. Unterschutz (2009). *Prawo pracy. Zarys instytucji*. WSAiB, Gdynia.

[16] OECD (2007). *Annual Report on the OECD Guidelines for Multinational Enterprises 2007. Corporate Responsibility in the Financial Sector*. http://www.oecdbookshop.org/en/browse/title-detail/Annual-Report-on-the-OECD-Guidelines-for-Multinational-Enterprises-2007/?K=5L4JHXPQN8XS (access: 10.05.2015).

[17] C. Daniel, J. Wilde-Ramsing, K. Genovese, V. Sandjojo (2015). *Remedy Remains Rare. An Analysis of 15 Years of NCP Cases and Their Contribution to Improve Access to Remedy for Victims of Corporate Misconduct*. OECD Watch, Amsterdam.

can be possible when the proceedings are impartial and access to remedies is facilitated. Remedies can be considered in various ways e.g. it could be compensation for harm, improvement of conditions for the victims of corporate abuse, improvement in the area of corporate policies and strategies[18], and finally judicial remedies provided in domestic law. It is worth noticing that the state is responsible for providing an effective domestic judicial mechanism, as well as non-judicial mechanisms when addressing corporate abuse.[19] Therefore, the effectiveness of NCPs can be considered through the lenses of state accountability. The analysis of functioning of OECD NCPs revealed that the model used by CEE countries (apart from the Czech Republic) carries the risks of promoting business interests over protection of potential victims. The NCP's structure can determine positive results with some remedy-related outcomes. That was the case of NCP operating as an independent expert body, tripartite structure, or oversight multistakeholder committee. Another weakness of the NCP were accessibility e.g. access to information, technical knowledge how to fill out the forms in a proper manner in order to get through the initial stage of processing the compliant; reliance on the statement of one party i.e. company. An important issue is also handling the situation when a company is reluctant to answer NCP's inquiry or refuses to join the mediation process. The analysis has shown that in some cases despite the existence of strong evidence of a company's misconduct and refusal to respond to the complaints, the NCPs tend to avoid giving MNC the non-compliant status in the final statement issued in the process of handling the grievance. The experience of the Norwegian NCP proved that the use of "non-compliant" determination was a strong motivation for companies to join the mediation rather than end-up with such a negative label.[20] Another finding indicates the rejection of allegations on future harms by NCPs. The revision of the OECD Guidelines in 2011 enables NCPs to prevent parties from further conflicts, facilitating dialogue and prevent business from causing potential, future harm. This approach was based on due diligence and human rights-related provisions introduced in the revised version of the OECD Guidelines recommending companies to assess the potential negative impact and risks associated with business operations.[21] Despite the clear guidance concerning avoidance of the potential harm, NCPs have often refused to accept the allegations associated with potential risks of actions planned by the MNCs.[22] Another accusation concentrates on high expectations in providing evidence of breaching the OECD Guidelines. Some NCPs required inappropriate evidence, impossible to deliver by the complainants. In this case the complaint was rejected at the initial stage without a chance to resolve the problem. This approach tends to create concession for corporate misconduct and may deepen confusion about the real role of NCP's in the area of dialogue facilitation and mitigation of conflicts.[23]

---

[18] *Ibidem.*
[19] United Nations, *op.cit.*
[20] C. Daniel, J. Wilde-Ramsing, K. Genovese, V. Sandjojo, *op.cit.*
[21] OECD (2011), *op.cit.*
[22] C. Daniel, J. Wilde-Ramsing, K. Genovese, V. Sandjojo, *op.cit.*
[23] *Ibidem.*

Despite the presented convergences in NCP's operations in CEE countries, the level of development of Czech, Hungarian, and Polish NCPs varies. The common weaknesses emerged in limited resources (financial and human) dedicated to these activities, relatively low public awareness of the OECD Guidelines which may negatively affect the prospects of long term stability of NCP development. However, some NCP improvement activities have been observed in CEE countries. Although the most significant steps in providing greater impartiality appear to be an introduction of a quadripartite structure of NCP in the Czech Republic, the risk of lack of cooperation between members of the Czech NCP was raised. Furthermore, all complaints were submitted before 2011, so it is hard to assess the effectiveness of the Czech NCP after the reform. Some changes have also been observed in the Polish NCP e.g. introduction of new procedures, organising educational and awareness raising activities in cooperation with the trade unions, employers, and civil society organisations. In the Polish NCP the issue of staff rotation and lack of multistakeholder oversight/advisory body or tripartite structure remains problematic. Political wiliness to the introduction of changes is needed in order to make a step forward. In all countries limited experience with mediation procedures is noted, therefore it is difficult to assess NCP effectiveness in this role. Hungary seems to be the country that still faces difficulties with rather basic activities. The available materials and publications are not widely translated into the national language which reduces the scope of impact and accessibility to educational resources for the companies and their stakeholders. All countries see some opportunities in further development, all of them have managed to establish relations with themselves and other NCPs worldwide, all of them are engaged in the process of education and development, nevertheless these cooperative attitudes are observed among NCPs' representatives/officers, but in order to achieve greater effectiveness they should be reflected in political decisions of institutions where NCP is housed.

CONCLUSIONS

The analysis of NCP's effectiveness from a civil society perspective does not depict an optimistic picture. For 250 complaints submitted in 15 years there was no compensation for the victims of corporate misconduct, in 1% of cases improvement of conditions for the victims was noted, 8% of cases led to improvement of corporate policies and in 8% of cases companies/ NCPs acknowledged business irresponsibility. Most of European complaints filed by representatives of society or individuals concentrated on human rights violations and came from United Kingdom and the Netherlands.[24] The number of cases submitted to NCPs by trade unions located in the CEE is relatively low in comparison to Western countries

---

[24] *Ibidem.*

e.g. France – 11 cases, Netherlands and the UK – 15 cases each (TUAC, n.d.). Explanatory factors emerging from the findings indicate a lack of knowledge on how to properly prepare the complaints, lack of impartiality resulting in lack of trust, bias in recognising the case and reliance on information provided by the company, lack of multistakeholder structures and effective cooperation between stakeholders, actions taken in favour of companies, fear of losing investors, etc. Establishing the OECD NCP is an obligation of the adhering country and the state decides how to fulfil its responsibility in providing effective dispute resolutions for conflicted parties. This however, requires more investment, dedicated budget, cooperation with social partners, civil society organisations, academic institutions, and most of all, decisive political steps.

The analysis shows that in some cases instead of effective mechanisms ensuring observance of the OECD Guidelines the state created only an illusion of accountability.[25] Although the practices of business are essential to ensure responsible behaviour of MNCs, the state has to provide a political, strategic, and operational framework executing and facilitating responsible business conduct and protecting citizens from corporate wrongdoing. This obligation lies in the state's responsibility for providing economic and social development of the country not only in the short term, but also in the long run.

References

Daniel C., Wilde-Ramsing J., Genovese K., Sandjojo V. (2015). *Remedy Remains Rare. An Analysis of 15 Years of NCP Cases and Their Contribution to Improve Access to Remedy for Victims of Corporate Misconduct*. OECD Watch, Amsterdam.

Dicken P. (2003*). Global Shift Reshaping the Global Economic Map in the 21ˢᵗ Century*. Sage Publication, London.

Dylus A. (2005). *Globalizacja, refleksje etyczne*. Zakład Narodowy im. Ossolińskich, Wrocław.

Enderwick P. (2005). *Attracting "desirable" FDI: Theory and evidence*. "Transnational Corporations", vol. 14, no. 2, pp. 93–119.

European Commission (2011). *Renewed EU strategy 2011–2014 for Corporate Social Responsibility*. European Commission, Brussels.

EY (2014), *EY's Attractiveness Survey Europe 2014. Back in the Game*. http://www.ey.com/GL/en/Issues/Business-environment/european-attractiveness-survey (access: 10.05.2015).

Ireland P. (2010). *Limited liability, shareholders rights and problem of corporate irresponsibility*. "Cambridge Journal of Economics", vol. 34, p. 837.

Marginson P. (2006). *Europeanisation and regime competition*. "Industrielle Beziehungen", vol. 13, no. 2, pp. 98–113.

Meeran R. (1999). *Liability of Multinational Corporations: A Critical Stage*. http://www.labournet.net/images/cape/campanal.htm (access: 20.02.2015).

Ministry of Economy (2015). *Nowe przepisy UE dotyczące ujawniania danych pozafinansowych*. http://www.mg.gov.pl/node/22566 (access: 21.01.2015).

OECD (2011). *OECD Guidelines for Multinational Enterprises, OECD Publishing*. http://dx.doi.org/10.1787/9789264115415-en (access: 10.05.2015).

---

[25] *Ibidem.*

OECD (2012). *2011 Update of OECD Guidelines for Multinational Enterprises. Comparative Table of Changes to the 2000 Texts*. https://mneguidelines.oecd.org/text/ (access: 10.05.2015).

OECD (2007). *Annual Report on the OECD Guidelines for Multinational Enterprises 2007. Corporate Responsibility in the Financial Sector*. http://www.oecdbookshop.org/en/browse/title-detail/Annual-Report-on-the-OECD-Guidelines-for-Multinational-Enterprises-2007/?K=5L4JHXPQN8XS (access: 10.05.2015).

Trade Union Advisory Committee (n.d.). *Trade Union Cases OECD Guidelines for Multinational Enterprises*. http://www.tuacoecdmneguidelines.org/Home.asp (access: 10.05.2015).

United Nations (2011). *Guiding Principles on Business and Human Rights*. United Nations New York – Geneva.

Unterschutz J. (2009). *Prawo pracy. Zarys instytucji*. WSAiB, Gdynia.

Andrea Benedek
Károly Róbert College
e-mail: beandi75@gmail.com

Katalin Takács-György
Károly Róbert College
e-mail: tgyk@karolyrobert.hu

EXAMINATION OF THE CORPORATE SOCIAL RESPONSIBILITY TO INTERNAL FACTORS OF CORPORATE MANAGERS

Abstract

Background. In the last few years not only the economists but also researchers from other fields such as law, media, etc. have been interested in corporate social responsibility. The relevance of the topic and the realisation of corporate responsibility were not only observed from a theoretical point of view, but also from practical points. Therefore, it can be clearly stated that CSR has become one of the most popular research topics in recent years, however, it seems that the competencies of the corporate leaders from CSR approach is a rather neglected research topic.

Methodology. The present research is devoted to this research topic through a quantitative primary research in order to have an insight into this area as well.

Findings. The detailed and complex study of the inner factors of the corporate leaders (both of their individual values and attitudes) reveals that self-enhancement shows a positive linear correlation with responsible corporate management among the Hungarian leaders of SMEs, and certain attitudes (altruistic benefit, moral benefit, and CSR≠PR attitudes) have determining roles, however, not exclusive.

Keywords: individual value, corporate social responsibility, CSR attitude, corporate managers.

INTRODUCTION

In the last few decades, especially in the 1990s, corporate social responsibility and business ethics have become important concerns in the global business world.

The topic has been examined from a different aspect, however, because of its constant change and development it remained a topic of interest in the scientific life. The social responsibility of corporations has become such a multidisciplinary science that many disciplines show interest in it e.g.: politics, political theory, media, finance, law, marketing, and business theory.[1] Topic related articles can be even read in the daily newspapers, while articles related to corporate social responsibility can be found in the issues of the Financial Times every second day.[2]

There are more and more corporations that voluntarily decide to take on such strict social and environmental regulations that go beyond the regulations of the country they operate in. It can be explained by the fact that corporate decisions not only influence the direct environment of the corporation, but also the society. CSR is a complex management approach, which has its impact on all aspects of business activities and on the competitiveness of the corporation.

The question is how to integrate CSR decision-making into the philosophy of the corporation, so that it does not contradict the corporation's classic principles, that is to emphasise the interest of the owner and profit maximisation.

The real practice depends on the behaviour of the organisation and the socially responsible attitude of the leader as the leader is the determining factor in the operation of any organisation.

There are many factors that influence the managers in their decision-making, these concerns include ethical, cultural, technical, ecological, and political issues, and the consequences of their decisions can immediately go public due to the Internet. The leaders are often involved in such situation where they are confronted with the stakeholders, not only in case of catastrophes (e.g. the Ajka alumina sludge spill or the oil spill in the Gulf of Mexico). The role and responsibility of corporations in the society has become a rather important issue, probably that is why so many corporations publicise their CSR-reports.

The relevance of the topic is also justified by the fact that several researchers refer to the importance of the manager's personality.[3]

There have been several researches carried out regarding corporate social responsibility in recent years, which results were published in specialist journals and

[1] C.A. Hemingway (2002). *An Exploratory Analysis of Corporate Social Responsibility: Definitions, Motives and Values. Research Memorandum 34*. Centre for Management and Organisational Learning Hull University Business School, Hull, UK, pp. 1–25.

[2] R. Aguilera, C. Williams, J.M. Conley, D.E. Rupp (2006). *Corporate governance and social responsibility: A comparative analysis of the UK and the US*. "Corporate Governance: An International Review", vol. 14, no. 3, pp. 147–158.

[3] E.g. Á. Angyal (2009). *Vállalatok társadalmi felelőssége. Műhelytanulmány*, working paper. Vállalatgazdaságtan Intézet, Budapest; A.B. Carroll, (1999). *Corporate social responsibility: Evolution of a definitional construct*. "Business and Society", vol. 38, no. 3, pp. 268–295; A. Chikán (2008). *Vállalati versenyképesség és társadalmi felelősség*. "Harvard Business Manager", vol. 11, pp. 6–13; K. Davis (1960). *Can business afford to ignore social responsibilities?* "California Management Review", vol. 2, pp. 70–76; M. Friedman (1970). *The social responsibility of business is to increase its profits*. "New York Times Magazine", vol. 9; K.E. Goodpaster, J.B. Matthews (1982). *Can a corporation have a conscience?* "Harvard Business Review", vol. 60, no. 1, pp. 132–141.

periodicals. There are research studies dealing with the correlation between individual values and business life[4], however, the number of those research studies that deal with specifically the relation between the practice of CSR and the individual values of corporate leaders[5] is low at an international level. There are not many research studies dealing with the management attitude of the CEO. Domestically, researchers only deal with the above mentioned topics separately, or with the subfield regarding the attitude of the CEO towards responsible management, in the SME sector. Hence there is a need to carry out research in the topic.

The present study deals with a less emphasized topic that is the relation between CSR and management attitudes among SMEs.

The main aim of the research was to examine the impact of the individual values of the general managers and CSR attitudes on the realisation of corporate social responsibility.

To define those specific values and attitudes that enjoy priorities in the personality of a CSR centred corporate leader. The research has formulated the following hypotheses.

H1: There is a positive relation between the higher value of self-transcendence and the realisation of CSR.

H1a: The self-enhancement value shows a strong positive linear correlation with the realisation of the CSR practice.

H2: The individual values of the company leaders are not the only factors having their direct impact on the realisation of the CSR, but also one or more mediator factors (CSR-attitude) play an important role.

H3: Out of the CSR attitudes the altruistic benefit attitude influences the realisation of the responsible corporate management to the greatest extent.

MATERIAL AND METHODS

The collection of data was realised through surveys. The quantitative survey can be divided into two parts. The core of the research were three groups of questions aiming to find out the correlation between the company leaders and the company. The personal values of the company leaders, their attitude to CSR, and the CSR practice of their company were approached first, so the realisation of CSR and the related factors were examined.

In the second part of the survey, the characteristics of the company and the demographic characteristics of the respondents were focused on.

The questions of CSR practice of the corporations focusing on the realisation of the CSR practice were grouped as follows:

---

[4] B.R. Agle, C.B. Caldwell (1999). *Understanding research on values in business*. "Business and Society", vol. 38, no. 3, pp. 326–387.

[5] Koivula N. (2008). *Basic Human Values in the Workplace*. University of Helsinki, Helsinki, pp. 1–141.

1) environment (environmental protection);
2) human factors (workplace relations, human rights, workplace safety, social questions, etc.);
3) community relations (cooperation with the concerned – partners, suppliers, consumers, etc., communication with the local community);
4) business environment (economy, ethical operation of the corporation, transparent operation of the corporation, lobbies).

The second group of questions focused on the *CSR attitudes of company leaders* and the third part of the questions focused on the *individual values of the leaders*.

Before formulating the questions, several research methods of international and national secondary research studies were examined.

Therefore, the 21-item-survey of the European Social Survey (ESS) was used in the survey of the individual values. This survey was successfully applied in 29 countries in representative research studies, out of which 27 were European. The value examination of the ESS is based on the Schwartz model, which plays an important factor in the secondary research of the present research. The Shalom Schwartz value test consists of statements (third person singular) regarding ten values.[6]

The questions regarded the usually examined features of companies i.e.: the number of employees, ownership, legal form, the characteristics of the branch, and the sales methods of the products and services of the company. As during the research the individual inner factors of the human personality are analysed, it was also necessary to ask certain questions regarding the demographic characteristics of the company leaders i.e.: gender, age, education, address-location, or marital status.

First the multitude was defined, the target multitude became the leaders of those companies which had at least 10 employees. It was decided to ask leaders of SMEs in my neighbourhood, that is Central Hungary and Northern Hungary (see figure 1).

By defining the sample the list of companies was the guideline. During the research one of the non-random sample methods the so-called snowball sampling and personal interview methods were used.

The interviewers were university students. In order to have a representative sample the students were asked to register the name and accessibility of the CEO of the manager to avoid duplicate appearance in my database. 416 CEOs were asked, however out of the survey only 202 could be used. The interviews were carried out during the autumn of 2013, and the spring of 2014.

So the research is therefore not representative, however, it contains interesting results. The results can be interpreted only in the context of the sample.

The itemised assessment scale method was used during the above mentioned research phases. The respondents were asked to evaluate the CSR practice of the company, the individual values and the attitudes on a six-level Likert item.

---

[6] S.H. Schwartz (2006). *Value orientations: Measurement, antecedents and consequences across nations* [in:] R. Jowell, C. Roberts, R. Fitzgerald, G. Eva (eds.), *Measuring Attitudes Cross-nationally – Lessons from the European Social Survey*. Sage, London.

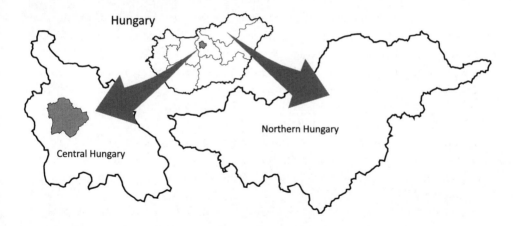

Figure 1. The regions of the sample
Source: own construction.

A reliability test was carried out and the guideline was considered to be above 0.6 Crombach's Alpha.

Although the research dealt with several sub-areas, the present study points out only those details that are relevant from the above mentioned point of view. It must be mentioned that although the research is not representative because of the lack of financial resources it still brought about important and interesting results.

RESULTS

Further on, a complex analysis was carried out to study the impact of the individual values on the CSR. Before the mediation analysis a rank correlation was carried out on the correlation of CSR attitude and CSR practice.

First the priorities of the generations were identified, where significant differences could be seen, the analysis was applied only to those base values that showed statistical differences.

The study of individual values of general managers

Based on the results of earlier researches of Schwartz and integrating his own studies he established his own value test. 21 human characteristics that carry individual values are shown in the third person singular out of which the respondent can indicate how characteristic the statement is on a six-point-scale.

In his studies he builds on the value test by Rokeach, however in his own research he denies the dichotomy of the goal and tool.[7] He is also interested in how values are organised in a system, so he illustrates it in a two-dimensional model. He believed that values respond to the needs of survival and welfare that are the results of biological and social interactions, based on this he assumed the existence of a value order of 8 values: prosocialist, conformist, hedonist, achievement-oriented, aiming for maturity, self-direction, security, and aiming for power.

Before establishing the value-model, an empirical study was carried out involving 5 continents, 20 countries, and 8 religions. Since then, several national and international studies have applied his value test including the European Social Survey (ESS) for ten years.

In his model 10 universal basic values were identified: achievement, benevolence, conformity, hedonism, power, security, self-direction, stimulation, tradition, and universalism; these values are organised under four higher value groups: self-transcendence, conservation, self-enhancement, and openness to change.

The values organised along the horizontal values: openness to change and conservation show similarities with the dichotomy of secular-rational and traditional studied by Inglehard.[8]

The values of self-transcendence and self-enhancement are to be found along the vertical axis.[9]

During the research of personal values of general managers the most important question was how much the value structure of the responding general managers fits to the chosen Schwartz-value model.

Table 1 shows the structure of the 21 items, which were linked to each other as assumed and studied by Schwartz, ten basic personal values were created. It also introduces how the 21 items connect to the basic and higher values, as well as it describes the main characteristics of each value.

The sample studied covered the general values (21 values) by 10 basic values, which are organised into 4 higher values (self-transcendence, self-enhancement, openness to change, and conservation) along a horizontal and vertical line.

Further on, the research studies the relation, connection of these ten basic personal values, the Euclidean distance was used for the accurate measurement of the distance. The relevance and interpretation of the results are justified by the s-stress indicator of 0.088.

According to the priority of values the competing values are positioned opposite each other thus creating the Schwartz model.

---

[7] S.H. Schwartz (2003). *A proposal for Measuring Value Orientations across Nations* [in:] *Questionnaire development report of the European Social Survey*, chap. 7. http://naticent02.uuhost.uk.uu.net/questionnaire/chapter_07.doc (access: 20.05.2013).

[8] R. Inglehart (1997). *Modernization and postmodernization-cultural and political change in 43 societies.* "New Jersey Journal", vol. 10, no. 1, Princeton University Press, pp. 53–68.

[9] S.H. Schwartz (2006). *Value orientations: Measurement, antecedents and consequences across nations* [in:] R. Jowell, C. Roberts, R. Fitzgerald, G. Eva (eds.), *Measuring attitudes cross-nationally – lessons from the European Social Survey.* Sage, London.

Table 1. The connection of the 21 items to the basic and higher values

Schwartz's individual higher values	Schwartz's individual basic values	Items	Questionnaires
openness to change	self-direction	pvalue01	Thinking up new ideas and being creative is important to him. He likes to do things in his own original way.
		pvalue11	It is important to him to make his own decisions about what he does. He likes to be free to plan and to choose activities for himself.
	stimulation	pvalue06	He likes surprises and is always looking for new things to do. He thinks it is important to do lots of different things in life.
		pvalue15	He looks for adventures and likes to take risks. He wants to have an exciting life.
self-enhancement	achievement	pvalue04	It is very important to him to show his abilities. He wants people to admire what he does.
		pvalue13	Being very successful is important to him. He likes to impress other people.
	power	pvalue02	It is important to him to be rich. He wants to have a lot of money and expensive things.
		pvalue17	It is important to him to be in charge and tell others what to do. He wants people to do what he says.
	hedonism	pvalue10	Having a good time is important to him. He likes to "spoil" himself.
		pvalue21	He seeks every chance he can to have fun. It is important to him to do things that give him pleasure.
self-transcendence	benevolence	pvalue12	It's very important to him to help the people who are under him. He wants to care for other people.
		pvalue18	It is important to him to be loyal to his friends. He wants to devote himself to people close to him.
	universalism	pvalue03	He thinks it is important that every person in the world be treated equally. He wants justice for everybody, even for people he doesn't know.
		pvalue08	It is important to him to listen to people who are different from him. Even when he disagrees with them, he still wants to understand them.
		pvalue19	He strongly believes that people should care for nature. Looking after the environment is important to him.
conservation	tradition	pvalue09	He thinks it's important not to ask for more than what you have. He believes that people should be satisfied with what they have.
		pvalue20	Religious belief is important to him. He tries hard to do what his religion requires.
	conformity	pvalue07	He believes that people should do what they're told. He thinks people should follow rules at all times, even when no-one is watching.
		pvalue16	It is important to him always to behave properly. He wants to avoid doing anything people would say is wrong.
	security	pvalue05	It is important to him to live in secure surroundings. He avoids anything that might endanger his safety.
		pvalue14	It is very important to him that his country be safe from threats from within and without. He is concerned that social order be protected.

s-stress indicator: 0.078
Euclidean distance was applied for accuracy.
Method: multidimensional scale, SPSS 21, PROXSCALE
Source: own construction, standard interview, autumn of 2013 and spring of 2014. N = 202.

One of the axis opposes the values of conservation with the openness to change, the normal axis contrasts the values of self-enhancement and self-transcendence.

The conservation value includes the values of tradition, security, and conformity, while openness to change includes self-direction, stimulation, and hedonism (see figure 2).

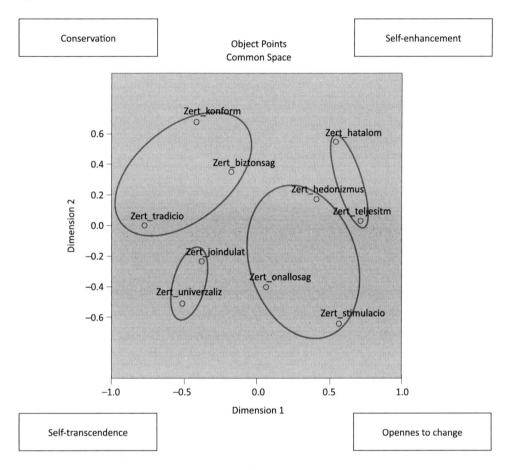

Figure 2. The grouping structure of the 10 basic values by Schwartz

Source: own construction, standard interview, autumn of 2013 and spring of 2014, N = 202.

It can be clearly seen that hedonism approached the self-enhancement higher value, which connects to the openness to change and self-enhancement in the original Schwartz model. Thus it is not surprising that this value (hedonism) strongly approaches the self-enhancement value category.

The other axis is between the self-transcendence and self-enhancement. At the self-transcendence end the universalism and benevolence values form the higher value while at the opposing end there is power and achievement forming self--enhancement.

The relation between the individual value of general managers and the practice of CSR

The study of personal values was continued by analysing the relation between the Schwartz kind of higher values and responsible management. Based on the results of the national and international empirical researches it is likely that only a few values show any kind of relation with the realisation of CSR practice. So, further on, those values were identified that showed a positive correlation with the realisation of the CSR.

The study of the Schwartz values relating the CSR practice

Studying the Schwartz higher values by statistical methods, the unambiguous influence of the self-transcendence and openness to change on CSR could be seen clearly. The Spearman rank correlation showed positive linear correlation ($rho = 0.317$, $p = 0.000$) between self-transcendence and positive correlation between openness to change ($rho = 0.210$, $p = 0.000$) and the CSR practice (table 2). This result is in line with those empirical research results that called the attention to the correlation of the environmental and social issues of self-transcendence and also H1 was proven.

✓ **H1:** There is a positive relation between the higher value of self-transcendence and the realisation of CSR.

On the other hand the research did not justify H1a.

✗ **H1a:** The self-enhancement value shows positive linear correlation with the realisation of CSR practice.

Table 2. Correlation of individual values by Schwartz and CSR practice

The examined variable pairs in the correlation	Correlational coefficients
Self-transcendence (benevolence, universalism) – CSR practice	0.317**
Conservation (tradition, conformity, security) – CSR practice	–
Self-enhancement (achievement, power, hedonism) – CSR practice	–
Openness of change (self-direction, stimulation) – CSR practice	0.210**

** (p = 0.000) shows significance
Source: own construction, standard interview, autumn of 2013 and spring of 2014, N = 202.

The one by one correlation study of the basic values of a personality showed the correlation of positive benevolence ($rho = 0.302$, $p = 0.000$) and positive universalism ($rho = 0.281$, $p = 0.000$) in the realisation of responsible behaviour. Correlation could be seen between hedonism belonging to openness to change and corporate social responsibility. Although this correlation was moderately positive, the connection is still significant. The correlation coefficient of the self-direction was ($rho = 0.152$, $p = 0.015$), while that of hedonism was ($rho = 168$, $p = 0.013$) (table 3). Correlation could be seen between self-direction and hedonism (openness to change) and realisation of CSR. It is not at all surprising that the basic values belonging to higher values show significant correlation with the CSR practice, however, they are not the only influential factor in the manifestation of responsible behaviour, other values also play their role.

Table 3. Correlation of individual values by Schwartz and CSR practice

The examined variable pairs in the correlation	Correlational coefficients
Benevolence – CSR practice	0.302**
Universalism – CSR practice	0.281**
Security – CSR practice	0.246**
Tradition – CSR practice	0.199**
Conformity – CSR practice	–
Achievement – CSR practice	–
Power – CSR practice	–
Self-direction – CSR practice	0.152*
Hedonism – CSR practice	0.168*
Stimulation – CSR practice	–

*** (p = 0.000) shows significance*
* (p < 0.05) shows significance
Source: own construction, standard interview, autumn of 2013 and spring of 2014, n = 202.

The security and tradition values (conservation) also indicated significant correlation ($p < 0.05$). The study proved positive linear correlation. The security value was ($rho = 0.246$, $p = 0.001$), while tradition ($rho = 0.199$, $p = 0.002$) was shown by the correlation coefficient.

The correlation of the personal values and the corporate responsible behaviour can be seen in table 4. In view of all the above, it is interesting to see the priorities of each values in the value system of the general managers.

Table 4. The correlation of the individual values and corporate responsible behaviour

Schwartz value	Self-enhancement		Openness to change			Self-transcendence		Conservation		
Correlational coefficients	–		0.210**			0.317**		0.217**		
Schwartz value	achieve-ment	power	self-direction	hedonism	stimu-lation	bene-volence	univer-salism	security	tradition	confor-mity
Correlational coefficients	–	–	0.152*	0.168*	–	0.302**	0.281**	0.246**	0.199**	–

*** (p = 0.000) shows significance*
* (p < 0.05) shows significance
Source: own construction, standard interview, autumn of 2013 and spring of 2014, N = 202.

The CSR attitudes of the general managers

An important aim of the research was to see whether the examined general managers can be segmented according to their CSR attitudes and if yes, whether the segmented groups can be unambiguously adapted according to the Quazi and O'Brien model.[10]

---

[10] A.M. Quazi-D.O'Brien (2000). *An Empirical Test of a Cross-national Model of Corporate Social Responsibility.* "Journal of Business Ethics", vol. 25, no. 1, pp. 33–51.

In order to research this topic, first the dimensions of the CSR attitudes needed to be established, and then the segments of the general managers will be introduced. Finally, the demographic features of the general managers' segment will be pointed out. In order to handle the variables the 21 item questionnaire was factor analysed. The questions of the survey were compiled based on previous research studies, so during the study a confirmatory analysis was carried out.

4 factors were identified by the factor analysis of the CSR attitudes of the general managers (table 5). Out of these the first and the explaining factor for the variation with the highest value is the CSR action in order to gain an *altruistic* benefit. The second factor is the factor of the rational advantages, this emphasises the importance of profit maximising and the unambiguous benefit from the CSR action, this is opposed to the modern approach of owner value, according to which cooperation with the stakeholders is the key to the increase of the owner's value. The statements connected with the moral benefit factor try to point out the long term theory of the CSR action. This factor basically includes the moral and ethical issues. These are those questions that are concerned with the non-direct benefits, but the theoretical issues of the CSR. During the study of the CSR-attitudes of corporate leaders, the factor analysis identified four factors, out of which the first is the altruistic factor which explains the spread with the highest values and is in the interest of the CSR activity which includes seven variables. The factors include all those statements that highlight the indirect and secondary advantages of the CSR. The CSR includes the positive approach in business and responsible thinking as well.

The first statement which is connected rather strongly to the factor, emphasises the loyalty of the employees of the corporation with CSR activity. Those scale questions are also strong that are connected with the indirect advantages that are ensured by CSR activity, which were the following: helps the sales of the product/services of a CSR company, strengthens the image of the corporation in the market, and attracts new consumers, competitors, and stakeholders. Those statements are also rather strong with high factor value that emphasise the good relationship with the stakeholders (suppliers, residents, consumers, business partners, etc.). So, this factor carries a modern owner approach, which offers the growth of the owner through cooperation. The realisation of the CSR is seen embedded in the operation of the company, in the interaction with the stakeholders. The second factor is the factor of the *rational* advantages to which four variables are connected, all of which received a high factor value. All the statements emphasise the primary importance of profit maximising, as well as the advantages of the CSR-activity and ignore the deeds that are not done in this direction. This factor is opposed to the modern approach of owner value, which sees the realisation in the cooperation of the stakeholders. The statements that are connected with the "moral benefit *factor* are those that tried to highlight the far reaching disciplines of the CSR activity. This factor includes moral and ethical questions. These questions are those that do not emerge with the advantages, but with the questions of CSR. The so-called conversed item got its place among the factors, however, it does not fit very well in the picture, which can be explained by the fact that this variable did not receive high values on other factor either, and the Cronbach's Alpha was not changed significantly likewise.

Table 5. The CSR attitude factors determined during the multi variant research. Items for Loadings from Confirmatory Factor Analysis

Item	Item Description	Component Loading			
		1	2	3	4
CSRattitude07	The performance of the employee of a corporation that is environmentally, ethically and socially responsible improves	.662	-.155	.126	.079
CSRattitude12	It is beneficial for a company to be socially responsible, environment conscious and ethical in its operation	.590	.205	.041	-.156
CSRattitude16	the ethical and reliable corporate behaviour that takes into consideration the social and environmental values with the suppliers is beneficial in the long term	.568	-.109	.314	-.026
CSRattitude04	The financial and non-financial contribution to the solution of the local problems and environment protection might mean profit for the corporation.	.561	-.171	.396	.094
CSRattitude05	Social responsibility is the expectation of the consumer, otherwise the interest in the products and services of the corporation might decrease and hence the profit might decrease as well.	.527	-.274	.332	.437
CSRattitude08	Several CEOs could do more for the natural and social environment and they only try to find an excuse when they refer to the lack of financial sources.	.492	.345	-.080	-.153
CSRattitude17	Corporations take into consideration the interest of the broader social and natural environment due to the pressure from their clients and partners.	.443	.331	.012	.056
CSRattitude10	A good CEO deals only little with such environmental and social problems that have no connection to gaining profit.	.040	.631	-.188	-.046
CSRattitude02	A society can only expect a corporation to solve social, environmental and economic problems if it is unambiguously profitable for the company as well.	-.371	.625	.001	.150
CSRattitude03	If a corporation observes the aims of the environmental protection and social problems, it often obstructs the business success.	-.200	.612	.145	.101
CSRattitude07	It is also the benefit of the employee if the profit is the priority of the corporation.	.233	.608	-.302	.216
CSRattitude13	Corporations must understand that they are part of a broader natural and social environment, so they need to react to social and environmental problems.	-.034	.136	.692	.092
CSRattitude09	If we would like the Earth to remain living space for the next generation, corporations should take the environment conscious management as top priority.	-.030	.046	.655	.067
CSRattitude21	The society can expect corporations to deal with social and environmental problems just as with their business activities.	.383	-.083	.644	-.022
CSRattitude14	Corporations take part in social responsibility only as others expect them to do so.	.295	.067	.550	.102
CSRattitude20	Hungarian consumers are neutral whether a corporation observes the natural and social environment.	.297	-.024	.136	-.126
CSRattitude11	It would be important that social responsibility is not only part of marketing communication (advertisement, PR etc.) but also absorbs the whole management and operation.	.351	-.200	.455	.737
CSRattitude19	In order to achieve a positive image of a corporation, it is essential to be socially responsible.	-.185	.234	-.020	.582
CSRattitude01	In order to create trust between the corporation and its consumers, the ethical operation and social responsibility play an important role.	.403	-.220	.167	.481

The relevance of the analysis is shown by the relevant KMO-index (.776). The whole explained variation is 49.465, the explained variations of each factor are the following: 36%, 11%, 8%, and 6%. The Bartlett-test is significant (p < 0.05).

Source: based on the output of SPSS 21, standard interview, autumn of 2013 and spring of 2014, N = 20

The *CSR ≠ PR factor* includes those items that deny the corporate image and the main role of the PR due to CSR action. Although the CSR-action is influenced positively this understanding is denied by the factor and emphasizes that the CSR is not marketing communication and PR.

The exception is the moral dimension, which includes those ideas that try to find a solution to the question of corporate responsibility not at micro- (company) level but at macro-(global) level.

The specialist literature identified further factors (beyond CSR attitudes): primary and secondary benefits, a broader understanding of responsibility of our own benefit, costs of social responsibility, responsibility beyond the legal rules, the companies do not only have business responsibility, the CSR practice, and the corporation does not only have business responsibility. The CSR action increases social expectations. These are not concerned with the topic. In summary it can be stated that the factor analysis of the CSR brought clearly understandable designs of which reliability was carried out by a reliability test.[11]

The study of the correlation of CSR attitude of the company leader and the CSR practice

The CSR attitude factors were separately examined. In case of leaders who achieved higher scores on the altruistic benefit and CSR≠PR attitude scale, their CSR practice was more significant. In case of the two mentioned factors Spearman's rank correlation showed a positive linear correlation (altruistic benefit CSR attitude: rho = 383, p = 0.000; CSR ≠ PR: CSR attitude: rho = 329, p = 0.000). The moral benefit attitude showed a positive correlation (rho = 274, p = 0.000) (table 6.) The rational benefit CSR attitude was not significant, so no further analysis was carried out in this field.

Table 6. Correlation of CSR attitude factors and CSR practice

The examined variable pairs in the correlation	Correlational coefficients
Rational benefit attitude – CSR practice	–
Altruistic benefit attitude – CSR practice	0.383**
CSR ≠ PR attitude – CSR practice	0.329**
Moral benefit attitude – CSR practice	0.274**

** *(p = 0.000) shows significance*
Source: own construction, standard interview, autumn of 2013 and spring of 2014, N = 202.

The research also focused on the fact whether certain CSR attitudes have a mediative role between individual values and CSR practice.

---

[11] A. Szabó-Benedek (2014). *A CSR-gyakorlat vizsgálata a vállalatvezetői értékek és attitűdök tükrében.* PhD értekezés Szent István Egyetem, Gazdálkodás és Szervezéstudományok Doktori Iskola.

The study of the mediative effect of the CSR attitude factors on self-enhancement and CSR practice

Based on the theoretical literature and the practice it is likely that there is a mediator between the individual values of the company leaders and the realisation of the CSR practice.

To explore the correlation between the variables mediation, an analysis was carried out in which three regression way analyses were needed. The relevance of the mediator can only be justified if all the three regression models are significant.[12]

The mediation analysis of the altruistic benefit

Before the mediation analysis, all the variables concerned were tested, and according to Spearman's rank correlation all the variables concerned (self-enhancement, altruistic attitude and CSR practice) have a positive linear correlation. The first route the self-enhancement and the CSR practice (rho=0.302, p=0.000), the second route the self-enhancement and altruistic benefit attitude (rho=0.399, p=0.000), and the third route the altruistic benefit attitude and CSR practice (rho=0.383, p=0.000) show an unambiguous positive correlation (table 7).

Table 7. Correlation among self-enhancement, CSR practice, and altruistic benefit attitude variables

The examined variable pairs in the correlation	Correlational coefficients
self-enhancement – CSR practice	0.302**
self-enhancement – altruistic benefit attitude	0.399**
altruistic benefit attitude – CSR practice	0.383**

*** (p = 0.000) shows significance*
Source: own construction, standard interview, autumn of 2013 and spring of 2014, N = 202.

Table 8 shows the results and routes of the analysis of the mediative impact of altruistic benefit attitude carried out by linear regression analysis.

Table 8. The mediative study of regressive route of self-enhancement and CSR practice

Regressive route	Standard beta
self-enhancement – altruistic benefit attitude	0.370**
altruistic benefit attitude – CSR practice	0.346**
self-enhancement – CSR practice	0.327**
self-enhancement – CSR practice (besides the control of altruistic benefit attitude)	0.230**

*** (p = 0.000) shows significance*
Source: own construction, standard interview, autumn of 2013 and spring of 2014, N = 202.

---

[12] R.M. Baron, D.A. Kenny (1986). *The moderator-mediator variable distinction in social psychological research: Conceptual, strategic, and statistical considerations.* "Journal of Personality and Social Psychology", vol. 51, pp. 1173–1182.

The results of the regressive routes were significant in each cases, so the analysis of the mediative route is also justified (see figure 3).

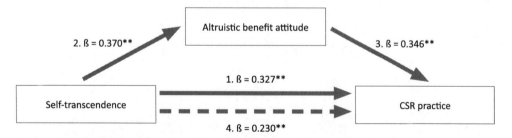

Figure 3. The altruistic benefit attitude as the mediator between self-enhancement and CSR practice

*** (p = 0.000) shows significance*

Source: own construction, standard interview, autumn of 2013 and spring of 2014, N = 202.

According to the Sobel test, the mediation is significant (Sobel z = 3.041; p < 0.01), 29.7% is explained by the self-enhancement and CSR practice correlation by the comparison of the standardized beta-coefficients.

The mediation analysis of the CSR≠PR attitude

In case of every variable the correlation was significant (positive linear correlation), even stronger correlation could be shown between self-enhancement and CSR ≠ PR attitude (table 9).

Table 9. Correlation among the variables of self-enhancement, CSR-practice and CSR≠PR attitude

The examined variable pairs in the correlation	Correlational coefficients
self-enhancement – CSR practice	0.302**
self-enhancement – CSR≠PR attitude	0.431**
CSR≠PR attitude – CSR practice	0.329**

*** (p = 0.000) shows significance*

Source: own construction, standard interview, autumn of 2013 and spring of 2014, N = 202.

Table 10 shows the three routes that are necessary to the mediation research, out of which the significant role of the mediator can be seen.

Table 10. The regressive route of the mediation

Regressive route	Standard Beta
self-enhancement – CSR≠PR attitude	0.426**
CSR≠PR attitude – CSR practice	0.306**
self-enhancement – CSR practice	0.327**
self-enhancement – CSR practice (besides the control of CSR≠PR attitude)	0.242**

*** (p = 0.000) shows significance*

Source: own construction, standard interview, autumn of 2013 and spring of 2014, N = 202.

According to the Sobel test, the mediation is significant (Sobel z = 2.55, p < 0.05), based on the comparison of standardised beta coefficients the CSR ≠ PR benefit attitude explains 26% of the correlation of the self-enhancement and CSR-practice (figure 4).

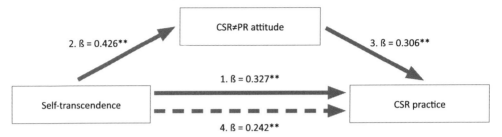

Figure 4. The CSR ≠ PR attitude as the mediator between self-enhancement and CSR practice

** (p = 0.000) shows significance
Source: own construction, standard interview, autumn of 2013 and spring of 2014, N = 202.

Mediation analysis of the moral attitude

However, the correlation between the moral attitude and the CSR practice is weak, positive, the correlation is still significant (p=.000), so this factor had to be analysed (table 11).

Table 11. Correlation between the variable pairs

Variable pairs in the correlation examined	Correlation coefficients
self-enhancement – CSR practice	0.302**
self-enhancement – moral benefit attitude	0.268**
moral benefit attitude – CSR practice	0.274**

** (p = 0.000) shows significance
Source: own construction, standard interview, autumn of 2013 and spring of 2014, N = 202.

The self-enhancement value significantly (p = 0.000) explains the CSR practice and the moral attitude. The moral attitude significantly explains the CSR practice (p = 0.000), so the power of the self-enhancement could be tested besides the control of the moral attitude (table 12).

Table 12. The regressive routes of the mediation

Regressive route	Standard beta
self-enhancement – moral benefit attitude	0.291**
moral benefit attitude – CSR practice	0.258**
self-enhancement – CSR practice	0.327**
self-enhancement – CSR practice (besides the control of the moral benefit attitude)	0.275**

** (p = 0.000) shows significance
Source: own construction, standard interview, autumn of 2013 and spring of 2014, N = 202.

As all the three regressive models were significant, the mediation could be shown. Based on the Sobel test, the mediation is significant (Sobel z = 2.212; p < 0.05), by the comparison of the standard beta coefficients the altruistic benefit attitude explains 15.9% of the correlation of the self-enhancement and CSR practice (figure 5).

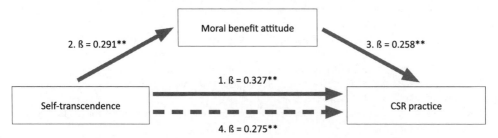

Figure 5. The moral attitude as the mediator between self-enhancement and CSR-practice

** (p = 0.000) shows significance
Source: own construction, standard interview, 2013 autumn of 2013 and spring of 2014, N = 202.

In conclusion it can be stated that the altruistic benefit, the moral benefit, and the CSR ≠ PR attitudes all mediate the effect of the self-enhancement on the CSR practice, hence H3 was justified.

✓ **H3:** The individual values of the company leaders are not the only factors having their direct impact on the realisation of the CSR, but also one or more mediator factors (CSR attitude) play an important role.

CONCLUSION

The result of the research indicated that out of the competencies of the corporate leaders the inner leader (the individual values and attitudes) plays important roles in responsible corporate management.

The individual values of the general managers and their correlation with the CSR practice were identified. The quantitative primary research results proved that from the CSR point of view in the value system of the general managers the self-enhancement enjoy the priority.

It was proved by complex methods (mediation) that the individual values have not only indirect effect on the realisation of CSR, but also have a significant role in the CSR attitudes. From among the attitudes, the altruistic benefit mediates the CSR practice to the greatest extent (almost 30%), then the CSR≠PR attitude (26%), and the moral benefit attitude (16%).

Although the research justified the correlation, the statistical results have also shown, that in the realisation of the CSR not only the inner factors of the leader play important roles. In the future the study of these factors would be rather important in order to receive a unified picture of the factors influencing the CSR practice.

References

Agle B.R., Caldwell C.B. (1999). *Understanding research on values in business.* "Business and Society", vol. 38, no. 3, pp. 326–387.

Aguilera R., Williams C., Conley J.M., Rupp D.E. (2006). *Corporate governance and social responsibility: A comparative analysis of the UK and the US.* "Corporate Governance: An International Review", vol. 14, no. 3, pp. 147–158.

Angyal Á. (2009). *Vállalatok társadalmi felelőssége.* Műhelytanulmány, working paper. Budapest, Vállalatgazdaságtan Intézet.

Baron R.M., Kenny D.A. (1986). *The moderator-mediator variable distinction in social psychological research: Conceptual, strategic and statistical considerations.* "Journal of Personality and Social Psychology", vol. 51, pp. 1173–1182.

Carroll A.B. (1999). *Corporate social responsibility: Evolution of a definitional construct.* "Business and Society", vol. 38, no. 3, pp. 268–295.

Chikán A. (2008). *Vállalati versenyképesség és társadalmi felelősség.* "Harvard Business Manager", vol. 11, pp. 6–13.

Davis K. (1960). *Can business afford to ignore social responsibilities?.* "California Management Review", vol. 2, pp. 70–76.

Friedman M. (1970). *The social responsibility of business is to increase its profits.* "New York Times Magazine", vol. 9.

Goodpaster K.E., Matthews J.B. (1982). *Can a corporation have a conscience?* "Harvard Business Review", vol. 60, no. 1, pp. 132–141.

Hemingway C.A. (2002). *An Exploratory Analysis of Corporate Social Responsibility: Definitions, Motives and Values.* Research Memorandum 34, Centre for Management and Organisational Learning Hull University Business School, Hull, UK, pp. 1–25.

Inglehart R. (1997). *Modernization and postmodernization – cultural and political change in 43 societies.* "New Jersey Journal", vol. 10, no. 1, Princeton University Press, pp. 53–68.

Koivula N. (2008). *Basic Human Values in the Workplace.* University of Helsinki, Helsinki, pp. 1–141.

Quazi A.M., O'Brien D. (2000). *An empirical test of a cross-national model of corporate social responsibility.* "Journal of Business Ethics", vol. 25, no. 1, pp. 33–51.

Schwartz S.H. (2006). *Value orientations: Measurement, antecedents and consequences across nations* [in:] R. Jowell, C. Roberts, R. Fitzgerald, G. Eva (eds.), *Measuring attitudes cross-nationally – lessons from the European Social Survey.* Sage, London.

Schwartz (2003). *A Proposal for Measuring Value Orientations across Nations* [in:] *Questionnaire Development Report of the European Social Survey,* chap. 7. http://naticent02.uuhost.uk.uu.net/questionnaire/chapter_07.doc (access: 20.05.2013).

Szabó-Benedek A. (2014). *A CSR-gyakorlat vizsgálata a vállalatvezetői értékek és attitűdök tükrében.* PhD értekezés Szent István Egyetem, Gazdálkodás és Szervezéstudományok Doktori Iskola.

Kristupas Žegunis
Klaipėda University
e-mail: kristupas@sportmedicine.lt
Rimantas Stašys
Klaipėda University
e-mail: rimantas.stasys@ku.lt

MANAGEMENT OF THE HEALTHCARE SYSTEM PERFORMANCE: CONCEPTS AND ISSUES

Abstract

Background. Statistical indicators show that the efficiency of the Lithuanian healthcare system is not good enough. Indices provided in the 2014 report of Euro Health Consumer Powerhouse, compared to the results of other EU Member States, are often assessed as moderate or satisfactory only. The 2015 conclusions provided by the Council of the European Union contain recommendations to improve the performance results of the Lithuanian healthcare system. Moreover, knowing that the healthcare performance is not efficient is not very helpful. The biggest issue for the policy makers is to determine the reasons of the bad performance. It means that the processes and the outcomes have to be analysed, therefore specific and measurable criteria must be introduced.

Research aims. Following the analysis of statistical data, to identify the problem areas of the healthcare system, to point out the possible reasons for the problems and anticipate the actions, which could help effectively improve the performance results of the healthcare system.

Methodology. Analysis of statistical indices of 2014 carried out by Euro Health Consumer Powerhouse and of the performance measurement criteria adaptability and usage. In addition, a survey of the executives of Lithuanian healthcare institutions was carried out; the results of the survey will be systematized and used to examine the issue.

Findings. Performance measurement provides the information about the efficiency of the healthcare services from the perspective of service providers, users, and policy makers. The most challenging issue is the assessment of the performance and setting up the roots of the adjustable processes and outcomes. The survey of the Lithuanian healthcare institutions confirms the statistical data and helps to identify the problems of the healthcare performance.

Keywords: healthcare performance, performance indicators, performance criteria, quality indicators.

INTRODUCTION

According to the data of Health Consumer Powerhouse (HCP), the quality of medical services in the EU Member States is gradually improving. This has been determined by the improvement of patients' knowledge about diseases and their treatment methods, more effective service accessibility, lower number and frequency of treatment-related and complication risks and better treatment outcomes. Nevertheless, there are still problems and perhaps it is time to stop using present and previous crises as a cover, because according to the HCP information, the correlation between the level of a country's economic development and the quality of medical services provided is very low.[1] Quality is more related to the rational management of finances, effective administration of healthcare institutions, organization of timely and effective services, good training of medical specialists, their maintenance, etc.

The Euro Health Consumer Index (EHCI), which is designed to measure medical service quality, was first used in 2005. Presently it is used in the 28 EU countries, as well as Norway, Switzerland, Macedonia, Albania, Iceland, Serbia, Montenegro, and Bosnia and Herzegovina. The EHCI measures the following health system performance criteria: patients' knowledge and their rights, accessibility to services, treatment results, the range of medical services provided, prevention, and pharmaceutical activity.

HCP assesses the results of the Lithuanian health system performance as satisfactory and places it 33rd out of 37. Having carried out a more detailed analysis of the statistical indices they indicate that the indices of the Lithuanian health system in many cases are seen as being moderate, satisfactory, or bad. Much is determined by the fact that Lithuania allocates only a small part of its budget to the health sector. With regard to this index, our country is ranked 27th. The level of corruption in the country is gradually decreasing; however, in the eyes of HCP, Lithuania is in 12th place, which is quite high, and a very negative evaluation. According to the details of EHCI, the number of physicians is 400/100,000 Lithuanian inhabitants, the same as in Sweden or Switzerland and even more than in the UK or Finland.[2]

Other important performance indices of the health system are related to the condition of patients' health, organisation of services, etc., and are evaluated as being moderate or satisfactory, in rare cases – as poor or very bad.

The fact that the number of doctors in Lithuania is relatively high but the queues to see a family physician or a doctor-specialist are long and that the waiting time for emergency medical aid is relatively long shows that the healthcare system is not efficiently organized. Significant results can only be achieved by making the procedure for providing medical services more efficient. This can be done if an equal distribution of specialists is ensured (currently, specialists are concentrated in big cities with the

---

[1] A. Bjornberg (2015). *Euro health consumer index 2014 report*. Health Consumer Powerhouse, 27.01.2015. http://www.healthpowerhouse.com/files/EHCI_2014/EHCI_2014_report.pdf (access: 14.09.2015).
[2] *Ibidem.*

provinces being poorly serviced). Implementing the e-medicine system which will allow doctors to issue electronic prescriptions, centrally reviewing and saving patient medical records will also lead to a more efficient system.

The results of the survey carried out by HCP demonstrate that patients do not know their rights, they are not informed of the possibilities to get treatment in other EU countries, it is comparatively complicated to get a second opinion/evaluation of a diagnosis and the prescribed treatment method without having to queue. The results confirm the lack of patients' awareness and education. More information on treatment opportunities and rights should be provided in public primary healthcare institutions.

The high index of corruption and the relatively low financing of the healthcare sector is signal instability in the political area and an insufficient level of economic development. The EHCI in Lithuania grew over the period from 2006 to 2013. However, since 2013 a significant fall in indices has been observed. Political decisions and continuous implementation of a health reform instead of just correcting it, should be the priority of the Lithuanian Government, which would also increase the funds allocated to the health system.

While observing the results the question remains: what must be done in order to improve the situation? Navigation is not possible without knowing the locations and the final destination. The same rule could be applied to the healthcare performance and management of the process. In order to make the right decisions the policy makers and all other actors of the healthcare system should evaluate the situation very carefully, in other words to determine the "status quo", to analyse the performance of the national healthcare system. The political decisions, which are taken by the policy makers, should be done very carefully.

DEVELOPING PERFORMANCE ASSESSMENT METHODOLOGY

The assessment of health system performance indices is an important process providing information about the efficiency of activity carried out, its quality, accessibility, and other significant criteria of qualitative performance parameters. Measurement of qualitative activity indices allows for more effective implementation of reforms and decision-making, which are safer and more beneficial economically. In improving healthcare quality all three main chains are included, namely, patients, physicians and managers, and, certainly, all authorities, Health and Finance Ministries, in particular.

The assessment of activity indices is a fairly new area and there has been no consensus on one single methodology; different countries apply different techniques. There are disagreements over what indices should be measured, what methods should be applied, etc. Dramatic changes which affected the assessment of indices were determined by the growth of patients' expectations, wide proliferation of information, the chance to be treated or to compare the methods of treatment used in foreign countries, as well as the development of information technology which has provided the opportunity to assess, compare and systemise as many different indices as possible.

Healthcare activity can be described in different ways: population health, effectiveness and quality of treatment, service accessibility, research opportunities and their accuracy, service price, etc. Huge progress has been made in diagnosing and treating acute health disorders and in the primary and public health sectors. However, a number of problems have been observed and this number continues to grow in the diagnosis and treatment of psychosomatic diseases. This might be related to modern lifestyle, frequent stresses and other risk factors, which are typical of today.

What should the performance assessment methodology be like? Perhaps, there is no single unique methodology, though some researchers think that one unique methodology of the performance management is possible to acquire. Engels proved that despite the differences of each country it is possible to set indicators of performance quality measurement.[3]. The basis for a methodology should be the concept of a specific region and a platform meeting the goals of the methodology, which would also allow for an effective measurement of health system performance indices.

Many researchers and practitioners in various levels of healthcare have discussed the assessment procedure. Campbell et al. exclude three issues of the development and application of the indicators[4]:

1. What aspects of healthcare are being measured?
2. Which stakeholder perspective(s) are the indicators intended to reflect?
3. What evidence is available?

According to Smith et al. the indicators of the performance measurement should follow six criteria[5]: reasonability, reproducibility, feasibility, reliability, sensitivity, and predictive validity. Special focus has to be put on the presentation of performance results and on how they will be evaluated by patients, managers, and doctors. Undoubtedly, assessment results constitute very valuable information. They often help choose the right activity direction, adapt performance methodologies and make other activity changes. Nevertheless, the risk remains that results may be wrongly interpreted; therefore, they should be assessed carefully and unambiguously.

Assessment results are very important for institutions responsible for the formation of the health policy. But it should also be understood that the healthcare system is very sensitive and the fulfilment of any changes related to assessment results should be performed in a coherent manner and with the measurement of all potential risks and alterations. Assessment of a health system helps determine the goals, shows how activity/work of individual healthcare institutions and physicians who work there are

---

[3] Y. Engels, *et al.* (2005). *Developing a framework of, and quality indicators for, general practice management in Europe.* "Oxford Journal, Family Practice", vol. 22, no. 2, pp. 215–222.

[4] S. Campbell, J. Braspenning, A. Hutchinson, M. Marshall (2002). *Research methods used in developing and applying quality indicators in primary care.* "Quality and Safety in Health Care", vol. 11, pp. 358–364.

[5] P.C. Smith, E. Mossialos, I. Papanicolas, S. Leatherman (2010). *Performance Measurement for Health System Improvement: Experiences, Challenges and Prospects.* Cambridge University Press, Cambridge.

evaluated by patients and what results are achieved by doctors in using one or other treatment techniques, etc. Authorities play a crucial role in the implementation of health reform and its performance assessment.

Defining and assessing performance

Healthcare systems are complex and complicated structures. Their operation is affected by individual national policies, organizations related to the health system and organization of its activity, patients, and doctors. The inter-relationships are depicted in figure 1.

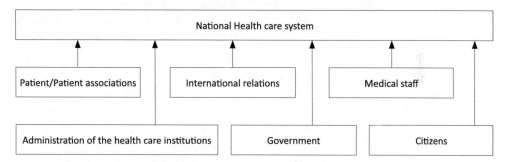

Figure 1. Algorithm of accountability relationships in a health system
Modified by author. Sources: P.C. Smith, E. Mossialos, I. Papanicolas, S. Leatherman (2010); V. Janušonis (2010); V. Janušonis (2012).

Two noticeable inter-relationships are: provision of information in all sorts of directions and on various levels, and acceptance and implementation of the information provided. Each individual structure has certain needs for specific information. For example, a patient who has to choose a health institution is interested in the capabilities of the healthcare institution to treat her/him, waiting time, the physicians who work there, their competence, etc. The main challenge in developing assessment systems is the ability to measure individual parameters taking into consideration different needs of individual institutions.

In practice, it is very hard to firmly and unambiguously state, who the true information users are, or how accurate their information needs are. Usually, a huge amount of concentrated information is provided with the hope that those who need it will find it, assess and draw corresponding conclusions. Information has to be provided, so that the users of every individual segment are satisfied given their needs. This can be done by providing information from the same source, but using different forms of presentation, adapted for a specific group of interested parties. The major challenge in assessing the performance of a health system is the ability to provide concentrated information, which is relevant for a certain specific group. Redundant information is not useful and may be incorrectly interpreted.[6]

---

[6] P.C. Smith, E. Mossialos, I. Papanicolas, S. Leatherman (2010). *Performance measurement for health system improvement: experiences, challenges and prospects*. Cambridge University Press, Cambridge.

Health system assessment is carried out by analysing the results of changes in separate indices. Some areas, such as public health, have certain well-founded and informative criteria, e.g. infant mortality rate or life expectancy. The major remaining challenge is how to link the activity of the health system to people's health. Scientists have developed a new method, which helps users determine avoidable mortality.[7] The quality of the health system is well reflected by the treatment results of clinical patients. These are probably one of the most frequently analyzed criteria, which quite accurately show the efficiency of individual treatment methods. A method often used is direct patient survey where patients are interviewed before and after treatment. Physicians can evaluate the course/development of the treatment process and patients' satisfaction with the services provided.[8]

Performance assessment can be carried out by analyzing processes and results. While both can be used, depending on the case, one or other may be more suitable. In many cases the assessment of the result is not informative enough. In such cases measures of the process become important signals for future success.[9] According to Smith both processes and the outcomes have the advantages and disadvantages and the use of one type of the criteria is determined by general research methodology and other factors.[10]

The assessment of productivity (efficiency) indices and effectiveness of performance is one of the most important and challenging fields.[11] The measurement of efficiency shows whether limited resources allocated to the maintenance and development of the health system are used in an efficient manner and helps determine inefficient providers. The experience of The World Health Report 2000 notes that the assessment of efficiency on a macro-economic level is a complex process.[12] The calculation of results and evaluation of resource consumption becomes even more important where assessments are carried out on a macro-economic level (e.g. provider organization), the clinical department, the practitioner, or – most challenging of all – the individual patient or person.[13]

Problems in applying performance assessment methodologies

To assess health system performance it is recommended to use as wide a range of assessment methods as possible including indicators, analytical methods, and presentation methods. No less important are data collection methods, such as, national

[7] W. Holland (1991). *An Community Atlas of 'Avoidable Death'*. Oxford University Press, Oxford; E. Nolte, M. McKee (2004). *Does Healthcare Save Lives? Avoidable Mortality Revisited*. The Nuffield Trust, London.

[8] R. Fitzpatrick, *et al.* (2000). *Framework for design and evaluation of complex interventions to improve health*. http://www.ncbi.nlm.nih.gov/pmc/articles/PMC1118564/ (access: 3.09.2015).

[9] A. Donabedian (1966). *Evaluating the quality of medical care*. "Milbank Memorial Fund Quarterly", vol. 44, no. 3, pp. 166–206.

[10] P.C. Smith, E. Mossialos, I. Papanicolas, S. Leatherman, *op.cit.*

[11] M.N. Baily, A.M. Garber (1997). *Health Care Productivity*. "Brookings Papers on Economic Activity: Microeconomics", pp. 143–215. http://nrs.harvard.edu/urn-3:HUL.InstRepos:11595722 (acess: 28.08.2015).

[12] *World Health Report 2000: Health Systems: Improving Performance* (2000). The World Health Organization. http://www.ctc-health.org.cn/file/whr00_en.pdf (access: 15.08.2015).

[13] A. Street, U. Hakkinen (2010). *Health system* [in:] P.C. Smith, *et al.* (eds.), *Performance measurement for health system improvement: experiences, challenges and prospects*. Cambridge University Press, Cambridge.

questionnaires, patient questionnaires and clinical details collected by the administrative database on a routine basis. When developing assessment systems, the concept, which includes all the main health sectors must be followed, as this establishes certain development priorities and determines the algorithms, which help avoid erroneous data and duplication of information/data. The Organization for Economic Cooperation and Development (OECD) Health Care Quality Indicators Project is a good example of a project, which was designed to collect/identify performance indicators typical of many countries, which carry out performance assessment.[14] In accordance with the Health Care Quality Indicators Project, since 2001 a set of indicators based on comparable data that can be used to investigate quality differences in healthcare among countries was developed. The five areas in which indicators are being collected are:

1. Patient safety.
2. Quality of mental healthcare.
3. Quality of health promotion.
4. Quality of diabetes care.
5. Quality of cardiac care.

Certain problems are encountered in trying to develop certain individual indicators. The main aims when developing performance analysis indicators are: accessibility, feasibility, reliability, sensitivity to change, and validity. Campbell et al. distinguished and systematised certain characteristics of good indicators/indices[15]: Face/content validity; Reproducibility; Acceptability; Feasibility; Reliability; Sensitivity; and Predictive validity.

Measuring and reporting performance offers one of the most powerful instruments for performance improvement, but so far it has been largely unexploited. Smith excludes the objectives of the performance measurement[16]:

- identifying good and bad practitioners;
- stimulating performance improvement;
- promoting choice for patients and purchasers;
- helping practitioners identify "what works";
- designing health system reform;
- regulating the health system;
- promoting accountability.

The outcomes of the performance measurement are used by management by securing better managerial control of the health services, professionals by securing better political control of the health system, service users by promoting user choice and empowerment, citizens by ensuring value of money and accountability, regulators by correcting market failures and researchers by helping them to identify "what works". The diversity of users implies interests in different aspects of performance and different levels of detail, different methods of analysis and presentations, different priorities attached to timeless comprehensiveness, precision etc. According the World health

---

[14] O.A. Arah, G.P. Westert, J. Hurst, N.S. Klazinga (2006). *A conceptual framework for the OECD Health Care Quality Indicators Project.* "International Journal for Quality in Health Care", September, pp. 5–13.

[15] S. Campbell, J. Braspenning, A. Hutchinson, M. Marshall, *op.cit.*

[16] P.C. Smith, E. Mossialos, I. Papanicolas S. Leatherman, *op.cit.*

report "healthcare performance comprises all organisations, institutions, and resources devoted to producing actions whose primary intent is to improve health".[17]

The performance measurement has been an object of the discussion for more than 250 years.[18] There are many domains of the performance measurement. According to Smith and Nerez the performance domains could be classified as[19]: *Population health, Clinical quality and appropriateness, Responsiveness, Financial protection, Equity,* and *Productivity.* It is very important to assure that the performance measures are valid and unbiased, they should properly adjust for external influences on performance, the data collection mechanism should be reliable and consistent, the data series should be consistent over time, the cost of data should be collected in proportionate way, and the performance measure should be vulnerable to perverse incentives. Risk adjustment for performance measurement is an approach that has been widely used to address the problem of attribution.

According to Iezzoni[20], risk adjustment is a statistical tool that allows data to be modified to control for variations in patient populations between providers, it makes possible to take patient differences into account when comparing the resource use and health outcomes of providers.[21] Risk adjustment is essential to assure fair comparison and clinical acceptability of comparisons and the methods that are used to justify the risk often remain highly contested. A typical risk adjustment algorithm might be definable like: *Risk adjusted adverts outcome = (observed events)/expected events).* Where the expected events usually depend on sample averages, given patient age, complexity, and social factors.

Finally, the performance measurement is best managed when it is based on clear scientific and statistical groundwork. The outcomes and processes of the healthcare system should be measured following the basic principles of the performance measurement and risk adjustment.

METHOD

To determine the outcomes of the findings presented by Health Consumer Powerhouse and the European Union Council, a survey of the executives of 22 Lithuanian healthcare institutions was carried out. The main and major country healthcare institutions were selected. The selection was done following the criteria:

---

[17] *World Health Report 2000, op.cit.*

[18] J.M. Loeb (2004). *The current state of performance measurement in health care.* "International Journal for Quality in Health Care", vol. 16, Suppl. 1, pp. i5–i9.

[19] P.C. Smith, E. Mossialos, I. Papanicolas, S. Leatherman, *op.cit.*; D.R. Nerenz, N. Neil (2001). *Performance Measures for Health Care Systems.* Michigan State University, Virginia Mason Medical Centre. Commissioned Paper for the Center for Health Management Research. http://www.hret.org/chmr/resources/cp19b.pdf (access: 2.08.2015).

[20] L.I. Iezzoni (ed.) (2012). *Risk adjustment for measuring health care outcomes.* "Health Administration Press", 4th edition, vol. 400.

[21] *Ibidem.*

1. Healthcare ministry or municipality subordination (private clinics did not match the Parameters of the study).
2. Accessibility of multi profile medical services.
3. Status of council, regional, or university hospital.

The criteria were developed in order to assure the equity of the respondents. For example privately owned clinics and state healthcare institutions face different issues because of differences of the funding, engaging medical personnel, and other processes. Local healthcare providers like outpatients' clinics or primary healthcare centers did not take part in the survey because of the narrow range of the provided medical services. However, many investigations on healthcare performance measurements are done to analyze the results and processes of the smaller (in the means of the range of the provided healthcare services) healthcare institutions. Therefore, the aim of the current study was to analyze the aspects of the healthcare issues relevant to county/region centre or university healthcare institutions.

RESULTS

The feedback from 15 hospitals (68 %) was received, 7 hospitals (32 %) did not return the completed surveys back. The questions of the survey were constructed considering the issues observed by Health Consumer Powerhouse. Only a few, but in our opinion, the most important issues, were included in the survey in the form of questions.

The summary of the results is presented in table 1.

Table 1. Survey results

No.	Question	Number of healthcare institutions, which responded to this question	%
1.	Lack of financing	14	93
2.	Ineffective management of the healthcare system	11	73
3.	Shortage of physicians and nursing personnel	6	40
4.	Insufficient qualifications of medical personnel	2	13
5.	Negative opinions about the healthcare system presented in public press	1	7
6.	Negative opinions about the healthcare performance expressed by people	1	7
7.	Strategic/political reasons exp.(?) lack of succession of the healtcare performance reform	4	27

Source: prepared by the article author.

The survey shows that insufficient funding, ineffective management of healthcare and a lack of medical personnel are one of the main reasons of ineffective performance. However, as it was discussed previously the outcomes do not show the exact situation and definitely the survey results must be analyzed much deeper using the right criteria to determine the false or inefficient processes and outcomes. The survey results might be a lighthouse navigating the policy makers and researchers to the right destination of the further and deeper researches.

DISCUSSION

The fundamental role of the performance is to promote the accountability within the health system. The performance should be measured and evaluated by following some rules and experience in other countries. Some outcomes and processes are still not an easy task to evaluate and scientists worldwide discuss the evaluation of the indicators and methods, which should be used for measuring performance. The influence of the external factors that influence our performance should be taken into account. The use of adequate risk adjustment methods and objectives that do not go beyond our measures also the avoided uncertainty in the reported measures, affect the validity of the comparisons and should be discussed very carefully.

The translation of the statistical data and surveys is critically important. Inappropriate or subjective interpretation of the records might lead to short and inadequate strategic decisions. The success of the strategy on the political level has a fundamental role. It should be discussed in the highest political level to avoid legislative recalls.

CONCLUSIONS

The statistical data reported by Health Consumer Powerhouse indicate mean or in some sectors bad results of the Lithuanian healthcare performance. The Council of the European Union recommends to improve the performance results of the Lithuanian healthcare system, therefore the policymakers and other actors of the sector must conduct further and deeper investigations of the healthcare performance processes and outcomes and to enact strategic decisions that would help to improve the performance.

A clear conceptual framework and a clear vision of the performance measurement system should be developed and should be aligned with the accountability relationships inherent in the health system. Definitions of the performance indicators should be clear and consistent and should fit into the conceptual framework. Indicators should aim at measuring concepts that are relevant to the need of specific actors and should not focus merely on measuring what is available or easy to measure. Performance measurement requires statistical risk adjustments to adjust for different circumstances of different entities.

A survey of the executives of Lithuanian healthcare institutions shows the guidelines and directions for the policymakers where deeper and more detailed investigations of the healthcare performance measurement should be done. The survey results reflect the problems of the healthcare system, but it does unlikely show the real reasons of the processes or outcomes. The lack of funding might be a reason of the economically inefficient productivity of the healthcare institutions. Some institutions face the deficiency of the medical staff. The university statistics report that there are enough specialists prepared every year. The problem might be that young specialists seek for the opportunities to stay in bigger university clinics and not to accept the proposals from healthcare institutions located peripherically.

References

Arah O.A., Westert G.P., Hurst J., Klazinga N.S. (2006). *A conceptual framework for the OECD Health Care Quality Indicators Project.* "International Journal for Quality in Health Care", September, pp. 5–13.

Baily M.N., Garber A.M. (1997). *Health Care Productivity.* "Brookings Papers on Economic Activity: Microeconomics", pp. 143–215. http://nrs.harvard.edu/urn-3:HUL.InstRepos:11595722 (access: 28.08.2015).

Bjornberg A. (2015). *Euro health Consumer Index 2014 Report.* Health Consumer Powerhouse, 27.01.2015. http://www.healthpowerhouse.com/files/EHCI_2014/EHCI_2014_report.pdf (access: 14.09.2015).

Campbell S., Braspenning J., Hutchinson A., Marshall M. (2002*). Research methods used in developing and applying quality indicators in primary care.* "Quality and Safety in Health Care", vol. 11, pp. 358–364.

Country Report Lithuania 2015 (2015). Brussels, 26.02.2015. SWD (2015) 34 final. http://ec.europa.eu/europe2020/pdf/csr2015/csr2015_lithuania_en.pdf (access: 22.07.2015).

Donabedian A. (1966). *Evaluating the quality of medical care.* "Milbank Memorial Fund Quarterly", vol. 44, no. 3, pp. 166–206.

Engels Y., et al. (2005). *Developing a framework of, and quality indicators for, general practice management in Europe.* "Oxford Journal, Family Practice", vol. 22, no. 2, pp. 215–222.

Fitzpatrick R., et al. (2000). *Framework for design and evaluation of complex interventions to improve health.* http://www.ncbi.nlm.nih.gov/pmc/articles/PMC1118564/ (access: 3.09.2015).

Holland W. (1991). *A Community Atlas of 'Avoidable Death'.* Oxford University Press, Oxford.

Iezzoni L.I. (ed.) (2012). *Risk adjustment for measuring health care outcomes.* "Health Administration Press", 4th edition, vol. 400.

Janušonis V. (2010). *Sveikatos priežiūra: vadyba ir kokybė. Mokslinių staripsnių rinkinys 1999–2009 metai.* Klaipėdos Universitetas, Klaipėdos Universitetinė ligoninė.

Janušonis V. (2012). *Sveikatos apsaugos sistemos organizacijų valdymas.* Klaipėdos Universitetas, Klaipėdos Universitetinė ligoninė.

Loeb J.M. (2004). *The current state of performance measurement in health care.* "International Journal for Quality in Health Care", vol. 16, Suppl. 1, pp. i5–i9.

Nerenz D.R., Neil N. (2001). *Performance Measures for Health Care Systems.* Michigan State University, Virginia Mason Medical Centre. Commissioned Paper for the Center for Health Management Research. http://www.hret.org/chmr/resources/cp19b.pdf (access: 10.08.2015).

Nolte E., McKee M. (2004). *Does healthcare save lives? Avoidable mortality revisited.* The Nuffield Trust, London.

Smith P.C., Mossialos E., Papanicolas I., Leatherman S. (2010). *Performance measurement for health system improvement: experiences, challenges and prospects.* Cambridge University Press, Cambridge.

Street A., Hakkinen U. (2010). *Health system* [in:] P.C. Smith, et al. (eds.), *Performance measurement for health system improvement: experiences, challenges and prospects.* Cambridge University Press, Cambridge.

World Health Report 2000: Health Systems: Improving Performance (2000). The World Health Organization. http://www.ctc-health.org.cn/file/whr00_en.pdf (access: 15.08.2015).

Julius Ramanauskas
Klaipėda University
e-mail: julius.ramanauskas@asu.lt
Rimantas Stašys
Klaipėda University
e-mail: rimantas.stasys@ku.lt
Ilona Osminina
Klaipėda University
e-mail: ilonaosm@gmail.com

THE IMPACT OF ORGANISATIONAL CULTURE ON THE PERFORMANCE OF A LITHUANIAN CLINICAL LAB

Abstract

Background. Lithuanian and foreign researchers have carried out extensive studies of the impact of an organisational culture on the performance of *business* enterprises. A strong organisational culture in a healthcare institution is also believed to lead to a good reputation of an institution and its better performance. However, it is not clear what quantitative parameters could be used to define the organisational culture in a healthcare institution and which specific performance indicators are affected by it.

Research problem. which quantitative parameters can be used to assess the organisational culture of the divisions of a clinical lab (hereinafter: Lab) and how does the performance of an institution depend on its organisational culture?

Research object. the organisational culture in the Lab divisions and their performance.

Research aims. to establish the impact of the organisational culture on the performance of the Lab divisions.

Methodology. analysis of internal and external information sources of the Lab by means of a questionnaire survey, a structured interview, and the processing and analysis of the findings.

Findings. As established, an organisational culture in a healthcare institution tends to inspire and motivate its staff to deal with common problems, to feel responsibility, and to pursue common goals of individual staff members and the organisation. Successful Lab divisions boast a strong organisational culture which makes a positive impact both on individual performance elements and on the overall performance. The Lab-declared policy is focused on quality performance as the most important value of the organisation. The better the organisational culture, the more intensive the activities of the Lab are, however, the dependence of the number of medical tests to be performed by one staff member on the organisational culture is weak.

Keywords: organisational culture, healthcare, impact, performance.

INTRODUCTION

An organisational culture shall be defined as the synthesis of art, science, and religion. It helps to guide the organisational activities in the right direction and covers the values of the organisation under which a satisfactory solution to the problem is found.[1] Contemporary executives have started to identify an organisational culture with a powerful strategic tool which directs people towards common goals, promotes initiative, and attracts and motivates people.

An organisational culture predetermines the lifestyle of the society and its traditions and values. However, to quote Steklova[2], just like any culture, an organisational culture is the "work of human hands", therefore, it forms on the basis of human relations, even though no specific action is taken. The presence of a coherent system of values and norms of behaviour allows an organisation to work out a goal pursuit schema and the development of the staff in the goal pursuit process.

To be able to successfully manage by means of an organisational culture, the executives of organisations ought to perform periodical comprehensive diagnostics.[3] In healthcare institutions, an exclusive organisational culture is generally formed, which features clearly formulated values and norms of behaviour based on moral principles, i.e. not to harm human health.

ASSESSMENT OF ORGANISATIONAL CULTURE IN HEALTHCARE INSTITUTIONS

An organisational culture exists in any organisation, regardless of its size and activity field. It forms the image of the organisation and its relations with patients, suppliers, colleagues, and partners. The institutions of the healthcare sector frequently form

---

[1] A. Kaziliūnas (2004). *Visuomenei teikiamų paslaugų kokybės ir organizacinės kultūros sąveika*. "Viešoji politika ir administravimas", vol. 9, pp. 71–78.

[2] O.E. Steklova (2007). *Organizacionnaja kul'tura*. UlGTU, Ul'janovsk.

[3] K. Ecko, H. Globa (2012). *Tipologija organizacionnyh kul'tur municipal'nyh bol'nic respubliki Moldova*. "Military and Political Sciences in the Context of Social Progress", "Problems and Ways of Modern Public Health Development": Materials Digest of the XV and XVI International Scientific and Practical Conferences.

a kind of an organisational culture where order and rules are recognized and valued by the majority of the staff, and organisational values are respected. In such institutions, the organisational culture is manifested not merely through the appearance of the medical staff, special clothing, cleanliness and sterility of the premises, and the scent, but also through the personal qualities of the staff: politeness, empathy, the style of communication with patients, professionalism, and a sincere wish not only to perform a delegated task, but also to contribute to the saving of a patient's life.

Organisational culture in a healthcare institution

Healthcare institutions consist of a complex of different structural divisions with a specific framework of relations, consequently a change in at least one element of their organisational culture may affect the whole organisational culture. Despite that, the organisational culture in healthcare institutions is difficult to change, as its members are reluctant to alter the system of values and the procedures established in the institution. The organisational culture in healthcare institutions usually changes gradually, with changes taking place in regulations, staff, executives, patient needs, and other elements.

A strong organisational culture in healthcare institutions evokes a wish to collaborate and work sincerely, while a weak culture can cause antipathy to work. Positive staff members usually respect their moral principles which are generally consistent with the organisational culture; however, it is not really easy to practically implement all the desired values and to achieve the most effective performance, as quite many activities in the organisation depend on the formed organisational culture and the understanding of its goals by the institution's staff. Although six dimensions of organisational culture were significantly related to organisational identification, employee morale emerged as the only significant predictor of employee identification.[4]

One of the specific characteristics in the activity of healthcare institutions is team work. A strong organisational culture in a healthcare institution can both improve the internal communication between the staff, ensure staff loyalty, and maintain team spirit. A staff member, who accepts the organisational culture of a healthcare institution, subconsciously memorises all the values, norms, aspirations, and goals of the organisation. The executives, who form the organisational culture on the basis of their perceptions, views, values, and moral principles, define the respective character of the institution activities and the rationale of its existence.

An organisational culture which emphasises important values of an institution can contribute to the achievement of the goals set by the team and to create conditions for the promotion of the relations of the staff and the development of the institution.[5] The stronger the organisational culture of an institution, the better its reputation is,

---

[4] P. Schrodt (2002). *The relationship between organizational identification and organizational culture: Employee perceptions of culture and identification in a retail sales organization.* "Communication Studies", vol. 53, no. 2, pp. 189–202.

[5] J. Palidauskaitė (2001). *Viešojo administravimo etika.* Technologija, Kaunas.

and consequently, it shall attract more patients. However, when patients come to a healthcare institution, they interact with specific service providers, therefore, each staff member has to perceive herself/himself as part of the institution, to understand its values, to form the responsibility for their own image, and to understand that the image of the whole organisation depends on them.

The organisational culture of a healthcare institution can be strongly affected by the external environment of the said institution. Simultaneously, individual organisations affected by the same environment can have very different cultures due to the fact that institutions try to solve two major problems in different ways. First, they try to adapt to the external environment and look for the solution to the work process organisation that would allow to overcome competition. Second, the institution seeks to increase its internal integration, so that internal institutional processes and relations would contribute to its adaptation to the external environment.

In the area of healthcare, work effectiveness and quality depend not merely on the recruited qualified specialists, the latest technologies, and organized work, but also on the ability to integrate it all in the right way. One of the main factors of work effectiveness is staff loyalty. To form it, a strong organisational culture is necessary. Each staff member is to understand the boundaries of their responsibilities and to deal with emerging issues in such a way as not to undermine the goals of the institution.

According to Ng'ang'a and Nyongesa[6], the three factors that seem to greatly contribute to the building up of a strong culture are: a founder or an influential leader who established desirable values, a sincere and dedicated commitment to operate the business of the institution according to those desirable values and a genuine concern for the well-being of the institution's stakeholders. From the foregoing discussion, there is no doubt that the type of culture prevailing in an institution has a great bearing on its performance. This calls for the development and perpetuation of a strong culture in an institution that supports high performance.

Hellriegel, Slocum, and Woodman[7] identify a strong organisational culture with high work productivity for three reasons: 1) a strong culture promotes coherence between culture and strategy, which is very important for the implementation of the strategy; 2) a strong culture motivates the staff to pursue the set goals; and 3) a strong culture makes the staff accept responsibility and motivates them. The stronger the culture in the institution, the less attention is to be paid to formal rules and regulations with the aim of controlling staff behaviour.[8]

Professionals (e.g. medical doctors) pay less attention to rules, procedures, and formal structures, and tend to focus on the diagnosis and the solutions to treatment problems. They turn to their colleagues for help and form teams which results in more effective, efficient, and quality performance; however, a complete absence of rules and

---

[6] M.J. Ng'ang'a, W. J. Nyongesa (2012). *The Impact of Organisational Culture on Performance of Educational Institutions*. "International Journal of Business & Social Science", vol. 3, no. 8, p. 211.

[7] D. Hellriegel, J.W. Slocum, R.W. Woodman (1998). *Organizational Behavior*, light edition. South Western College Publishing, Ohio, p. 635.

[8] I. Gurkov (1998). *Mil'ner B. Z. Theory of Organizations*. "Voprosy Economiki", vol. 11.

procedures or non-compliance to them can lead to a chaos. Thus, the executives of institutions are to find a balance between the rules, restrictions, and the medical staff discretion. In the institutional activities, especially in the relations with the staff, all the rules, principles of conduct, and other aspects are to be transparent and specific, and to leave as little as possible space for ambiguities and misunderstandings.[9]

An organisational culture also plays an important role in the process of adaptation. It is difficult for a newcomer to adapt to such large organisations as hospitals or polyclinics, therefore, the professional adaptation of medical staff takes longer than that of the staff in industrial companies. To integrate the newcomers, experienced and qualified staff are mainly appointed, but that is risky, as the quality of work suffers when qualified staff put their effort into the training and control of other staff instead of pursuing institutional goals or the welfare of patients. According to Shahzad et al.[10], a strong organisational culture helps new employees to adopt the organisational culture and to get the competitive advantage under particular conditions.

Medical staff in healthcare institutions face human suffering, pain, fear, and death, more frequently than others experience nervous breakdowns and find themselves in stressful situations, moreover, they encounter a lack of time and the necessity to make decisions with incomplete information. The quality and effectiveness of work also depend on staff qualifications and their personal qualities and principles. Increased moral responsibility of the staff, with respect to patients and colleagues, is positively affected by the organisational culture.

The impact of organisational culture on performance

Most of the researchers who deal with the issues of an organisational culture agree that it has a strong impact on the long-term performance of an institution.[11] The findings imply that when individuals are satisfied with their roles and feel that their supervisor or leader provides them with support, their contextual performance is expected to increase.[12] A number of Lithuanian authors explored the impact of an organisational culture on the staff of business organisations and their performance. To quote Paužuolienė and Trakšelys[13], the values of an organisational culture make a positive impact on the staff, provide its members with a sense of identity, strengthen the trust of the staff in their organisation, and distinguish the organisation from other organisations.

[9] I. Pikturnaitė, J. Paužuolienė (2013). *Organizacinės kultūros Institucionalizavimas*. "Tiltai", vol. 4, pp. 93–108.

[10] F. Shahzad, R.A. Luqman, A.R. Khan, L. Shabbir (2012). *Impact of organizational culture on organizational performance: An overview*. "Interdisciplinary Journal of Contemporary Research in Business", vol. 3, no. 9, pp. 975–985.

[11] S.M. Irfan, T. Hussain, I. Yousaf (2009). *Organizational culture: Impact on female employees' job performance*. "Journal of Quality and Technology Management", vol. V, no. 1, pp. 1–16.

[12] S. Sinha, A. Singh, N. Gupta, R. Dutt, *op.cit.*

[13] J. Paužuolienė, K. Trakšelys (2009). *Komunikacijos reikšmė organizacinėje kultūroje*. "Vadyba", vol. 14, no. 2, pp. 157–162.

Priorities and values in an institution form for a long time and turn into a culture merely when all the members of the organisation understand and observe them. As stated by Šimanskienė[14], organisational culture provides a sense of identity, develops loyalty to the mission of the organisation, becomes a key management tool, helps to take into account the needs of clients and staff, ensures the recognition of the value of each individual, creates friendly relations with colleagues, and defines and establishes the standards of behaviour.

In accordance with the character of social identity, an individual depends on the organisational culture and simultaneously influences the changes in the organisational culture.[15] An organisational culture forms as a response to an entirely new situation for the organisation (within the organisation and outside it). That allows the organisation to adapt to changing conditions and to pursue its goals. In response to a new situation, organisational culture makers may change the general language and specific working terminology, to facilitate the rules and requirements for the process of work, establish informal and formal relationships between the members of the organisation, divide work in a different way, and approve the systems of promotion, or motivation.

The impact of the organisational culture is also related to its institutionalisation: the more different cultural aspects recorded in various documents, brochures, and other forms, the more that affects the staff of the organisation.[16] Leaders, heroes, and stories mean the personification of cultural values and examples to be emulated by the staff of the organisation. It is important to share information and to hand on the rules and requirements of the organisation. Myths and stories about important events or individuals who play significant roles in the organisation can create an atmosphere of a harmonious and united team which pursues the same goals and seeks the welfare of the organisation.

Workplace design, the presence of symbolic elements, slogans, workplace layout, style, either strict and "official" or "convenient", rigorous procedures, or creative disorder also make an impact on the formation and maintenance of an organisational culture. However, each element of culture has to be individualised. Thus, e.g., strict introduction of a formal dress code in a company which is mainly engaged in arts may result in the reduction of productivity and the emergence of an internal conflict.[17] Tuľchinskij[18], as well as Stephen and Robbins[19], agree that organisational traditions and rituals play an important role in the building up of organisational culture and its use in the pursuit of the desired goals. That means an opportunity for the staff to become closer, dream about the future together, and resolve contradictions, and for the head

[14] L. Šimanskienė (2008). *Organizacinės kultūros poveikis organizacijų valdymui.* "Management Theiry and Studines for Rural Business and Infrastrukture Development", vol. 15, no. 4, pp. 175–180.

[15] O.E. Steklova, *op.cit.*

[16] I. Pikturnaitė, J. Paužuolienė, *op.cit.*

[17] A.S. Dudin (2007). *Korporativnaja kuľtura.* "Professija Direktor", vol. 6, pp. 96–100.

[18] G.L. Thulcinkij (2001). *PR firmy: Tehnologija i jeffektivnosť.* Aletejja, Sankt-Peterburgskij gosudarstvennyj universitet kuľtury i iskusstv, Sankt-Peterburg, p. 294.

[19] P. Stephen, S.P. Robbins (2003). *Organizacinės elgsenos pagrindai.* „Poligrafija ir informatika", UAB, pp. 285–288.

of the organisation, to once again strengthen her/his authority and to inculcate some important ideas, since informally communicated ideas are perceived better.

In Pikčiūnas'[20] opinion, the prevailing symbols not only predetermine the way how the organisation members perceive their organisation, but also how they introduce their organisation to independent users. In that context, two things are worth noting. First, symbols are to be used as frequently as possible and spread as widely as possible. Second, not all the staff and users can be sure about the meaning of one or another symbol. To achieve the aims effectively and fluently, it is necessary to choose staff members who possess certain specific knowledge and skills for the performance of the delegated tasks. One cannot expect to recruit a new staff member and to observe an immediate increase in work productivity. Before the newcomer is adapted to the organisation and learns all about its rules, requirements, values, and traditions, she/he is of little use for the organisation, therefore, organisations are interested in the involvement of each staff member in their activities as fast as possible. An organisational culture can be an important factor in predicting the behaviour of the organisation members. The said characteristics cover both the structural aspects and the aspects of the organisation members' behaviour.[21]

Measurement of the impact of organisational culture on performance

Researchers propose different ways for the quantitative measurement of an organisational culture based on staff-recognized norms, views, and values. However, according to Matsumoto[22], the said assessment methods are not comprehensive, since they assess the culture on an individual staff member level and neglect the impact of the organisational culture of individual divisions. Cameron and Quinn[23] propose to analyse the basic values and beliefs on the basis of the Competing Values Framework which reflects the response of respondents to the importance of different scenarios for their organisational culture. The said methodology of qualitative assessment has been recognised internationally. By means of it, the most important aspects of an organisation can be assessed, while the organisational culture can be analysed on several levels.

The methodology includes two types of measurement: those of the content and of the example. The content measurements are assigned to the cultural aspects of an organisation whose role implies hints in scenarios that help the staff to identify cultural values in their organisation. The example measurements are assigned to the profile of the organisational culture which is established by means of scoring in compliance with a certain methodology.

[20] A. Pikčiūnas (2002). *Organizacijos ryšių sistema*. Vytauto Didžiojo universiteto leidykla, Kaunas.

[21] I. Gurkov, *op.cit.*

[22] D. Matsumoto (2002). *Methodological requirements to test a possible ingroup advantage in judging emotions across cultures: Comments on Elfenbein and Ambady and evidence*. "Psychological Bulletin", vol. 128, pp. 236–242.

[23] K.S. Cameron, R.E. Quinn (1999). *Diagnosing and Changing Organizational Culture: Based on the Competing Values Framework*. Addison-Wesley, Reading, MA.

Cameron and Quinn (1999) proposed 6 dimensions which together represent the fundamental values of an organisational culture. They include[24]: 1) dominant organisational characteristics; 2) leadership style; 3) management of employees; 4) organisational glue; 5) strategic emphasis; and 6) criteria for success which demonstrate how to define achievement and what shall be encouraged and awarded. As stated by the authors, the collection is not complete, however, sufficient for the establishment of the type of an organisational culture.

In accordance with the staff answers to the content questions, one can identify the organisational culture or a mix of cultures that provide its basis. By means of that methodology, the current and the target organisational cultures shall be measured in parallel. The outcomes shall be displayed on a special coordinate system. The coordinate axes present the common values of the organisational culture (flexibility and discretion; stability and control; internal focus and integration; and external focus and differentiation). Each quadrant of the coordinate system corresponds to a certain type of culture, while the coordinate points are calculated as the means of the scores marked by the respondents at each type of culture (separately for the current and the target culture). That kind of a graphical depiction is convenient and visual, and the profile of organisational culture allows to quickly assess both the current and the target culture and relationships.[25]

METHODOLOGY OF THE STUDY

To assess the organisational culture of the Lab divisions and its impact on the Lab performance, a study was carried out which used both quantitative and qualitative analysis methods. During the qualitative analysis (a semi-structured interview), the executives of the Lab were surveyed. By means of the interview method, their views on the organisational culture of the Lab division and its performance were established. By means of the quantitative analysis, the weight coefficients of the organisational culture elements of the Lab divisions were calculated (table 1).

Table 1. Weight coefficients of the organisational culture elements of the Lab divisions

No.	Elements of organisational culture	Element weight coefficient, scores
1.	Staff turnover	8
2.	Staff loyalty	6
3.	Conflicts at work	14
4.	Overall image of the organisation	8
5.	Adaptation at the workplace	12
6.	Service quality	10
7.	Lab development	12

Source: own construction.

---

[24] *Ibidem.*
[25] L. Šimanskienė, *op.cit.*

The studies of the views of the staff of the Lab divisions on the elements of the organisational culture aimed to establish what values and behavioural norms predominated in the organisation and what values were desirable for the members of the organisation, as well as whether the declared values corresponded to those really existing in the division. The data were processed, systematized, and graphically displayed by means of Microsoft Office Excel and SPSS software. For the establishment and assessment of the statistical relationships of the variables, McNemar's Chi-square and a number of degrees of freedom tests were used. The calculation of the rank-order correlation coefficient was performed under Spearman's rank variable formula. The statistical differences between the respondent groups were assessed under the (p) significance level coefficient. Provided $p < 0,05$, the differences between the attributes were considered to be statistically significant.

The study was conducted in 2015, and the site of the study was a clinical lab in Lithuania with its 16 divisions in different cities. The lab performed tests for the patients of healthcare institutions, and the patients who were not directed by their doctors and wished to have tests done were provided with paid services. The Lab was guided by the policy which included the principal aims set for the good of the staff, patient, and society. New tests and methods were continually introduced, and the quality of testing was improving.

The sample of the study was the staff of the Lab divisions: employees and executives. The sample was calculated in accordance with V.I Paniotto's formula at 5% error. The number of the respondents was 93.

To assess the elements of the organisational culture, identified by the executives of the Lab, the author-derived formulas were used.

The staff turnover indicator:

$$D_{sk} = \frac{A_{sk}}{D_{vid.sk}} \cdot 100\% \qquad (1)$$

where D_{sk} was the staff turnover indicator; A_{sk} was the number of dismissals over the period; and $D_{vid.sk}$ was an average number of the staff over the period.

The staff loyalty index:

$$D_{si} = \frac{D_{sp}}{D_{sn}} \cdot 100\% \qquad (2)$$

where D_{si} was the staff stability index; D_{sp} was the number of the staff who worked in the Lab for one year; and D_{sn} was the number of the staff hired a year ago.

The situation of conflicts in the divisions:

$$K_{sk} = \frac{K_{sk}}{R_{sk}} \qquad (3)$$

where K_{sk} was the number of conflicts per staff member a year; K_{sk} was the number of conflicts in units; and R_{sk} was the number of the staff in the division.

Adaptation at the workplace:

$$A_{d.v.} = A_{laikas} * N_{sk.periode} \qquad (4)$$

where $A_{d.v.}$ was newcomer adaptation; A_{laikas} was the time of training per staff member; and $N_{sk.periode}$ was the number of newcomers hired over one year.
Service quality:

$$P_{kokybe} = \frac{T_{sk}}{I_{sk}} \qquad (5)$$

where P_{kokybe} was the relative quality of the Lab services; T_{sk} was the number of tests a year; and I_{sk} was the number of individual patient visits to an institution a year.

RESULTS AND DISCUSSION

To assess the organisational culture of each division of the Lab, seven weight coefficients of the elements of the organisational culture established by the executives (experts) of the Lab were applied (see table 1).

The element of conflicts was identified by the executives of the Lab divisions as the least desired and the most harmful to the organisation. The least weight coefficient was ascribed by the executives to staff loyalty, which can be accounted for by an excess of the Lab staff nationally. On the basis of the weight coefficients of the elements of organisational culture, the meanings of the elements of the organisational culture in the Lab divisions were derived (see table 2):

Successful organisations boast a strong organisational culture which makes a positive impact on their performance. As established, 89% of the respondents believed they worked in a successfully performing lab. 67,35% of the staff agreed with the definition of a successful lab and defined the performance of the Lab as high quality (R = 0.658, p < 0.05).

As established, the principal value of a clinical lab was the quality of performance (92% of the respondents). The service quality policy declared by the Lab corresponded to the current one, therefore, both the service providers and the Lab administration were strongly focussed on the performance quality.

The development of the Lab, as witnessed by comparison of the scope of the services provided in the period of 2013 to 2014, was positive in all 16 Lab divisions. The highest indicators belonged to Klaipėda Division (from 43.9 to 103.5 thousand units).

The common indicator of the staff stability amounted to 38%: 13 staff members were hired, and 5 of them stayed for one year. The annual staff turnover in the Lab was 28%. The highest turnover (60%) was observed in Šilalė Division.

Table 2. Meanings of the organisational culture in the Lab divisions

No.	Division	Elements of the organisational culture							Total scores
		1	2	3	4	5	6	7	
1.	Zarasai	200	0	−98.0	68.0	50.6	165.0	228.0	213.6
2.	Naujoji Akmenė	−320	0	−28.0	75.2	50.6	171.0	288.0	236.8
3.	Ignalina	0	0	−14.0	76.0	50.6	213.0	9.6	335.2
4.	Vilnius (Division 1)	−264	300.0	−99.4	65.6	50.6	342.0	0.88	395.7
5.	Kretinga	0	0	−84.0	80.0	50.6	91.0	330.0	467.6
6.	Vilnius (Division 2)	−144	300.0	−36.4	75.2	50.6	206.0	20.9	472.3
7.	Tauragė	−88	300.0	−58.8	67.2	50.6	167.0	54.0	492.0
8.	Mažeikiai	−136	0	−19.6	72.0	50.6	378.0	253.2	598.2
9.	Vilnius (Division 5)	0	0	−105.0	72.0	50.6	320.0	309.6	647.2
10.	Vilnius (Division 3)	−264	600.0	−46.2	72.0	50.6	184.0	90.0	686.4
11.	Vilnius (Division 4)	0	0	−84.0	64.0	50.6	284.0	52.8	367.4
12.	Panevėžys	−264	396.0	−119.0	54.0	50.6	874.0	180.0	1171.6
13.	Šiauliai	−224	600.0	−98.0	72.8	50.6	183.0	818.4	1402.8
14.	Klaipėda	−224	0	−159.6	70.4	50.6	145.0	1620.0	1502.4
15.	Šilalė	−480	600.0	−53.2	68.8	50.6	273.0	1531.2	1990.4
16.	Utena	0	600.0	−2.0	80.0	50.6	94.0	1200.0	2022.6

Source: own construction.

It is worth noting that the dependence of the number of tests on the number of individual patient visits in 2014 ($R^2 = 0.8048$), in comparison with 2013, grew in all the divisions, however, the number of tests per one patient grew merely in 8 divisions out of 16.

The period of newcomer adaptation per 1 staff member was 4,22 months, after which they started working independently, however, a number of the respondents agreed that the newcomer's knowledge and motivation were also important (38,8%). 65,3% of the respondents tended to rather agree than disagree with the statement that newcomers adapted easily and soon became part of the team when they were received in a warm and friendly manner. Merely 12,7% of the respondents believed that it was difficult for the newcomers to adapt, and the staff productivity was reduced, as the newcomers impeded the process of work.

The total number of conflicts in the Lab amounted to 5,5 conflicts per person a year. The largest number of conflicts a year was observed in the Klaipėda Division (11,4 conflicts per person), and the smallest, in Ignalina Division (1 conflict per person). As proved by the survey, 37% of the Lab staff agreed that conflict situations were rare and forgettable.

The performance of the Lab divisions was assessed in two aspects: the development of the Lab over the period of 2013 to 2014 (in %) and the scope of the activities of the Lab network, i.e. the number of tests per one staff member (in thousands of units, see table 3).

Table 3. Performance of the Lab divisions

No.	Division	The development of the Lab network over the period of 2013 to 2014	The number of tests (thousands of units per staff member)
1.	Zarasai	(0.08)	18925.5
2.	Naujoji Akmenė	15.0	24012.2
3.	Ignalina	4.5	18235.4
4.	Vilnius (Division 1)	(1.9)	12154.5
5.	Kretinga	27.5	10105.0
6.	Vilnius (Division 2)	21.1	13045.6
7.	Tauragė	0.8	15930.0
8.	Mažeikiai	7.5	11023.3
9.	Vilnius (Division 5)	4.4	8070.0
10.	Vilnius (Division 3)	25.8	9701.5
11.	Vilnius (Division 4)	68.2	20620.5
12.	Panevėžys	135.0	14790.4
13.	Šiauliai	19.0	5997.5
14.	Klaipėda	24.0	11912.4
15.	Šilalė	127.6	9613.0
16.	Utena	100.0	3975.5

Source: own construction.

As proven by the data of table 3, the development of individual Lab divisions over the period of 2013 to 2014 was very different. Some divisions made significant progress (the number of performed tests increased), however, some other divisions acquired advanced equipment and reduced the number of staff, consequently, the number of tests per staff member increased.

The established dependence of the performance of the Lab divisions on the level of the organisational culture in the divisions is presented in figure 1.

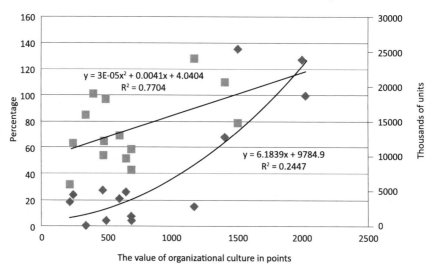

Figure 1. The impact of the organisational culture on the performance of the Lab divisions

Source: own construction.

As seen in figure 1, the higher the level of the organisational culture, the faster the development of Lab divisions' performance is. The relationship is rather significant ($R^2 = 0.7704$). Among 16 divisions, the strongest impact on the development of the Lab performance was felt in the Klaipėda, Šilalė, Šiauliai, and Utena Divisions, and the weakest, in the Panevėžys and Vilnius (1, 2, 3, 4) Divisions. Even though the assessment in the organisational culture in the said divisions was among the highest, the network performance development was rather slow. That could be accounted for by the following reasons:

- reduction in the flow of patients, e.g. low incidence in the town;
- some healthcare institutions stopped collaboration with the Lab and did not send tests;
- poor marketing failed to attract new clients/patients.

It was assumed that the better the organisational culture, the larger the number of tests per staff member. However, as proved by our study, the relationship was weak ($R^2 = 0.2447$). It can be accounted for by the predominance of other business factors:

- a lack of equipment. An advanced and fully automated division which employed two people performed twice more tests than the division that did not have automated equipment and employed the same number of staff;
- the complexity and the type of tests. Some newly set up divisions that started work in 2014 had not yet started working at full capacity and fully using their technological possibilities; they could not perform a wide range of tests.

CONCLUSIONS

An organisational culture makes an impact on the performance and the general corporate climate of organisations, while a strong culture tends to enhance the impact and guides it in the right direction. An organisational culture inspires and motivates the staff to solve common problems, to feel responsibility, and to pursue common individual and organisational goals.

The successful Lab divisions boasted a strong organisational culture, which made a positive impact both on the overall organisational performance and on its individual elements. The Lab declared-policy focused on quality performance as the fundamental value of the organisation.

The better the organisational culture, the faster the development of the Lab performance ($R^2 = 0.7704$) was, however, the dependence of the number of tests performed by one staff member was weak ($R^2 = 0.2447$).

References

Cameron K.S., Quinn R.E. (1999). *Diagnosing and Changing Organizational Culture: Based on the Competing Values Framework*. Addison-Wesley, Reading, MA.

Dudin A.S. (2007). *Korporativnaja kul'tura*. "Professija Direktor", no. 6, pp. 96–100.

Ecko K., Globa H. (2012). *Tipologija organizacionnyh kul'tur municipal'nyh bol'nic respubliki Moldova*. "Military and Political Sciences in the Context of Social Progress", "Problems and Ways of Modern Public Health Development": Materials Digest of the XV and XVI International Scientific and Practical Conferences.

Gurkov I. (1998). *Mil'ner B. Z. Theory of Organizations*. "Voprosy Economiki", vol. 11.

Hellriegel D., Slocum J.W., Woodman R.W. (1998). *Organizational Behavior*, light edition. South Western College Publishing, Ohio.

Irfan S.M., Hussain T., Yousaf I. (2009). *Organizational culture: Impact on female employees' job performance*. "Journal of Quality and Technology Management", vol. V, no. 1, pp. 1–16.

Kaziliūnas A. (2004). *Visuomenei teikiamų paslaugų kokybės ir organizacinės kultūros sąveika*. "Viešoji politika ir administravimas", vol. 9, pp. 71–78.

Matsumoto D. (2002). *Methodological requirements to test a possible ingroup advantage in judging emotions across cultures: Comments on Elfenbein and Ambady and evidence*. "Psychological Bulletin", vol. 128, pp. 236–242.

Ng'ang'a M.J., Nyongesa W.J. (2012). *The Impact of Organisational Culture on Performance of Educational Institutions*. "International Journal of Business & Social Science", vol. 3, no. 8, pp. 211.

Palidauskaitė J. (2001). *Viešojo administravimo etika*. Technologija, Kaunas.

Paužuolienė J., Trakšelys K. (2009). *Komunikacijos reikšmė organizacinėje kultūroje*. "Vadyba", vol. 14, no. 2, pp. 157–162.

Pikčiūnas A. (2002). *Organizacijos ryšių sistema*. Vytauto Didžiojo universiteto leidykla, Kaunas.

Pikturnaitė I., Paužuolienė J. (2013). *Organizacinės kultūros Institucionalizavimas*. "Tiltai", vol. 4, pp. 93–108.

Shahzad F., Luqman R.A., Khan A.R., Shabbir L. (2012). *Impact of organizational culture on organizational performance: An overview*. "Interdisciplinary Journal of Contemporary Research in Business", vol. 3, no. 9, pp. 975–985.

Schrodt P. (2002). *The relationship between organizational identification and organizational culture: Employee perceptions of culture and identification in a retail sales organization*. "Communication Studies", vol. 53, no. 2, pp. 189–202.

Šimanskienė L. (2008). *Organizacinės kultūros poveikis organizacijų valdymui*. "Management Theiry and Studines for Rural Business and Infrastrukture Develipment", vol. 15, no. 4, pp. 175–180.

Šimanskienė L., Gargasas A., Ramanauskas K. (2015). *The role of organizational culture in the organization's activities*. "Management Theory and Studines for Rural Business and Infrastrukture Development", vol. 37, no. 2, pp. 310–320.

Shahzad F., Luqman R.A., Khan A.R., Shabbir L. (2012). *Impact of organizational culture on organizational performance: An overview*. "Interdisciplinary Journal of Contemporary Research in Business", vol. 3, no. 9, pp. 975–985.

Sinha S., Singh A., Gupta N., Dutt R. (2010). *Impact of work culture on motivation and performance level of employees in private sector companies*. "Acta Oeconomica Pragensia", vol. 2010, no. 6, pp. 49–67.

Steklova O.E. (2007). *Organizacionnaja kul'tura*. UlGTU, Ul'janovsk.

Stephen P., Robbins S.P. (2003). *Organizacinės elgsenos pagrindai*. „Poligrafija ir informatika", UAB, pp. 285–288.

Thulcinkij G.L. (2001). *PR firmy: Tehnologija i jeffektivnost'*. Aletejja, Sankt-Peterburg GUKI.

Barbara Kożuch
Jagiellonian University
e-mail: barbara.kozuch@uj.edu.pl

Regina Lenart-Gansiniec
Jagiellonian University
e-mail: regina.lenart-gansiniec@uj.edu.pl

Katarzyna Sienkiewicz-Małyjurek
Silesian University of Technology
e-mail: katarzyna.sienkiewicz-malyjurek@polsl.pl

SHAPING TRUST IN PUBLIC SCHOOLS

Abstract

Background. The rationale behind the selection of the topic are the shifts that occur in education institutions. The uncertainty of the environment, progressive demographic decline, and the requirement of remaining competitive are driving schools to seek new ways to survive and present an attractive prospectus. One of the challenges faced by schools, and at the same time a legal obligation imposed by the legislation governing education, is the openness of schools to the environment – understood as the establishment of collaboration by the school with its local environment. The literature emphasises that openness to the environment proves to be one of the factors strengthening trust in the organisation. Trust is crucial in shaping mutual relationships between an organisation and its environment. The paper assumes that the prerequisite for engendering trust on the part of candidates and their parents is the appropriate fulfilment of the mission by schools through their efficient management, which may be easily discerned when observing the quality of education.

Research aims. The paper strives to assess the impact of trust in schools on the enrolment results and to identify which principal contributors to trust are used in the practice of Polish schools.

Methodology. Accomplishing the objective of the paper was made possible by an analysis of the body of literature devoted to public trust, complemented by empirical studies. The studies were conducted on a targeted sample selected in an expert manner, comprising public upper-secondary schools located in the territory of the Silesian agglomeration. These studies used a structured interview methodology. The survey covered students in the first year of three upper-secondary schools (N = 15), their parents (N = 30), and principals of upper-secondary schools (N = 3). While selecting students for the survey, winners and finalists of Olympiads and competitions for schools were taken into consideration.

Key findings. The research process led to the conclusion that trust in schools has a direct impact on their enrolment results. Moreover, the findings show the degree to which the primary trust factors are harnessed in upper-secondary education institutions. Further in-depth research requires identification of interdependencies between trust and enrolment success of the school in the context of its ongoing collaboration with partners. After all, trust management constitutes a promising field of challenges for further detailed scientific research.

Keywords: public trust, trust creation, secondary schools, education.

INTRODUCTION

A high level of competitiveness and shifts in the environment present new challenges for organisations. For many organisations it implies a need to search for new ways to survive and flourish. The issue of trust currently receives ample attention from the aspect of organisational theory and research. Trust is both the core and the most useful resource in the organisation. In essence, it generates the value, determines and streamlines team work, drives interpersonal relationships as well as diminishing translational costs and shaping relational capital.[1] Moreover, the area where public trust is shaped and maintained was identified.

Despite research in trust, many questions remain unanswered. Specifically, relatively scant attention has been devoted to building public trust. This paper attempts to fill this research gap by analysing factors that foster trust and linking it with the success of the specific venture. The research problem addressed aims at expanding the current knowledge on trust management.

Educational institutions are subject to manifold changes that take place in all domains. Tremendous importance is given to social, political, and economic transformations that trigger a new manner by which organisations operate across all their aspects. Therefore, under these circumstances, the requirements for educational institutions also alter. Voices have been raised to tailor principles guiding the operations of educational institutions to suit the new requirements. Thus, to survive on the market of educational services, schools need to resort to the management theory and effect changes in their management methods. As a result, the outcome may be seen in the form of successful fulfilment of the school mission due to more effective management. This process may be easily recognised by reviewing teaching standards at a given school.

The literature assumes that the establishment of long-term relationships may become the key for each organisation and act as a remedy to the crisis. Underlying this

---

[1] B. Kożuch, Z. Dobrowolski (2014). *Creating Public Trust. An Organisational Perspective.* Peter Lang GmbH, Frankfurt am Main.

approach lies the idea of building trust.[2] Without trust, it is difficult to expect collaboration with internal as well as external relations of daily operations in the organisation. Hence, trust surges to prominence in contemporary management.

The paper focuses on key aspects concerned with the factors driving effective trust. At the same time, it fits into mainstream contemporary trends in research on inter-organisational relationships and collaboration. When trust is investigated from the perspective of the organisation, it may be structured into: interpersonal, organisational, intra- and inter-organisational trust. This paper puts organisational trust under the spotlight.

To be more specific, the objective of the paper is to empirically assess the impact of trust in schools among students and their parents on the school's enrolment success and to identify the primary trust-building factors which are applied in the practice of educational institutions, illustrated using the example of the upper-secondary school level. In particular, focus was brought to students, and particularly the winners/finalists of Olympiads and competitions for schools. These students enjoy more choice opportunities than the typical candidates. On the whole, they choose a school in a more rational way. Narrowing the research focus to upper-secondary institutions results from the closure of these types of schools which is already underway. According to figures provided by the Central Statistical Office of Poland (GUS), there is a decline in the number of these schools by 12% on an annual basis.[3] Coupled with this, over recent years the number of candidates for schools is lower than the number of school places offered. Due to the considerable shrinking in population, the market for educational services becomes increasingly competitive.

The paper comprises three sections. The first part provides a critical overview of the literature on the specifics embedded in trust from the organisational perspective. The second part discusses the primary trust-building factors. The third and last section shows the findings from the empirical research conducted among first-year students at upper-secondary schools as well as the parents supporting their decisions and the principals of these schools. The research was explanatory in its nature. The research process yielded the conclusion that trust in schools has a relatively high impact on their enrolment results.

---

[2] A. Wójcik-Karpacz (2014). *Zaufanie w relacjach międzyorganizacyjnych: substytucja i komplementarność.* "Prace Naukowe Uniwersytetu Ekonomicznego we Wrocławiu", vol. 366; B. Kożuch (2014). *Organizacyjna perspektywa zaufania publicznego. Zarys koncepcji* [in:] Ł. Sułkowski, A. Woźniak (eds.), *Przedsiębiorczość i zarządzanie,* "Zarządzanie Humanistyczne", vol. XV, no. 11, part III; B. Kożuch, K. Sienkiewicz-Małyjurek (2015). *Dimensions of Intra-organisational Trust in Local Public Administration.* Proceedings International Research Society For Public Management Conference, Birmingham.

[3] GUS (2014). *Oświata i wychowanie w roku szkolnym 2013/2014.* Warszawa.

CONCEPT AND ESSENCE OF TRUST

Trust, both in common language as well as in the reference literature is defined and understood differently. As a consequence, many definitions of trust occur, and when analysing them, it is possible to identify a certain common basis for interpreting this concept. Frequently, the emphasis is placed on the issue of characteristics related to uncertainty[4], interdependency, sensitivity[5], credibility[6] as well as reliability, predictability, readiness for collaboration, goodwill, and responsibility.[7] Importantly, definitions of trust also include aspects of trust concerned with: the credibility of the other party[8] and willingness to trust the other party connected with a sensitivity to its activities.[9]

Trust is broadly understood to mean the conviction about the credibility and benevolence of the trusted entity and the decision to take risks with respect to future behaviours displayed by another person (or persons) in a situation of interdependencies and lack of control. From a slightly different perspective, trust tends to be associated with predicting positive effects generated by the activities of others, which is belief in the good intentions and expectation that others will deliver on their promises.[10] More broadly, trust is a subjective perception by a specific individual, being a spinoff of their judgements. It rests on the willingness to trust in the other party, raising awareness of sensitivity to its activities following assessment of the other party's credibility.[11]

Essentially, a great many typologies of trust may be traced in the literature. The paper omits a full exemplification of trust typology, because these may be found in the other works cited above. Attention should be devoted to the form of organisational trust. Basically, organisational trust is defined as the "perceived credibility of an organisation estimated by dimensions of transparency, integrity, competence, benevolence, and reliability, and based on information from the third party (reputation), personal experience, and compatibility of values (identification)".[12]

---

[4] A. Josang, S.L. Presti (2004). *Analysing the relationship between risk and trust* [in:] *Proceedings of the Second International Conference on Trust Management.* Springer-Verlag, Berlin–Heidelberg, pp. 135–145.

[5] R.B. Handfield, C. Bechtel (2004). *Trust, power, dependence, and economics: Can SCM research borrow paradigms?.* "International Journal of Integrated Supply Management", vol. 1, no. 1.

[6] R. Hardin (2006). *Trust.* Polity Press Cambridge.

[7] B. Kożuch, *op.cit.*

[8] S.B. Sitkin, N.L. Roth (1993). *Explaining the limited effectiveness of legalistic remedies for trust/distrust.* "Organization Science", vol. 4; K. Blomqvist, P. Stahle (2000). *Building Organizational Trust.* 16th Annual IMP Conference, Bath, UK; L.G. Zucker (1986). *Production of trust: Institutional sources of economic structure.* "Organizational Behavior", vol. 8; A. Zaheer, B. McEvily, V. Perrone (1998). *Does trust matter? Exploring the effects of interorganizational and interpersonal trust on performance.* "Organization Science", vol. 9; B. Kożuch, Z. Dobrowolski, *op.cit.*

[9] R.C. Mayer, J.H. Davis, F.D. Schoorman (1995). *An integrative model of organizational trust.* "Academy of Management Review", vol. 20, p. 712.

[10] W.M. Grudzewski, I.K. Hajduk, A. Sankowska, M. Wańtuchowicz (2009). *Zarządzanie zaufaniem w przedsiębiorstwie.* Wolters Kluwer, Kraków.

[11] A. Sankowska (2011). *Wpływ zaufania na zarządzanie przedsiębiorstwem. Perspektywa wewnątrzorganizacyjna.* Difin, Warszawa, p. 34.

[12] M. Pirson (2008). *Facing the Trust Gap Measuring and Managing Stakeholder Trust.* SVH, Saarbrucken, p. 60.

Trust has an immense significance for an organisation's operations. First, trust is seen as the reason for establishing relationships and collaboration.[13] Trust is a force facilitating and simplifying coordination of social interactions and processes. Trust promotes collaboration while accomplishing the objectives set, and emerges as the requirement for integration, effective learning, and exchange of knowledge and experience.

Second, trust is a contributor to the reduction of transactional costs[14], risk[15], as well as uncertainty in terms of the organisation's operations in an unstable and unpredictable environment.[16]

Third, trust has key implications for interpersonal contacts inside the organisation. Overall, this refers to relationships, it inspires reciprocity and may enhance the quality and quantity of social interactions.[17]

As previously noted, organisational trust is a specific manifestation of an organisational climate.[18] Principally, this is associated with credibility, and more specifically, with the conviction about credibility represented by the other party. Thus, when deliberating the concept and essence of trust, it is vital to take into account its implications for generating collaborations, based on benevolence and integrity.

SHAPING TRUST IN PUBLIC ORGANISATIONS

The identification of the drivers of trust affects the manner by which the problems concerned with organisational trust are addressed.[19] Essentially, these drivers are volatile, they continually evolve and advance, thereby creating new solutions for a specific problem. Of importance, however, are two conditions that constitute a specific toolbox. When structuring them, it should be kept in mind that trust is largely

---

[13] P.C. Early (1986). *Trust, perceived importance of praise and criticism, and work performance: An examination of feedback in the United States and England.* "Journal of Management", vol. 12; J.L. Badaracco (1991). *The Knowledge Link: How Firms Compete Through Strategic Alliances.* Harvard Business School Press, Boston, MA; J.L. Bennett (1996). *Building Relationships for Technology Transfer.* "Communications of the ACM", vol. 39, no. 9; G. Hamel (1991). *Competition for Competence and Inter-Partner Learning within International Strategic Alliances.* "Strategic Management Journal", no. 12; J. Paliszkiewicz (2013). *Zaufanie w zarządzaniu.* PWN, Warszawa.

[14] C. Handy (1995). *Trust and the virtual organization.* "Harvard Business Review", vol. 73, no. 3.

[15] P.S. Adler (2001). *Market, hierarchy, and trust: The knowledge economy and the future of capitalism.* "Organization Science", vol. 1, no. 2, p. 217.

[16] R.M. Morgan, S.D. Hunt (1994). *The commitment-trust theory of relationship marketing.* "Journal of Marketing", vol. 58, no. 3, July, pp. 24–38.

[17] *Ibidem.*

[18] A. Sankowska (2013). *Further understanding of links between interorganisational trust and enterprise innovativeness – from a perspective of an enterprise.* "International Journal of Innovation and Learning", vol. 13, no. 3, p. 9.

[19] S. Bibb, J. Kourdi (2004). *Trust Matters for Organizational and Personal Success.* Palgrave Macmillan, New York, pp. 161–167; B. Kożuch, *op.cit.*

based on the subjective conviction that the other party will not harness its advantage. At that point, elements related to the sense of safety and voluntary participation come to the foreground.

Drivers of trust may be divided by diverse criteria. Given the fields of their application, the following are distinguished: those concerned with (1) competences, (2) intra-organisational circumstances and (3) collaboration with the environment (table 1). Though, it is increasingly stressed that trust is built upon compliance with the reciprocity basis while exchanging values. For instance, Zucker argues that the following factors are significant: previous exchange, reputation, professionalization, and authority of institutions.[20] Other authors point out: attractiveness, dynamism, expertise, belief, intentions, reliability, and social responsibility.[21] It is revealed that core to organisational trust are the attitudes shown by senior management staff and employees towards clients.[22] From among numerous studies, the work by R.C. Mayer et. al. should receive attention.[23] From these authors three common factors have been identified: ability, benevolence, and integrity.

Competences[24] are a combination of different abilities, including capabilities of acquiring knowledge, which is crucial for the creation of competitive advantage, reputation, participation in projects, awards, mentions, new technologies, holding membership in organisations, or recommendations.[25] Of notable significance are reputation and opinions, as found in publicly available sources such as: mass media, publications issued by consumers' organisations, and certification authorities. Equally important are also individual sources of information, i.e.: friends, family, or acquaintances.[26]

Ability to inspire others[27] stems from the fact that superiors have a high impact on building trust in the organisation. All in all, providing the patterns for positive relationships starts from the top management and then permeates through

---

[20] L.G. Zucker, *op.cit.*

[21] W. Grudzewski, I.K. Hejduk, A. Sankowska, M. Wańtuchowicz (2007). *Zarządzanie zaufaniem w organizacji wirtualnej.* Difin, Warszawa, p. 136.

[22] L. Young, G. Albaum, (2003). *Measurement of trust in salesperson-customer relationships in direct selling.* "Journal of Personal Selling and Sales Management", vol. 24, no. 3, pp. 253–269.

[23] R.C. Mayer, J.H. Davis, F.D. Schoorman, *op.cit.*

[24] R.C. O'Brien (1995). *Employee involvement in performance improvement: A consideration of tacit knowledge, commitment and trust.* "Employee Relations", vol. 17, no. 3; A.K. Mishra (1996). *Organizational responses to crisis: The centrality of trust* [in:] R.M. Kramer, T.R. Tyler (eds.), *Trust in Organizations: Frontiers of Theory and Research.* Sage, Thousand Oaks, CA; K. Blomqvist (1997). *The many faces of trust.* "Scandinavian Journal of Management", vol. 13, no. 3.

[25] J. Rokita (2005). *Zarządzanie strategiczne. Tworzenie i utrzymywanie przewagi konkurencyjnej.* PWE, Warszawa, p. 143; W. Czakon (2009). *Przedsiębiorstwo oparte na wiedzy w kontekście międzyorganizacyjnym* [in:] R. Krupski (ed.), *Zarządzanie strategiczne. Problemy kierunki badań.* Prace Naukowe Wyższej Szkoły Zarządzania i Przedsiębiorczości. Wydawnictwo Wałbrzyskiej Wyższej Szkoły Zarządzania i Przedsiębiorczości, Wałbrzych, p. 289.

[26] M. Sander, B. Weywara (2006). *Markenvertrauen im Rahmen des Markenmanagements, Konsumentenvertauen: Konzepte und Andwendungen für ein nachhaltiges Kundenbindungsmanagement.* Vahlen Franz Gmbh, München, p. 254.

[27] S.M. Covey (2009). *How the best leaders build trust. Leadership now.* http://www.leadershipnow.com/CoveyOnTrust.html (access: 22.11.2015).

Table 1. Factors in building trust

Author/authors	Factors	Manifestation
O'Brien 1995 Mishra 1996 Sydow 1998 Kożuch, Sienkiewicz-Małyjurek 2015	Capabilities	Technological capability
		Business capability
		Meta ability to cooperate
Covey 2009	Ability to inspire others	Benevolent atmosphere
		Security and stability
		Honesty
Luhmann 1995 Ståhle 1998 Dodgson 1992 Sydow 1998 Creed and Miles 1996 Jones and George 1998 Zucker 1986 Nonaka 1996 Tyler, Kramer 1996 Hardy et al. 1998	Goodwill	Credibility
		Reciprocity
		Common values
		Accepted code of behaviour
		Personal mutual liking:
		Organisational identity
		Organisational culture
Luhmann 1979 O'Brien 1995 Mishra 1996 Das and Teng 1998 Sydow 1998 O'Brien 1995 Swan 1995 Whitener et al 1998 Jones and George 1998	Specific competences and experience	Sharing knowledge
		Internal communication
		Direct meetings
		Continuous interaction
		Transfer of key personnel
		Involvement

Source: own development based on literature.

middle management level and finally affecting behaviours among employees. This has a particular influence on sharing knowledge, fair conduct while competing, and no resistance to decisions made. Whereas, the ability to exert an influence by superiors and to inspire others is closely linked to the benevolent atmosphere prevailing in the company.

Goodwill is related to building the climate and culture of trust which includes, among others: structural factors[28], comprising: normative cohesion, organisation's transparency, stability of the social order, and employees' responsibility. Normative cohesion may be understood to mean a lasting system of applicable rules that determine the sense of order among the members of the organisation and their certainty of their identity with the company.[29] The literature highlights the conviction

---

[28] P. Sztompka (2002). *Socjologia. Analiza społeczeństwa.* Znak, Kraków, pp. 318–319.

[29] M. Maccoby (2003). *To Build Trust, Ethics Are Not Enough.* "Research Technology Management", vol. 46, no. 5, p. 60.

that interpersonal trust positively affects the quality of the group communication, their abilities to work at and solve problems, their involvement and their propensity to share knowledge.[30] Overall, this enhances the predictability of their partner's behaviours.

Interactions and experience **are** connected with opening the organisation to its environment. Its level is gauged based on the communication with the environment[31], network links, sharing knowledge and ideas[32], partnership[33], and personal relationships.[34] Also, this refers to personal involvement, sense of belonging, mutual support, and learning from partners.

Recognising the manners by which trust is built and created principally gains in prominence in the context of public trust. This is due to a steady erosion of trust in public institutions. After all, it is widely assumed that public trust may become conducive to not only forging collaboration with partners and accomplishing common goals[35], but also in streamlining the management of contemporary public organisations. It should however be remembered that trust is not a goal in itself for an organisation, but rather a means to achieve and accomplish goals.[36]

Inherent to public trust is the fact that it is produced on the basis of the delivery of public services. Overall, public organisations are involved in the fulfilment of public tasks, the rights of citizens, as well as the satisfaction of their needs and the delivery of services in their favour. Public trust is reflected in internal relations as well as in relationships between citizens and those performing public services. Fundamentally, this is concerned with their belief that public organisations are competent, open, function in compliance with the law and accomplish public goals to the highest standards. Accordingly, public trust is manifested in relationships between public organisations and their stakeholders.

A natural consequence of recognising the importance of trust to the operations run by public organisations is to ensure suitable conditions that facilitate its generation. In conclusion, in the light of the body of literature to date – a variety of factors are seen as necessary for trust to occur in the organisation: starting from appropriate competences[37],

---

[30] L.G. Zucker, *op.cit.*

[31] R.C. O'Brien, *op.cit.*

[32] L.G. Zucker, *op.cit.*

[33] W. Creed, R. Miles (1996). *Trust in organizations: A conceptual framework linking organizational forms, managerial philosophies, and the opportunity costs of controls* [in:] *Trust in Organizations: Frontiers of Theory and Research*. SAGE Publications, Thousand Oaks, CA, pp. 16–39.

[34] L.G. Zucker, *op.cit.*

[35] M. Bugdol (2010). *Zaufanie jako element systemu wartości organizacyjnych*. "Współczesne Zarządzanie", no. 2, p. 28; R. Lenart (2014). *Zarządzanie wiedzą w tworzeniu konkurencyjności szkoły*. Wolters Kluwer, Warszawa.

[36] B. Kożuch, K. Sienkiewicz-Małyjurek, *Dimensions...*

[37] R.C. O'Brien, *op.cit.*; A.K. Mishra, *op.cit.*; J. Sydow (1998). *Understanding the constitution of interorganizational trust in trust within and between organizations* [in:] Ch. Lane, R. Bachman (eds.), *Conceptual Issues and Empirical Applications*. Oxford University Press, Oxford; B. Kożuch, K. Sienkiewicz-Małyjurek (2014). *New requirements for managers of public safety systems*. "Procedia – Social and Behavioral Sciences", no. 149; B. Kożuch, K. Sienkiewicz-Małyjurek, *Dimensions...*

through coordination mechanisms[38], and stewardship of essential resources[39], to a positive attitude to stakeholders.[40] From the list, the latter takes on particular saliency. Public trust may be analysed when taking into account the relationships between a public organisation and citizens. This, in turn, requires trust.

RESEARCH METHODOLOGY

The research completed was explanatory in its nature and focused on determination of the impact exercised by trust in schools on their enrolment results and identification of which primary instruments intended to create trust are being leveraged in the practice of Polish schools. The survey covered a targeted sample selected in an expert manner, comprising public upper-secondary schools located on the territory of the Silesian agglomeration. When selecting the sample for the survey, the results of the "National Ranking of Upper-Secondary Schools 2015" guided the inclusion decisions.

The survey was conducted consistently with case-study methodology, propelled by the need to define, understand, and interpret trust instruments. As revealed, the survey was of a pilot nature, and thus the authors overlook the problem of sample representativeness. The survey covered 48 respondents, constituting three groups: principals of public schools (N = 3), students (N = 15) and parents (N = 30). When selecting the students for the survey, the highest scores on the lower secondary school graduation certificate as well as winners and finalists of Olympiads and competitions for schools were taken into account. All interviews were carried out in the premises of the educational institutions. Interviews took from 30 up to 45 minutes, while the answers provided by the participants were entered in interview questionnaires on an ongoing basis.

Measurement of public trust presents a challenging task. The challenge is further compounded by the fact that trust is a complex phenomenon. The literature contains numerous approved and recognised methods for gauging trust, including

---

[38] R.C. O'Brien, *op.cit.*; A.K., Mishra *op.cit.*; J. Sydow, *op.cit.*

[39] N. Luhmann (1995). *Social Systems*. Stanford University Press, Stanford, CA; P. Ståhle (1998). *Supporting a System's Capacity for Self-Renewal*. A Doctoral Dissertation, Research Reports 190, University of Helsinki; J. Sydow, *op.cit.*; R. Creed, W. Miles, *op.cit.*, pp. 16–39; G.R. Jones, J.M. George (1998). *The experience and evolution of trust: Implications for cooperation and teamwork*. "Academy of Management Review", vol. 23, no. 3, pp. 531–546; L.G. Zucker, *op.cit.*; R.M. Kramer, T.R. Tyler, (1996). *Trust in Organizations: Frontiers of Theory and Research*. Sage Publications, California; C. Hardy, N. Phillips, T. Lawrence (1998). *Distinguishing trust and power in interorganizational relations: Forms and facades of trust in trust within and between organizations* [in:] Ch. Lane, R. Bachman (eds.), *Conceptual Issues and Empirical Applications*. Oxford University Press, Oxford.

[40] B. Kożuch, *op.cit.*

organisational trust.[41] As a result, in the context of management sciences it is suggested to principally bring focus on to the processes of management and the organisation's operations as well as its formulation and attainment of goals when investigating public trust. Put differently, public trust requires integrity.

Therefore, the analysis of existing methods designed to measure trust leads to the conclusion that there is no tool that fully corresponds to the specifics rooted in works of schools. In consequence, the tool proposed by S.K. Hacker and M.L. Willard was adopted for gauging organisational trust.[42] The research was conducted in September 2015 and it was split into two phases: In the first phase, the survey embraced first-year students of public upper-secondary schools and their parents. The second phase of the survey took place among the principals of public schools located in the Silesian Province.

TRUST IN UPPER-SECONDARY SCHOOLS – SURVEY FINDINGS

The surveys were intended to empirically assess the impact of trust in schools among students and their parents to the enrolment success and to identify primary trust-building factors applied in the practice of educational institutions, illustrated with the example of the upper-secondary level and were conducted in three upper-secondary schools across the Silesian Province.

The first aspect of the survey was to determine the degree to which trust affects the enrolment success achieved by educational institutions. Success is commonly associated with victory, prosperity, or positive outcomes of efforts. However, it is difficult to unequivocally define the term. It is rather more about defining certain factors that illustrate the complexity underpinning the term. The measure of success may be the degree by which internal conditions are aligned to external conditions[43], and above all, the capability of collaboration.[44]

---

[41] L.L. Cummings, P. Bromiley (1996). *The organizational trust inventory (OTI): Development and Validation* [in:] R.M. Kramer, T.R. Tyler (eds.), *Trust in Organisations: Frontiers of Theory and Research.* Sage, Thousand Oaks, CA, pp. 302–331; B.D. Adams, J. Sartori (2006). *Validating the Trust in Teams and Trust in Leaders Scales.* DRDC No. CR-2006-008. Defence Research & Development, Toronto; H. Tan, A. Lim (2009). *Trust in co-workers and trust in organization.* "The Journal of Psychology", vol. 143, no. 1, pp. 45–66; R.B. Shaw (1997). *Trust in the Balance: Building Successful Organizations on Results, Integrity, and Concern.* Jossey-Bass, San Francisco; S.K. Hacker, M.L. Willard (2002). *The Trust Imperative: Performance Improvement through Productive Relationship.* American Society for Quality, Milwaukee, Wisconsin; G.L. De Furia (1997). *Facilitators Guide to the Interpersonal Trust Surveys.* Pfeiffer & Co, London; M. Pirson, *op.cit.*; D.R. Spitzer (2007). *Transforming Performance Measurement: Rethinking the Way we Measure and Drive The Organizational Success.* Amacon, New York, pp. 230–231.

[42] S.K. Hacker, M.L. Willard, *op.cit.*

[43] A. Pabian (1998). *Uwarunkowania sukcesu przedsiębiorstwa na rynku. Zarys problematyki.* Wydawnictwo Politechniki Częstochowskiej, Częstochowa, p. 7.

[44] B. Kożuch, W. Zaremba (2005). *Czynniki sukcesu organizacji publicznych.* "Prace i Materiały Wydziału Zarządzania Uniwersytetu Gdańskiego", vol. 4, pp. 125–135.

In accordance with the guidelines released by the Ministry of National Education, winners of school Olympiads are awarded the privilege of priority in their selection of a public upper-secondary school. Some schools set their own admission examinations as the basis of entry in a bid to assesses the abilities required by the school.

The analysis of the demographic projections[45] shows that changes occurring in the size of the available student population considerably influences the enrolment process, thereby affecting the network of schools. A decrease in the number of children has been, and will continue to be the reason for the closure of some schools. According to data published by the Educational Research Institute, the major cause underlying the closure of schools is the demographic decline. The number of candidates available to schools over recent years is lower than the number of school places being offered. Due to the significantly diminished population of pupils, the market of educational services is becoming increasingly diversified (table 2).

Table 2. The number of students at the school surveyed over 2010–2015

School year	Number of first-year students			Number of winners of theme competitions/ school Olympiads among first-year students		
	School X	School Y	School Z	School X	School Y	School Z
2010/2011	100	80	50	50	65	29
2011/2012	98	80	50	50	65	25
2012/2013	80	78	45	55	60	30
2013/2014	50	55	40	35	29	35
2014/2015	45	60	30	40	30	29

Source: own survey 2015.

In the first place, the survey centred on the propensity of parents and students to make a decision on the choice of the upper-secondary school surveyed. Students and their parents were asked which factors had influenced their choice of school. These were open questions and the respondents were not given any criteria or factors. They provided their own factors of choice (figure 1). Interviews were conducted individually: with students first and then with their parents.

The initial overview of data corroborates a relatively high number and diversity of listed factors that determine the school selection by both students and their parents. In the responses, parents indicated from 2 up to 6 factors. Some of factors listed, due to their similarity, were classified in common groups. When analysing and assessing values distinguished, it is likely to produce several synthetic evaluating criteria. The first criterion is designed by a positive attitude and consistency of values expressed and the organisational practices of the school. Respondents-parents underlined the relevance of credibility and organisational transparency which manifested itself in recommendations and references in favour of the educational institution. The second criterion applies to competences and attitude to stakeholders, which is related to a high level of management skills and technical expertise.

---

[45] GUS, *op.cit.*

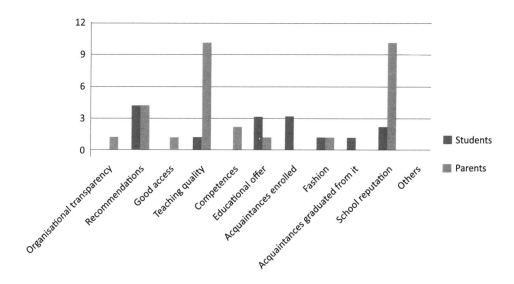

Figure 1. Factors driving selection of the school
Source: own study.

The survey findings provided support to conclusions arising from the theoretical discussion on the relevance of trust. As many as 90% of parents surveyed reported that the choice of school depends on many factors. One factor is trust built through positive opinions and recommendations voiced by persons frequently referred to as opinion leaders. Those surveyed were mostly guided by diverse aspects in their school selection. For parents, over 33% of the respondents recognised the impact of teaching quality and school reputation on their selection of a specific school. Whereas, more than 13% of the participants pointed out the importance of recommendation. The lowest number of parents surveyed were driven by the factors such as: good access, educational offer, and social fashion, when selecting the school.

Prior to making a decision on school selection, a respondent-student often inquired about the opinions held by acquaintances, colleagues, and friends. Importantly, views about the school reverberating in the local environments also mattered, though not only were positive opinions relevant, but also unfavourable opinions voiced by students of the school and their parents. Principally, this information was sought on the Internet. Equally significant were the educational offer and school reputation. The respondents also indicated the level of education, extracurricular activities, and achievements boasted by the school. Frequently, student respondents checked the comparative rankings of upper-secondary schools, specifically in terms of the graduation (secondary school final examinations) rate at an advanced level and admission for higher education institutions.

The findings from empirical studies seem to validate the arguments set out in the literature.[46] Central to the creation of public trust are factors concerned with credibility

---

[46] R.C. O'Brien, *op.cit.*; A.K. Mishra, *op.cit.*; J. Sydow, *op.cit.*; B. Kożuch, K. Sienkiewicz-Małyjurek, *New Requirements…, op.cit.*

and competences. Hence, trust originates (derives, results from) assessment of credibility, which may be considered as the willingness to take risks and raise awareness of its operations.[47]

It was found that parents and students did not use the term "trust" in their responses. Nevertheless, respondents-parents said that the selection of the school had been made by the whole family. They rely on their childrens' opinions and other parent's impressions. They trust that the effect of school's operations will be appropriate, enabling their children to be promoted to the next grade and move to the subsequent educational stage. During the interviews, respondents-parents highly esteemed the quality of the service offered, positive opinion on the market as well as knowledge, competence and resources held, and recommendation of the school by a trusted partner. The respondents drew attention to references earned and a partnership approach to collaboration. At that point it is noteworthy that parents-respondents distinguish two aspects of trust: trust in the teaching level of the school and trust in the system of values advocated by the school.[48] It is necessary to emphasise the fact that institutional trust has its origins in personal trust and the authority of the school as an institution. The latter is the outcome of effects and the work style displayed by the principal and teaching staff.

The results obtained confirm the theoretical presumptions on the relationship between trust and enrolment success and more specifically, the choice of a school by parents of students; particularly among winners of school Olympiads and competitions. Overall, relationships based on trust generate increased profits from the collaboration. Trust may be manifested as an effect of a positive reputation of the school, its capabilities, and brand. Those parents, who trust the educational institution, are driven by the conditions of work quality as well as the teachers' reliability, their professional, methodical, and educational competences. For the respondent's parents, the possibility of establishing collaboration with the school emerges a natural consequence of recognising the importance of trust.

Another aspect of the research concerned the identification of trust-building factors utilised by upper-secondary schools. The respondents included the principals of schools. Previous studies show that organisations cannot exist without collaboration which, in turn, requires trust.[49] For that reason, it is necessary to create specific conditions that allow stakeholders to become engaged, while organisations attain their planned intentions and goals.[50] As noted in the literature, an underlying factor in building trust is a procedural justice that pertains to consistent, rational, and objective decision-making based on legal regulations observed.[51] This issue was incorporated

[47] N. Gillespie, G. Dietz (2009). *Trust repair after an organization-level failure.* "Academy of Management Review", vol. 34, no. 1, pp. 127–145.

[48] M.J. Szymański (1998). *Młodzież wobec wartości.* Wydawnictwo Instytutu Badań Edukacyjnych, Warszawa, pp. 9–21.

[49] B. Kożuch, *op.cit.*

[50] R.C. Mayer, J.H. Davis (1999). *The effect of the performance appraisal system on trust for management: A field quasi-experiment.* "Journal of Applied Psychology", vol. 84, pp. 123–136.

[51] B. Kożuch, A. Kożuch (2015). *Zarządzanie partycypacyjne* [in:] B. Kożuch, Ł. Sułkowski (eds.), *Instrumentarium zarządzania publicznego.* Difin, Warszawa.

while designing the research tool. When asked whether the school harnesses any tools or methods to create trust – 68% of the respondents replied in the affirmative "definitely yes". Therefore, it may be concluded that the school surveyed attaches great importance to active efforts, being aware of building trust. The respondents realise that trust is crucial for fostering a lasting and long-term collaboration with their clients (both students as well as parents are regarded as clients).

During the research process, the respondents were asked about the use of selected trust-building tools in practice. The respondents could choose from among thirteen answers or give their own response. However, the selected factors were previously characterised for the group surveyed and their practical application in the educational institution was demonstrated. Such a move was made on purpose, because it appears that the respondents report a variety of factors, yet they do not have any theoretical knowledge in this field and may be lacking in the relevant terminology (table 3).

Table 3. Application of selected tools in building trust in the views held by the respondents – principals of schools – qualitative comparative analysis

Features	In whole			In partial			In general		
	X	Y	Z	X	Y	Z	X	Y	Z
Empathy	✓	✗	✗	✓	✓	✗	✗	✗	✗
Formal agreements/contracts	✗	✗	✗	✗	✗	✗	✓	✓	✓
Quality of information	✓	✓	✗	✓	✗	✗	✗	✗	✗
Competences	✗	✗	✗	✓	✗	✗	✓	✓	✗
Confidentiality	✗	✗	✗	✓	✓	✗	✗	✓	✗
Predictability	✗	✓	✓	✗	✓	✗	✗	✗	✗
References	✗	✓	✓	✗	✓	✗	✗	✗	✗
Style in which operations are conducted	✓	✓	✓	✗	✗	✗	✗	✗	✗
Successes	✓	✓	✗	✓	✗	✗	✗	✗	✗
Candour	✗	✗	✗	✓	✓	✗	✓	✗	✗
Integrity	✓	✓	✓	✗	✗	✗	✗	✗	✗
Credibility	✓	✓	✓	✗	✗	✗	✗	✗	✗
Fulfilment of expectations	✗	✓	✗	✓	✓	✗	✗	✗	✗

Source: own study.

In the ranking of instruments driving trust, credibility and the style in which operations are conducted come into the spotlight. The latter element was specified in-depth by the respondents as openness to the environment, transparency in operations and involving all stakeholders in ongoing activities of the school. At that point, the transparency of operations and decisions made assume prominence. Attention should be also given to the role of references or recommendations, which may imply their significance in building trust. In this situation, support was provided for the previous supposition that interactions and organisation of events integrating the local community constitute an important trust-building tool. On the whole, it is crucial to ensure that there is an opportunity for the students and their parents to meet with school leaders ahead of the school selection decision phase. School strategies governed by the principle of "open doors" facilitate trust building and help to reassure that they will conduct the partnership in a fair manner at the phase of more advanced collaboration when partners have relevant knowledge about each other.

CONCLUSIONS

The findings from literature and empirical research lead to the formation of the following conclusions.

1. Trust in educational institutions constitutes an essential factor in establishing of collaboration and long-term relationships, forging and building interactions intended to coordinate activities, yet the activities performed may result in their survival on the market and weathering the current crisis.

2. Trust is a phenomenon marked by features of subjectivity. Its creation relies on several key activities – their distinction depends on the manner in which an educational institution is managed. In the respondents' opinion, reliability and competences are significant.

3. Reliability and openness to the environment constituted the main factors driving the selection of the specific educational institution. The respondents attach the greatest importance to open and transparent communication with the environment, ensuring feedback and stepping up the collaboration at specific stages. It may be assumed therefore, that the key imperative for the selection of the place where education will be obtained is trust in the specific school, because out of 30 elements examined, 20 were tied to trust.

The studies completed are not free from certain confinements, notably stemming from the size of the research sample, and thus principally resulting in an absence of opportunities for generalisations. Taken together, the research was rather supposed to delineate the extensive and complex issues that underpin the creation of trust-building tools in public educational institutions. Thus, an additional direction set for further scientific explorations may be the launch of research carried out on a larger, representative sample of educational institutions. The authors argue that research devoted to interdependencies in building trust in relation to the current phase of collaboration between partners may be equally interesting. Nonetheless, trust management constitutes an inspiring area of challenges for further, detailed scientific research.

References

Adams B.D., Sartori J. (2006). *Validating the Trust in Teams and Trust in Leaders Scales*. DRDC No. CR-2006-008. Defence Research & Development, Toronto.

Adler P.S. (2001). *Market, hierarchy, and trust: The knowledge economy and the future of capitalism*. "Organization Science", vol. 1, no. 2.

Badaracco J.L. (1991). *The Knowledge Link: How Firms Compete Through Strategic Alliances*. Harvard Business School Press, Boston, MA.

Bennett J.L. (1996). *Building Relationships for Technology Transfer*. "Communications of the ACM", vol. 39, no. 9.

Bibb S., Kourdi J. (2004). *Trust Matters for Organizational and Personal Success*. Palgrave Macmillan, New York.

Blomqvist K. (1997). *The many faces of trust*. "Scandinavian Journal of Management", vol. 13, no. 3.

Blomqvist K., Stahle P. (2000). *Building Organizational Trust*. 16th Annual IMP Conference, Bath, UK.

Bugdol M. (2010). *Zaufanie jako element systemu wartości organizacyjnych*. "Współczesne Zarządzanie", no. 2.

Covey S.M. (2009). *How the best leaders build trust*. Leadership now. http://www.leadershipnow.com/CoveyOnTrust.html (access: 22.11.2015).

Creed W., Miles R. (1996). *Trust in organizations: A conceptual framework linking organizational forms, managerial philosophies, and the opportunity costs of controls* [in:] *Trust in Organizations: Frontiers of Theory and Research*. SAGE Publications, Thousand Oaks, CA.

Cummings L.L., Bromiley P. (1996). *The organizational trust inventory (OTI): Development and Validation* [in:] R.M. Kramer, T.R. Tyler (eds.), *Trust in Organisations: Frontiers of Theory and Research*. Sage, Thousand Oaks, CA.

Czakon W. (2009). *Przedsiębiorstwo oparte na wiedzy w kontekście międzyorganizacyjnym* [in:] R. Krupski (ed.), *Zarządzanie strategiczne. Problemy kierunki badań*. Prace Naukowe Wyższej Szkoły Zarządzania i Przedsiębiorczości. Wydawnictwo Wałbrzyskiej Wyższej Szkoły Zarządzania i Przedsiębiorczości, Wałbrzych.

De Furia G.L. (1997). *Facilitators Guide to the Interpersonal Trust Surveys*. Pfeiffer & Co, London.

Early P.C. (1986). *Trust, perceived importance of praise and criticism, and work performance: An examination of feedback in the United States and England*. "Journal of Management", vol. 12.

Gillespie N., Dietz G. (2009). *Trust repair after an organization-level failure*. "Academy of Management Review", vol. 34, no 1.

Grudzewski W., Hejduk I.K., Sankowska A., Wańtuchowicz M. (2007). *Zarządzanie zaufaniem w organizacji wirtualnej*. Difin, Warszawa.

Grudzewski W.M., Hajduk I.K., Sankowska A., Wańtuchowicz M. (2009). *Zarządzanie zaufaniem w przedsiębiorstwie*. Wolters Kluwer, Kraków.

GUS (2014). *Oświata i wychowanie w roku szkolnym 2013/2014*. Warszawa.

Hacker S.K., Willard M.L. (2002). *The Trust Imperative: Performance Improvement through Productive Relationship*. American Society for Quality, Milwaukee, Wisconsin.

Hamel G. (1991). *Competition for Competence and Inter-Partner Learning within International Strategic Alliances*. "Strategic Management Journal", no. 12.

Handfield R.B., Bechtel C. (2004). *Trust, power, dependence, and economics: Can SCM research borrow paradigms?*, "International Journal of Integrated Supply Management", vol. 1, no. 1.

Handy C. (1995). *Trust and the virtual organization*. "Harvard Business Review", vol. 73, no. 3.

Hardin R. (2006). *Trust*. Polity Press, Cambridge.

Hardy C., Phillips N., Lawrence T. (1998). *Distinguishing trust and power in interorganizational relations: Forms and facades of trust in trust within and between organizations* [in:] Ch. Lane, R. Bachman (eds.), *Conceptual Issues and Empirical Applications*. Oxford University Press, Oxford.

Jones G.R., George J.M. (1998). *The experience and evolution of trust: Implications for cooperation and teamwork*. "Academy of Management Review", vol. 23, no. 3.

Josang A., Presti S.L. (2004). *Analysing the relationship between risk and trust* [in:] *Proceedings of the Second International Conference on Trust Management*. Springer-Verlag, Berlin–Heidelberg, pp. 135–145.

Juchnowicz M. (2007). *Zaufanie organizacyjne*. "Kwartalnik Nauk o Przedsiębiorstwie", vol. 2, no. 3.

Kożuch B. (2014). *Organizacyjna perspektywa zaufania publicznego. Zarys koncepcji* [in:] Ł. Sułkowski, A. Woźniak (eds.), *Przedsiębiorczość i zarządzanie*. "Zarządzanie Humanistyczne", vol. XV, no. 11, part III.

Kożuch B., Dobrowolski Z. (2014). *Creating Public Trust. An Organisational Perspective*. Peter Lang GmbH, Frankfurt am Main.

Kożuch B., Kożuch A. (2015). *Zarządzanie partycypacyjne* [in:] B. Kożuch, Ł. Sułkowski (eds.), *Instrumentarium zarządzania publicznego*. Difin, Warszawa.

Kożuch B., Sienkiewicz-Małyjurek K. (2014). *New requirements for managers of public safety systems*, "Procedia – Social and Behavioral Sciences", no. 149.

Kożuch B., Sienkiewicz-Małyjurek K. (2015). *Dimensions of Intra-organisational Trust in Local Public Administration*. Proceedings International Research Society For Public Management Conference, Birmingham.

Kożuch B., Sułkowski Ł. (2015). *Instrumentarium zarządzania publicznego*. Difin, Warszawa.

Kożuch B., Zaremba W. (2005). *Czynniki sukcesu organizacji publicznych*. "Prace i Materiały Wydziału Zarządzania Uniwersytetu Gdańskiego", vol. 4.

Kramer R.M., Tyler T.R. (1996). *Trust in Organizations: Frontiers of Theory and Research*. Sage Publications, California.

Lenart R. (2014). *Zarządzanie wiedzą w tworzeniu konkurencyjności szkoły*. Wolters Kluwer, Warszawa.

Luhmann N. (1995). *Social Systems*. Stanford University Press, Stanford, CA.

Mayer R.C., Davis J.H. (1999). *The effect of the performance appraisal system on trust for management: A field quasi-experiment*. "Journal of Applied Psychology", vol. 84, pp. 123–136.

Mayer R.C., Davis J.H., Schoorman F.D. (1995). *An integrative model of organizational trust*. "Academy of Management Review", vol. 20.

Mishra A.K. (1996). *Organizational responses to crisis: The centrality of trust* [in:] R.M. Kramer, T.R. Tyler (eds.), *Trust in Organizations: Frontiers of Theory and Research*. Sage, Thousand Oaks, CA.

Maccoby M. (2003). *To Build Trust, Ethics Are Not Enough*. "Research Technology Management", vol. 46, no. 5.

McAllister D.J. (1995). *Affect- and cognition-based trust as foundations for interpersonal cooperation in organizations*. "Academy of Management Journal", vol. 38.

Morgan R.M., Hunt S.D. (1994). *The commitment-trust theory of relationship marketing*. "Journal of Marketing", vol. 58, no. 3, July.

Morgan R.M., Shelby D.H. (1994). *The commitment-trust theory of relationship marketing*. "Journal of Marketing", no. 58.

O'Brien R.C. (1995). *Employee involvement in performance improvement: A consideration of tacit knowledge, commitment and trust*. "Employee Relations", vol. 17, no. 3.

Pabian A. (1998). *Uwarunkowania sukcesu przedsiębiorstwa na rynku. Zarys problematyki*, Wydawnictwo Politechniki Częstochowskiej, Częstochowa.

Paliszkiewicz J. (2013). *Zaufanie w zarządzaniu*. Wydawnictwo Naukowe PWN, Warszawa.

Pirson M. (2008). *Facing the Trust Gap Measuring and Managing Stakeholder Trust*. SVH, Saarbrucken.

Prognoza ludności na lata 2008–2035 (2014). Główny Urząd Statystyczny, Warszawa.

Rokita J. (2005). *Zarządzanie strategiczne. Tworzenie i utrzymywanie przewagi konkurencyjnej*. PWE, Warszawa.

Sander M., Weywara B. (2006). *Markenvertrauen im Rahmen des Markenmanagements, Konsumentenvertauen: Konzepte und Andwendungen für ein nachhaltiges Kundenbindungsmanagement*. Vahlen Franz Gmbh, München.

Sankowska A. (2011). *Wpływ zaufania na zarządzanie przedsiębiorstwem. Perspektywa wewnątrzorganizacyjna*. Difin, Warszawa.

Sankowska A. (2013). *Further understanding of links between interorganisational trust and enterprise innovativeness – from a perspective of an enterprise*. "International Journal of Innovation and Learning", vol. 13, no. 3.

Shaw R.B. (1997). *Trust in the Balance: Building Successful Organizations on Results, Integrity, and Concern.* Jossey-Bass, San Francisco.

Sitkin S.B., Roth N.L. (1993). *Explaining the limited effectiveness of legalistic remedies for trust/distrust.* "Organization Science", vol. 4.

Shockley-Zalabak P.S., Morreale S., Hackman M. (2010). *Building the High-Trust Organization: Strategies for Supporting Five Key Dimensions of Trust.* Jossey-Bass, San Francisco.

Spitzer D.R. (2007). *Transforming Performance Measurement: Rethinking the Way we Measure and Drive The Organizational Success.* Amacon, New York.

Ståhle P. (1998). *Supporting a System's Capacity for Self-Renewal.* A Doctoral Dissertation, Research Reports 190, University of Helsinki.

Sydow J. (1998). *Understanding the constitution of interorganizational trust in trust within and between organizations* [in:] Ch. Lane, R. Bachman (eds.), *Conceptual Issues and Empirical Applications.* Oxford University Press, Oxford.

Szulczewski G. (2003). *Zaufanie z perspektywy pragmatyczno-transcendentalnej koncepcji porozumienia.* "Prakseologia", vol. 143.

Szymański M.J. (1998). *Młodzież wobec wartości.* Wydawnictwo Instytutu Badań Edukacyjnych, Warszawa.

Sztompka P. (2002). *Socjologia. Analiza społeczeństwa.* Znak, Kraków.

Tan H., Lim A. (2009). *Trust in co-workers and trust in organization.* "The Journal of Psychology", vol. 143, no. 1.

Young L., Albaum G. (2003). *Measurement of trust in salesperson-customer relationships in direct selling.* "Journal of Personal Selling and Sales Management", vol. 24, no. 3.

Wójcik-Karpacz A. (2014). *Zaufanie w relacjach międzyorganizacyjnych: substytucja i komplementarność.* "Prace Naukowe Uniwersytetu Ekonomicznego we Wrocławiu", vol. 366.

Zaheer A., McEvily B., Perrone V. (1998). *Does trust matter? Exploring the effects of interorganizational and interpersonal trust on performance.* "Organization Science", vol. 9.

Zucker L.G. (1986). *Production of trust: Institutional sources of economic structure.* "Organizational Behavior", vol. 8.

Paulina Kubera
Poznan University of Technology
e-mail: Paulina.Kubera@put.poznan.pl

THE CHALLENGES OF IMPACT ASSESSMENT OF INNOVATION POLICY

Abstract

Background. Evaluation of public support for innovation poses serious methodological challenges. The reason for this lies in the systemic character of the innovation process and the need for more knowledge about the actual impacts of public interventions.

Research aims. The paper examines the specificity of the innovation process and the rationale behind public intervention in this field. It identifies the areas, which are crucial from the point of view of effective functioning of the innovation system and which should be recognised in evaluation. Systems thinking seems to be relatively new in the field of evaluation which has traditionally favoured more linear framework approach. Hence, the problem that deserves more consideration is: how to respond to the changing paradigms of innovation in the evaluation field.

Methodology. The method comprises a literature review, an analysis of the European Commission and OECD working papers, as well as a statistical analysis.

Findings. The paper distinguishes various approaches for impact assessment of the innovation policy: linear approach, based on input-output variables; an innovation system framework approach, which draws on the systemic understanding of the innovation process where many actors, their relations, and institutions affect the emergence of innovation; and a dynamic innovation system approach, which maps the processes (functions) of the innovation system over time in order to gain more insights to the dynamics of the innovation system. These different approaches build on each other and are the answer to identified shortcomings of the previous one as well as the growing need for more accurate assessment of the efficiency of public interventions.

Keywords: evaluation, impact assessment, public intervention, innovation.

INTRODUCTION AND BACKGROUND

Stimuli in public intervention impact analysis are growing. Due to the scarcity of public funds and growing societal expectations combined with the demand for greater government accountability, the focus of policy makers tends to be placed on the development of a systematic investigation of the effectiveness of public interventions. Monitoring and evaluation of public interventions provides feedback on their actual results and outcomes and it can be argued that they are a necessary precondition for a public organisation to be described as a learning organisation.[1]

Although the rationale behind the evaluation of public interventions is hardly undermined by the academics and practitioners alike, the mode of action poses serious methodological challenges. This refers, among other, to identifying and measuring of the impact of intervention. First, as it is about much more than the direct effects of intervention. Impact does not have to be intended or beneficial. Second, due to the increasing interest in more complex outcomes such as well-being, behaviour change etc.

Research and innovation policies are very complex and multidimensional. In order to evaluate this type of public actions one should recognise the specificity of the innovation process, its complex and systemic nature and put the evaluated operations in a broader context (e.g. in the regional, sectoral context or in a context of the whole system of innovation).[2] At the same time, innovation is at the centre of modern theories of economic growth. It is high on the political agenda at both national and the EU level. Therefore, it is all the more crucial to learn how the maximum leverage of public interventions in the field of research and innovation can be obtained.

The specificity of the innovation process

The term 'innovation' comes from the Latin word 'innovare', and means 'to make something new'.[3] One of the most frequently cited definitions of the innovation is that formulated in the *Oslo Manual*. The Manual defines innovation as 'the implementation of a new or significantly improved product (goods or services), or process, a new marketing method, or a new organisational method in business practices, workplace, organisation or external relations'. It can be radical or incremental. The innovative firm is a firm which has introduced an innovation during the period that is under review.[4]

---

[1] E. Stern (2005). *What do we know about the utilization of evaluation?*, I Evaluation conference "Evaluation of the Socio-economic Programmes Financed by Structural Funds, Warsaw 16.09.2005, Ministry of Economic Affairs and Labour, Polish Agency for Enterprise Development.

[2] M. Miedziński (2008). *Wybrane zagadnienia ewaluacji polityki innowacyjnej* [in:] K. Olejniczak, M. Kozak, B. Ledzion (eds.), *Teoria i praktyka ewaluacji interwencji publicznych*. Wydawnictwo Akademickie i Profesjonalne, Warszawa, pp. 480–498.

[3] D. Amidon (2003). *The Innovation Highway*. Butterworth-Heinemann, Boston.

[4] OECD and Eurostat (2005). *The Measurement of Scientific and Technological Activities. Proposed Guidelines for Collecting and Interpreting Technological Innovation Data. Oslo Manual*. A joint publication of OECD and Eurostat.

However, depending on policy or research needs the definition of innovation can be specified, taking into consideration selective types of innovation (e.g. product, process innovation), the degree of novelty (new to the firm, to the market – regional, national, or global), a specific sector, etc. It is important to define the key concepts and terms before the analysis, so that all stakeholders understand and use the terminology consistently.

The challenges of impact assessment of the innovation policy come from the fact that innovation is a complex process which is difficult to quantify. There are several critical aspects of the innovation process that should be recognised by policy-makers in order to address innovation problems in an appropriate way.

The linear approach to the innovation process has been abandoned in favour of the systemic approach. The linear model of innovation has turned out to be oversimplified and insufficient to explain the complete phenomena of innovation. It views innovation as an orderly and one-way process, starting with the discovery of new knowledge, moving through various development steps and emerging in a final viable form. This path from research, development to product, implies the 'technical push' as opposed to the 'market pull'.[5] However, the systemic approach to innovation implies that, to understand the specific challenges and opportunities with respect to innovation, it is critical to examine the way in which various actors, institutions, and structures interact and thereby influence the driving forces and capabilities for innovation.[6] Individual organisations rarely possess all the knowledge necessary for the whole process of innovation. Therefore, a greater emphasis in evaluation of innovation policies should be placed on the interactions among many actors, (including companies, universities, and research institutes) as well as the relevant knowledge flows.

Consequently, it is argued that innovation is not merely the result of science and technology. Innovation is a lot more than R&D. It means a shift of attention from research and the supply of science and technology, towards the whole system of innovation, in which research is only one element. The innovation process tends to involve continuous feedback loops between the different stages, the interplay between supply sources of science, and the demand forces of the market place.

Rationale for public innovation support – the market and systemic failure concepts

In neoclassical economic theory, the rationale for public initiatives to foster innovation is the recognition that the private rate is often too low to induce firms to engage in innovative activities that would be beneficial from a societal standpoint. This 'market failure' rationale is an important factor taken into consideration while assessing the admissibility of state aid for research, development, and innovation activities. In

---

[5] S. Kline (1985). *Innovation is not a Linear Process.* "Research Management", vol. 28, no. 4, pp. 36–45.

[6] T. Andersson, J. Appelquist, S. Serger (2004). *Public Research and Innovation Policy for the Good of Society: How to Assess the Way Forward?* Background Paper at joint IKED/INNOVA seminar. November 8, 2004. Berns, Salonger, Stockholm.

accordance with the Communication from the Commission: Framework for State aid for research and development and innovation (2014) in order to consider an aid measure to be compatible with the internal market it 'must be targeted towards a situation where aid can bring about a material improvement that the market cannot deliver itself, for example by remedying a market failure or addressing an equity or cohesion concern' (par. 36). It should be noted that State aid is an advantage conferred on a selective basis to undertakings by national public authorities, (as opposed to general public measures). In literature, there are several major market failures identified which may have a significant impact on the innovation process. Gustafsson and Autio argue that underinvestment in knowledge creation is due to[7]:

1) uncertainties and risks in innovation efforts;
2) insufficient appropriability (innovators have difficulty in realising the full benefits of their own innovation and new knowledge);
3) information asymmetries;
4) failure of markets to assign values to externalities (impacting knowledge diffusion) and
5) undervaluation of public good technologies in firm strategies.

Crusem and Hollenders emphasise the significance of the non-proprietary nature of knowledge (potential leaks) and the uncertainty in the exploration of new knowledge, as grounds for underinvestment in innovation activity by market operators.[8] They indicate the public good nature of knowledge that explains the second mover advantage. Firms, in order to avoid risks and high exploration costs, more often than not, are more willing to wait for other actors to invest in knowledge creation.

However, the market failure is not sufficient enough to provide a strong policy rationale for specific innovation support measures. The fact is, that not only markets fail to deliver optimal results. Too low investments in innovation can be put down to the lack of a favourable business environment for innovation, which is referred to as 'systemic failures'. It can be argued that this concept is broader in nature. 'Beyond simply addressing market failures that lead to underinvestment in R&D and innovation, [the systemic failure concept] aims at ensuring that the innovation system works effectively as a whole, by removing blockages that hinder the effective networking of its components.[9] The focus is on 'units' interactions in knowledge exploration and exploitation'.[10] Arnold identifies four types of systemic failures[11]:

[7] R. Gustafsson, E. Autio (2006). *Grounding for Innovation Policy: The Market, System and Social Cognitive Failure Rationales, Innovation Pressure – Rethinking Competitiveness, Policy and the Society in a Globalised Economy.* International ProACT Conference, Tampere, Finland, March 15–17, 2006.

[8] A. van Cruysen, H. Hollanders (2008). *Are Specific Policies Needed to Stimulate Innovation in Services?* INNO Metrics 2007 Report. European Commission, DG Enterprise, Brussels.

[9] European Commission (2014). *Communication from the Commission: Framework for State Aid for Research, Development and Innovation* (2014/C 198/01).

[10] A. van Cruysen, H. Hollanders, *op.cit.*

[11] R. Arnold (2004). *Evaluating research and innovation policy: a system world needs systems evaluation.* "Research Evaluation", vol. 13, no. 1, pp. 3–17.

1) 'capability failures', which refer to inadequacies in a firms' ability to act for their own advantage due to i.e. managerial deficits, lack of technological understanding, learning skill, or 'absorptive capacity';
2) 'failures in institutions', which refer to inadequacies in other social institutions, such as universities, research institutions, or patent offices, e.g. rigid disciplinary orientation in universities, lack of adequate investment in knowledge institutions;
3) 'network failures', which refer to problems in interaction among various actors in the innovation system, due to e.g. low trust, isolation of universities from their social context, transition failures, or 'lock-in' failures[12];
4) 'framework failures', which refer to deficiencies in the regulatory framework, intellectual and industrial property law, and other background conditions such as culture and social values.

Providing rationale for public innovation support, the concepts may entail different types of public policy measures. The market failure concept justifies public intervention for R&D and innovation at the level of target groups, while the systemic failure concept aims to enhance the functioning of the whole system of innovation; therefore the focus is on the bottlenecks and the weakest links of the innovation system.[13] Consequently, the former leads to more specific types of intervention, and the latter usually involves more generic types of intervention.

METHOD

The method comprises a literature review of both theoretical and practical studies and an analysis of the working papers issued by the European Commission and OECD in support of innovation policy making and implementation.

RESULTS

The systemic nature of the innovation process poses a serious challenge in terms of evaluation. The process is significantly more complicated and difficult to quantify than it had been previously thought. It is commonly measured using two basic families of statistics.[14] First, by the spending on research and development activities. An indicator

---

[12] K. Smith (2000). *Innovation as a systemic phenomenon: Rethinking the role of policy*, "Enterprise and Innovation Management Studies", vol. 1, no. 1, pp. 73–102.

[13] M. Miedziński, *op.cit.*

[14] OECD and Eurostat (2005). *Oslo Manual. Guidelines for Collecting and Interpreting Innovation Data*, 3rd edition.

that is easy to use and which fits in well with the linear approach to the innovation process. However, it does not reflect the actual innovation performance of the re-searched object, a firm, or a country. It has been criticised for being an input variable that is insufficient to tell about the actual implementation of a new or significantly improved product or process, (as well as a new marketing or organisational method).[15] According to the Eurostat data, government R&D financing underpins a small part of all R&D, in particular in reference to countries with the highest R&D-intensity. (The R&D intensity for a country is defined as the R&D expenditure as a percentage of the gross domestic product.). The countries with the highest R&D intensity, namely: Finland (3.55%), Sweden (3.41%), and Denmark (2.99%) (compared to the EU av-erage which amounts to 2.06%), are at the same time countries with relatively high ratio of business expenditure on R&D to GDP [Eurostat: gross domestic expenditure on R&D by source of funds, code: tsc00031]. However, the ratio of GERD to GDP is a key Europe 2020 Strategy indicator. The target level is 3% of GDP to be invested in the research and development activity by the year 2020, with two thirds of this objective coming from the business sector.

The figures suggest that the actual effects of public R&D financing depend on other factors, such as existing relations and leverage between public and private innovation efforts. The true effectiveness of government R&D financing is unclear. The question is: what additionally is achieved by government R&D financing, does it stimulate the total R&D activity in the private sector, or substitute private financing? There were a number of studies carried out[16]. Most of them proved the complementary effects, however, substitute effects have also been found. Nevertheless, policy-makers should acknowledge the systemic character of the innovation process and the fact that inno-vation is a lot more than R&D.

The second indicator frequently used in innovation policy assessment is the number of patents obtained. This is an indicator of the output of innovation activities, however, not all innovations are patentable and not all patentable innovations are patented. Moreover, there are three significant sources of bias in patent counts: differences across countries, among technologies and sectors in reference to the importance of patents as protection against imitation and among firms in propensity to patent.[17] In order to overcome these problems, the Innovation Union Scoreboard, a tool used to assess the research and innovation performance of the EU member states, instead of the patents granted takes into account the patent applications filed in the frame of the Patent Cooperation Treaty (PCT). This exempts the patent statistics from the above

---

[15] M.L. Flor, M.J. Oltra (2004). *Identification of innovating firms through technological innovation indicators: an application to the Spanish ceramic tile industry*. "Research Policy", vol. 33, pp. 323–336.

[16] For a survey, see: Ali-Yrkkö J. (2005). *Impact of public R&D financing on private R&D. Does financial constraint matter?*. "European Network of Economic Policy Research Institutes. Working Paper", no. 30; P. David, B. Hall, A. Toole (2000). *Is public R&D a complement or substitute for private R&D? A review of the econometric evidence*. "Research Policy", vol. 29, pp. 497–529.

[17] K. Pavitt (1988). *Uses and abuses of patent statistics* [in:] A.F.J. van Raan (ed.), *Handbook of Quantitative Studies of Science and Technology*. Elsevier Science Publishers, Amsterdam; from: B. Hall (2013). *Using Patent Data as Indicators*. http://eml.berkeley.edu/~bhhall/papers/BHH13_using_patent_data.pdf (access: 11.12.2015).

mentioned bias effects to a large extent. In order to make figures more comparable internationally, the number of patent applications are expressed per billion GDP (in PPP). And once again, Finland, Sweden, and Denmark are on the top of the ranking where Finland and Sweden are statistical outliers with more than 9 patent applications per billion GDP (in comparison to the EU average which accounts to 3.8).

Obviously no single indicator is sufficient to provide a full picture of impact of innovation efforts and must be combined with other indicators with careful consideration given to the dissimilarities resulting from different levels of analysis, sectors, and regions researched etc. Moreover, examining indicators requires the conceptual framework, which can be described as the system of fundamental premises and concepts that supports and informs the study.[18] In particular, without a conceptual framework it is impossible to establish causality, which is a key issue when evaluating public interventions.[19] Causality implies that between the cause (public intervention) and the effect there is a casual relationship. Establishing causality is difficult, but not impossible, it requires the construction of a counterfactual.[20]

Based on the assumption that the innovation process is non-linear, from investment to impact, but systemic in nature, the Council of Canadian Academies (2013) proposed five crucial components (the aggregate behaviours) for analysing the effectiveness of the innovation system with a firm placed at the centre.[21] By analysing the state of these five aggregate behaviours it would be 'possible to pinpoint the bottlenecks in the system – whether sectoral[22], regional[23], or national[24] – that hinder innovation; and to identify leverage points to drive innovation[25]. The proposed approach has been dubbed 'the innovation ecosystem approach' and harks back to the similarity between firms and organic life which in order to sustain must obtain energy, water, and other mineral inputs from the biological system. Similarly, firms need knowledge, capital, adequate regulatory conditions, and market demand forces to innovate.

---

[18] J.A. Maxwell (2005). *Qualitative Research Design: An Interactive Approach.* SAGE Publications, Thousand Oaks, CA.

[19] J. Górniak, S. Mazur (2012). *Zarządzanie strategiczne rozwojem.* Ministerstwo Rozwoju Regionalnego, Warszawa.

[20] For more details see: e.g. R. Trzciński (2009). *Wykorzystanie techniki, propensity score matching w badaniach ewaluacyjnych.* Polska Agencja Rozwoju Przedsiębiorczości, Warszawa.

[21] Council of Canadian Academies (2013). *Innovation Impacts: Measurement and Assessment.* The Expert Panel on the Socioeconomic Impacts of Innovation Investments, Council of Canadian Academies.

[22] F. Malerba (2005). *Sectoral systems: How and why innovation differs across sectors* [in:] J. Fagerberg, D. Movery, E. Nelson, *The Oxford Handbook of Innovation.* Oxford University Press, Oxford.

[23] H. Bathelt, A.K.Munro, B. Spigel (2011). *Social foundations of regional innovation and the role of university spin-offs.* "Industry and Innovation", vol. 18, no. 5, pp. 461–486.

[24] J.L. Furman, M.E. Porter, S. Stern (2002). *The determinants of national innovative capacity.* "Research Policy", vol. 31, no. 6, pp. 899–933.

[25] J.S. Metcalfe (2005). *Systems failure and the case for innovation policy* [in:] P. Llerena, M. Matt (eds.), *Innovation Policy in a Knowledge Based Economy.* Springer, Berlin; Council of Canadian Academies 2013, pp. 45–46.

Table 1. The five components (the aggregative behaviours) of the innovation ecosystem and indicators to assess their state

COMPONENTS OF INNOVATION ECOSYSTEM	INDICATORS
KNOWLEDGE GENERATION (scientific research and education)	• Spending on R&D and Innovation • Publications • Patents • Highly cited scientists • Stock of R&D personnel • University graduates
INNOVATION FACILITATION (financial support and networking capabilities)	• Direct financial support (at the program level, application decision time etc.) • Innovation intermediary in-kind support (resource allocation within innovation intermediaries, the overhead of innovation intermediaries) • Private financial support (venture capital and angel funds, leveraged funds, foreign direct investment, tax credits) • Mentoring, advice, and access to global market based on the client-based surveys • Level of collaboration (i.e. public-private) • New venture collaboration (contracts and intellectual property agreements, spin-off companies)
POLICY-MAKING (policies and regulations, esp. in six areas: (1) competition policy, (2) trade policy, (3) intellectual property policies, (4) sector-specific regulations, (5) good governance, transparency and corruption, and (6) public innovation platforms	• No set of readily available indicators; this requires a benchmarking exercise
DEMAND (needs and preferences of consumers)	• Apart from the data on public procurement expenditures, there are no readily available indicators; a benchmarking exercise is required
FIRM INNOVATION (the distribution of firms and how they are influenced by the innovation system)	• Rate of new venture creation • Leading R&D firms • New or improved products • Aggregate productivity • GDP

Source: own description based on: Council of Canadian Academies (2013).

Another example of a systemic tool utilised for impact assessment of innovation policy is the Innovation Union Scoreboard. The Scoreboard also rests on the assumption that for firms to innovate, important are: the availability of a highly skilled and educated workforce; open, competitive research system; as well as financial support for firms' innovation projects. These determinants are called the 'Enablers' and capture external factors that drive innovation. An effective innovation policy should have an impact on them. They are measured by the following indicators: new doctorate graduates, population aged 30–34 with tertiary education, youth with at least upper secondary education, international scientific co-publications, top 10% most cited publications, non-EU doctorate students, R&D expenditure in public sector and venture capital investments. (Little attention is paid in the Scoreboard to the innovation intermediary in-kind support.)

The next two groups of indicators included in the Scoreboard are; the "Firm activities' and the 'Outputs.' The former is to capture the firm's innovation efforts, the latter to capture their effects. A firm's innovation efforts are assessed taking into account: firm investments (R&D and non R&D innovation expenditures), linkages and entrepreneurship (SMEs innovating in-house, innovative SMEs collaborating with others, public-private co-publications), and the intellectual assets (PCT patent applications, Community trademarks and Community designs). The Outputs, in turn, are measured by the share of SMEs that have introduced innovation, the employment in fast-growing firms of innovative sectors as well as economic indicators such as: employment in knowledge-intensive activities, the contribution of medium and high-tech product exports to the trade balance, knowledge-intensive services exports, sales due to innovation efforts, license and patent revenues from selling technologies abroad.

However, the applicability of the innovation system framework approach is questionable in reference to the analysing of the technological changes. It is argued that the innovation system framework approach, although it assists the policy-making process using a more holistic perspective, is rather static or qusi-static in nature. It is based on the theories of interactive learning and evolutionary economics, but due to the great number of actors involved, network relations, and the system's complexity, its focus is more on the current structure of national system innovation. Hence, there are postulates put forward for more insights in the dynamics of innovation systems (functions of innovation system).[26]

A widely recognized fact is that technologies are subject to the lock-in effect, i.e. technologies and technological systems as well follow specific paths that are difficult and costly to escape. This is a matter of a better understanding at the user side and the adaptation of the socio-economic environment: accumulated knowledge, capital outlays, available skills, infrastructure, production routines, or social norms,[27] For this reason, insights in system structure alone are not sufficient to understanding technological changes. This requires gaining insights in the relations between the existing technology and innovation systems in relation to the emerging technology and emerging innovation systems.

Hekkert et al. proposed a framework for systematically mapping the processes that are significant for a well performing innovation system (a dynamic innovation system approach).[28] These processes (functions) are activities in the innovation system that influence the goal of the innovation system which is to develop, apply, and diffuse new technological knowledge. System change occurs when certain threshold fulfilment of

---

[26] E.g. M.P. Hekkert, R.A.A. Suurus, S.O. Negro, S. Kuhlmann, R.E.H.M. Smits (2007). *Functions of innovation systems: A new approach for analysing technological change.* "Technological Forecasting & Social Change", vol. 74; A. Bergek, S. Jacobssen, B. Carlsson, S. Lindmarki, A. Rickne (2008). *Analysing the functional dynamics of technological innovation systems.* "Research Policy", vol. 37, pp. 407–429; C. Storz (2008), *Dynamics in innovation system: Evidence from Japan's game software industry.* "Research Policy", vol. 37, no. 37, pp. 1480–1491.

[27] R. Kemp (1994). *Technology and the transition to environmental sustainability – the problem of technological regime shifts.* "Futures", vol. 26, no. 10, pp. 1023–1046.

[28] M.P. Hekkert, R.A.A. Suurus, S.O. Negro, S. Kuhlmann, R.E.H.M. Smits, *op.cit.*, p. 413–432.

functions is reached. Therefore, the researcher's attention should also be placed on the order and sequence of these functions.

In this approach, the significant events for the technology specific innovation are tracked down over time. These events are, as Hekkert et al. put it[29]: 'what the central subjects do or what happens to them'. Information on the events are reported at the system level and may be found in newspaper archives and professional journals. The events are mapped and allocated to one of the seven functions (as a positive or negative contributor) and plotted in figures. These seven functions are: entrepreneurial activities, knowledge development, knowledge diffusion through network, guidance of the search, market formation, resources mobilisation, and creation of legitimacy/counteract resistance to change. The focus is on extracting general patterns and gaining insights what functions perform well and when.

CONCLUSIONS

With the recognition of the systemic character of the innovation process, public interventions in this field have become more complex, from single-action interventions concentrated on the sub-optimal level of R&D investment to portfolios of actions targeted at bottlenecks and weak chains in the innovation system. The benefits from thinking beyond a particularistic, piecemeal approach to policy have long been realised. However, in order to gain the capacity to address problems that hinder innovation, the conceptual framework for mapping and measuring impact of the innovation policy is needed.

The innovation system framework approach is more practical than standard prescriptive policy guidelines. It offers a more holistic perspective, which identifies various actors: firms, government, universities, etc., their environment and the relationships between them to explain the performance of the innovation system. The most often utilised indicators are: R&D spending, patents, university-industry collaborations, university graduates, or venture capital availability. However, the applicability of the innovation system framework approach is questionable in reference to the analysing of the technological changes. Due to its complexity, its focus is more on the current structure of national system innovation. Therefore, more recent studies are not limited to descriptive understanding of innovation systems but they analyse the dynamics of innovation systems to gain more insights in the underlying mechanisms that influence a technological change.

---

[29] *Ibidem.*

References

Ali-Yrkkö J. (2005). *Impact of public R&D financing on private R&D. Does financial constraint matter?* "European Network of Economic Policy Research Institutes. Working Paper", no. 30.

Amidon D. (2003). *The Innovation Highway*. Butterworth-Heinemann, Boston.

Andersson Appelquist Serger (2004). *Public Research and Innovation Policy for the Good of Society: How to Assess the Way Forward?* Background Paper at joint IKED/INNOVA seminar. November 8, 2004. Berns, Salonger, Stockholm.

Arnold R. (2004*). Evaluating research and innovation policy: A system world needs systems evaluation.* "Research Evaluation", vol. 13, no. 1, pp. 3–17.

Bergek A., Jacobssen S., Carlsson B., Lindmarki S., Rickne A. (2008). *Analysing the functional dynamics of technological innovation systems.* "Research Policy", vol. 37, pp. 407–429.

Council of Canadian Academies (2013*). Innovation Impacts: Measurement and Assessment.* The Expert Panel on the Socioeconomic Impacts of Innovation Investments, Council of Canadian Academies.

Cruysen A. van, H. Hollanders (2008). *Are Specific Policies Needed to Stimulate Innovation in Services?* INNO Metrics 2007 Report. European Commission, DG Enterprise, Brussels.

David P., Hall B., Toole A. (2000). *Is public R&D a complement or substitute for private R&D? A review of the econometric evidence.* "Research Policy", vol. 29, pp. 497–529.

Desroches P. (1998). *On the abuse of patents as economic indicators.* "Quarterly Journal of Austrian Economics", vol. 1, no. 4, pp. 51–74.

European Commission (2009). *Making Public Support for Innovation in the EU More Effective.* Commission Staff Working Document SEC (2009), 1197, 09/09/2009.

European Commission (2014). *Communication from the Commission: Framework for State Aid for Research, Development and Innovation* (2014/C 198/01).

Flor M.L., Oltra M.J. (2004). *Identification of innovating firms through technological innovation indicators: an application to the Spanish ceramic tile industry.* "Research Policy", vol. 33, pp. 323–336.

Furman J.L., Porter M.E., Stern S. (2002). *The determinants of national innovative capacity.* "Research Policy", vol. 31, no. 6, pp. 899–933.

Górniak J., Mazur S. (2012). *Zarządzanie strategiczne rozwojem*. Ministerstwo Rozwoju Regionalnego, Warszawa.

Gustafsson R., Autio E. (2006). *Grounding for Innovation Policy: The Market, System and Social Cognitive Failure Rationales, Innovation Pressure – Rethinking Competitiveness. Policy and the Society in a Globalised Economy.* International ProACT Conference, Tampere, Finland, March 15–17.

Hall B. (2013). *Using Patent Data as Indicators.* http://eml.berkeley.edu/~bhhall/papers/BHH13_using_patent_data.pdf (access: 11.12.2015).

Hekkert M.P., Suurus R.A.A., Negro S.O., Kuhlmann S., Smits R.E.H.M. (2007). *Functions of innovation systems: A new approach for analysing technological change.* "Technological Forecasting & Social Change", vol. 74, pp. 413–432.

Kemp R. (1994). *Technology and the transition to environmental sustainability – the problem of technological regime shifts.* "Futures", vol. 26, no. 10, pp. 1023–1046.

Kline S. (1985). *Innovation is not a linear process.* "Research Management", vol. 28, no. 4, pp. 36–45.

Malerba F. (2005), *Sectoral systems: How and Why Innovation Differs Across Sectors* [in:] J. Fagerberg, D. Movery, E. Nelson, *The Oxford Handbook of Innovation.* Oxford University Press, Oxford.

Maxwell J.A (2005). *Qualitative Research Design: An Interactive Approach.* SAGE Publications, Thousand Oaks, CA.

Metcalfe J.S. (2005), *Systems failure and the case for innovation policy* [in:] P. Llerena, M. Matt (eds.), *Innovation Policy in a Knowledge Based Economy*, Springer, Berlin.

Miedziński M. (2008). *Wybrane zagadnienia ewaluacji polityki innowacyjnej* [in:] K. Olejniczak, M. Kozak, B. Ledzion (eds.), *Teoria i praktyka ewaluacji interwencji publicznych.* "Podręcznik Akademicki". Wydawnictwa Akademickie i Profesjonalne, Warszawa, pp. 480–498.

OECD and Eurostat (2005). *Oslo Manual. Guidelines for Collecting and Interpreting Innovation Data*, 3rd edition.

OECD and Eurostat (2005). *The Measurement of Scientific and Technological Activities. Proposed Guidelines for Collecting and Interpreting Technological Innovation Data*. Oslo Manual. A joint publication of OECD and Eurostat.

Pavitt K. (1988). *Uses and abuses of patent statistics* [in:] A.F.J. van Raan (ed.), *Handbook of Quantitative Studies of Science and Technology*. Elsevier Science Publishers, Amsterdam.

Smith K. (2000). *Innovation as a systemic phenomenon: Rethinking the role of policy*. "Enterprise and Innovation Management Studies", vol. 1, no. 1, pp. 73–102.

Stern E. (2005). *What do we know about the utilization of evaluation?* I Evaluation conference, Evaluation of the Socio-economic Programmes Financed by Structural Funds, Warsaw, 16.09.2005, Ministry of Economic Affairs and Labour, Polish Agency for Enterprise Development.

Storz C. (2008). *Dynamics in innovation system: Evidence from Japan's game software industry*. "Research Policy", vol. 37, no. 37, pp. 1480–1491.

Trzciński R. (2009). *Wykorzystanie techniki propensity score matching w badaniach ewaluacyjnych*. Polska Agencja Rozwoju Przedsiębiorczości, Warszawa.

Justyna Bugaj
Jagiellonian University
e-mail: j.bugaj@uj.edu.pl

STRATEGY OF ORGANISATIONAL DEVELOPMENT – A CASE STUDY OF UTRECHT UNIVERSITY

Abstract

Background. Contemporary universities functioning in the conditions of intensifying globalisation and competition are looking for effective methods of increasing their competitive advantages. A clearly defined and consistently implemented SHRM strategy plays an important role in this process.

Research aims. The objective of this paper is to identify good practices of European universities in the area of strategic human resources management. The author has tried to acquire answers to two basic questions: On the basis of published documents, is it possible to identify examples of the execution of specific HRM strategies at European universities? What elements should such strategies comprise, so that universities could combine the fulfilment of their fundamental functions with modern management techniques?

Methodology. The analysis is based on the results of the author's study of literature on the subject as well as qualitative research based on a particular case. The research presented in this paper constitutes a part of a wider research programme.

Findings. The conducted research has allowed the identification of a specific HRM strategy in the area of organisational development at Utrecht University. The paper discusses the elements and stages of this strategy. In conclusion, the author emphasises that, in the Polish conditions, such a strategy would require considerable modifications.

Keywords: strategic HRM (SHRM), organisational development (OD), university management.

INTRODUCTION

Effective management of a university in the 21st century is an enormous challenge for managers which results, among other things, from the changes in economic, social, and demographic processes as well as the development of new and innovative sectors of the economy. This challenge obliges university managers to develop and implement strategic activities which will guarantee an institution's organisational development irrespective of changes in its environment. The adoption of an organisational development strategy may ensure great prestige and competitive advantage for a university in the long term. An organisation acquires involvement, attachment, and loyalty of its employees, while the latter are provided with a possibility of safe employment, better working conditions, and development opportunities.

Within the context of approach, *Strategic Human Resource Management* was developed as an instrument of executing a business strategy at a functional level and was a logical consequence of the development of the concept of *Organisational Development* (OD), which gives priority to man and the principle of promoting values in the processes of change. This is confirmed by the opinions of numerous theoreticians, practitioners, and consultants, although so far their deliberations have concerned business organisations, and not higher education institutions.

The objective of this paper is to present an organisational development strategy employed at one of Europe's public universities. In order to achieve this objective, the author has used the methods of content analysis and participatory observation, pursuing answers to the following questions: On the basis of published documents, is it possible to identify examples of the execution of specific human resource management strategies at European universities? What elements should such strategies comprise, so that universities could combine the fulfilment of their fundamental (research, scholarly, didactic, and social) functions with modern management techniques?

Human Resource Management

The end of the 1980s witnessed the birth of a new concept of human resource management (HRM) consisting in searching for ways of unlocking employees" potential as well as increasing their efficiency and operating effectiveness.[1] Postulated changes were not limited only to burdening line managers with new responsibilities, a new approach to traditional positions, which started to be understood more broadly in terms of roles, or perceiving employees as assets[2], but also to delegating duties to organisational units with the simultaneous centralisation of administrative tasks. Their consequences included a higher level of employees" involvement and their perception as a source of capital, i.e. values contributed by the employees to organisations.[3]

In many cases, the economic situation forced organisations, on the one hand, to cut costs, restructure operations generating losses, and reduce employment, and, on the other hand, to recruit or outsource new employees. This generated conflicts among

---

[1] P. Relly, T. Williams (2012). *Strategiczne Zarządzanie Zasobami Ludzkimi*. Oficyna Wolters Kluwer business, Warszawa, pp. 12–15.

[2] M. Armstrong (2011). *Zarządzanie zasobami ludzkimi*. Oficyna Wolters Kluwer business, Warszawa, pp. 43–58.

[3] R.G. Ehrenberg, R.S. Smith (1994). *Modern Labor Economics*. Harper Collins, New York.

employees and hindered the functioning of organisations as a coherent whole. Counteracting these negative phenomena, organisations started to appreciate employees more, not only to improve their effectiveness and efficiency, but also to keep them in employment. These phenomena resulted in the addition of a strategic dimension to the HRM concept: Strategic Human Resource Management (SHRM)[4], which lays special emphasis on the development of employees in organisations, the building of an organisational culture oriented towards values, and the development of an organisational system of learning.

The strategy- and capital-based approach to employees in an organisation accompanied by the model of involvement[5] was based on the following principles[6]:

- Employees develop their occupational competencies and involvement if this is facilitated by the work environment.
- The interests of an organisation and its employees can be aligned thanks to open communication which builds trust and involvement.
- Employees are involved if they participate in solving organisational problems.

Guest confirmed that, through adequate HRM practices, employees involvement and behaviour translated directly into organisational values.[7]

Strategic Human Resource Management

Strategic human resource management defines a manner in which an organisation achieves its objectives through people, means of an HR strategy, as well as integrated operational principles and practices related to HR.[8] It consists in initiating activities and making decisions which apply to employees and in the long term determine the direction of personnel-related activities, and are of primary importance for an organisation.[9] On the one hand, it stresses the building of interpersonal relations in the management process, highlighting the need for continuous development, involvement, communication, work quality, and balance between professional life and personal life[10]; on the other hand, it focuses on employees' results achieved in consequence of investment in their development.

[4] N.M. Tichy, C.J. Fombrun, M.A. Devanna (1982). *Strategic human resource management.* "Sloan Management Review", vol. 23, pp. 47–61; J. Strużyna (2010). *Ewolucja strategicznego zarządzania zasobami ludzkimi.* „Zarzadzanie Zasobami Ludzkimi", vol. 3–4, pp. 12, 18–20.

[5] M. Beer, B. Spector, P.R. Lawrence, D. Quinn Mills, R.E. Walton (1984). *Managing Human Assets.* The FreePress, New York.

[6] O. Lundy, A. Bowling (2001). *Strategiczne zarządzanie zasobami ludzkimi,* Dom Wydawniczy ABC – Oficyna Ekonomiczna, Kraków.

[7] D.E. Guest (1997). *Human resource management and performance: A review and research agenda.* „The International Journal of Human Resource Management", vol. 8, June.

[8] M. Armstrong (2010). *Strategiczne zarządzanie zasobami ludzkimi.* Oficyna Wolters Kluwer business, Warszawa.

[9] T. Listwan (1995). *Kształtowanie kadry menedżerskiej firmy.* Kadry, Wrocław.

[10] J. Storey (1989). *Introduction: From personel management to human resource management* [in:] J. Storey (ed.), *New Perspectives on Human Resource Management.* Routledge, London.

Research conducted by Armstrong and Baron confirmed the existence of many variants of HR strategies in business organisations[11]: from very general and intentional ones to very detailed ones addressing particular aspects of human resource management such as recruitment, development, or remuneration.[12] Comprehensive HR strategies present manners of employee management, including providing employees with development opportunities; attracting, maintaining, and motivating employees; and building employees"involvement. Examples of such comprehensive strategies include high-performance management, high-involvement management, and high-commitment management.[13] Meanwhile, specific strategies determine what an organisation intends to achieve in selected HR areas, for example in recruitment, development, talent management, remuneration, or the development of employees' relations.

Human Resource Development

The concept of *Human Resource Development* (HRD) also developed in the 1980s, from narrowly understood training activities to a comprehensive approach.[14] It concerned the most frequent issues related to "individual and organisational learning, knowledge enhancement, the improvement of skills and abilities, and the shaping of people's values and attitudes in the work environment".[15] Hence HRD is associated with such notions as: "training, employee development, career, talent management, learning, education, but also work effectiveness improvement at the individual, group, and organisational levels". As a new concept, HRD was developed by G.N and L. McLean.[16]

HRD is generally understood as "intentional configurations of undertakings aimed at knowledge enhancement, talent development, the shaping of values, attitudes, motivation, and skills".[17] Two approaches can be distinguished within HRD. In one of them, development is treated as a part of processes related to human resource management; in the other, development is perceived as a separate process. In the case of both approaches, HRD can be analysed at the levels of a whole organisation, teams, individual employees, or as four interdependent functions: *organisation development* (OD); *career development* (CD); *training and development,* (T&D) and *performance improvement* (PI).[18]

---

[11] M. Armstrong, A. Baron (2002). *Strategic HRM: The Route to Improved Business Performance.* CIPID, London.

[12] M. Armstrong, *Strategiczne…*

[13] *Ibidem.*

[14] A. Pocztowski (2007). *Zarządzanie zasobami ludzkimi. Strategie, procesy, metody.* PWE, Warszawa, pp. 273–274.

[15] *HRM. Human Resource Management* (2013). From the editors. "Institute of Labor and Social Studies", vol. 6, no. 95(13), p. 7.

[16] G.N. McLean, L. McLean (2001). *If we can't define HRD in one country, how can we define it in an international context?,* "Human Resource Development International", vol. 4, no. 3, p. 322.

[17] A. Pocztowski, *op.cit.*; T. Listwan (2010). *Rozwój badań nad zarządzaniem zasobami ludzkimi w Polsce* [in:] S. Lachiewicz, B. Nogalski (eds.), *Osiągnięcia i perspektywy nauk o zarządzaniu.* Oficyna Wolters Kluwer business, Warszawa, pp. 237–240.

[18] D. McGuire, M. Cseh (2006). *The development of the field of HRD: A Delphi study.* „Journal of European Industrial Training", vol. 30, no. 8, pp. 653–667; H. Abdullah (2009). *Definitions of HRD: Key concepts from a national and international perspective.* "Journal of European Social Sciences", vol. 10, no. 4, pp. 486–495.

Human Resource Strategy for Researchers (HRS4R)

The *Human Resources Strategy for Researchers* (HRS4R) programme is recommended for implementation in all organisations employing academics and researchers.[19] It is connected with the management improvement processes within *the European Higher Education Area*. Participation in the programme makes it possible for a research institute:
- to take part in periodic meetings of international public and non-public organisations employing academics and researchers;
- to share information and experiences among institutions and to use internal documents related to the implementation of an HRS4R programme;
- to enter the international Internet platform connected with the European Commission, to use the quality mark of *HR Excellence in Research*;
- to improve a university"s image as an exceptional employer, in particular on the international arena.

The right to use the logo of *HR Excellence in Research* is granted to institutions supporting the creation of a work environment friendly for academics and researchers. The programme provides opportunities for the implementation of academic reforms, simultaneously strengthening an organisation's prestige and increasing its chances for a better position in international rankings.

Organisations joining the HRS4R programme are obliged to conduct an internal analysis of their previous practices in the area of human resources and subsequently prepare a plan of changes and a strategy of their implementation. Such activities should be the result of an assessment of an organisation's internal processes and a procedure of planned changes determined in order to adjust the organisation to the principles and values presented in *the Charter and Code*. If the *European Commission* accepts the planned and implemented changes, the organisation is awarded with the logo of *HR Excellence in Research*. The HRS4R programme motivates university managers to take measures aimed at their institutions' internal reforms in the personnel area.

The Charter and the Code allow researchers to identify universities operating in accordance with a similar set of principles and values irrespective of their country of origin. Since the adoption of the Commission"s recommendations in 2005 more than 1200 institutions in 35 countries in Europe and around the world have expressed their support for *The Charter and the Code,* while 102 acquired the mark of *HR Excellence in Research*.

---

[19] Human Resources Strategy for Researchers. http://ec.europa.eu/euraxess/index.cfm/rights/strategy-4Researcher (access: 7.01.2015).

METHOD

Management sciences are a set of various disciplines, subdisciplines, specialisations, research trends, and perspectives which force researchers to work intensively on determining a research method appropriate for a particular problem under analysis. Their paradigm is a practical problem, and *the principle of problem orientation requires the understanding and formulation of problems going beyond the limits of disciplines.*[20] In this paper, the author relies on the *interpretative and symbolic* paradigm (a dominant paradigm based on qualitative research)[21], which shows interdependencies in complex social and organisational structures and is most often used in the areas of personnel management and strategic management. The author uses a *case study,* i.e. a research procedure representing the *idiographic approach*, together with such methods as *documentation analysis, observations, interviews, and projective tests.*[22]

The popularity of *good practices* results from the need for access to the best models and for a reflection on *what can be done better, and how.* They consist in an organised presentation of the whole system (or its part) in a particular institution and a formulation of generalising conclusions[23], although particular good practices effective in one university do not necessarily deliver expected benefits in another.

Silverman distinguished two types of case selection[24]: *intentional* and *theoretical*, while Czakon distinguished five such types[25]: *grammaticality* (data availability); *an extreme character of a case* (extreme, but unambiguous in an interpretation of a case); *diversity* (different or opposing cases); *a critical phenomenon* (whose unusual and unexpected course allows the formulation of generalisations); *a metaphor* (allows the adoption of a particular position or a particular course of a studied phenomenon). The importance of a case study is determined by the application of exploratory methods (by assumption – many methods) in order to understand a studied phenomenon best.[26]

In February and August 2015, the author conducted an analysis of the websites of the European public universities. The analysis was based on the following three basic

---

[20] H. Steinmann, G. Schreyögg (1995). *Zarządzanie. Podstawy kierowania przedsiębiorstwem. Koncepcje, funkcje, przykłady.* Oficyna Wydawnicza Politechniki Wrocławskiej, Wrocław, pp. 43–44.

[21] Ł. Sułkowski (2011). *Struktura teorii naukowej w zarządzaniu* [w:] W. Czakon (ed.), *Podstawy metodologii badań w naukach o zarządzaniu.* Oficyna Wolters Kluwer business, Warszawa, pp. 169–175.

[22] J. Niemczyk (2011). *Metodologia nauk o zarządzaniu* [w:] W. Czakon (ed.), *Podstawy metodologii badań w naukach o zarządzaniu.* Oficyna Wolters Kluwer business, Warszawa, p. 24.

[23] B.R. Kuc. *Jak sformułować i rozwiązać problem badawczy?.* http://wydawnictwoptm.pl/content/8-artykuly-naukowe (access: 7.01.2015).

[24] D. Silverman (2008). *Prowadzenie badań jakościowych.* Wydawnictwo Naukowe PWN, Warszawa, pp. 171–175.

[25] W. Czakon (2011). *Zastosowanie studiów przypadków w badaniach nauk o zarządzaniu* [in:] W. Czakon (ed.), *Podstawy metodologii badań w naukach o zarządzaniu.* Oficyna Wolters Kluwer business, Warszawa, pp. 46–56.

[26] R.K. Yin (2003). *Case Study Research. Design and Methods.* Sage Publications, Thousand Oaks – London – New Delhi, pp. 21–27.

criteria: availability, possibility of adaptation to the Polish conditions, and diversity. The more detailed criteria included the following:

- it is possible to use a given experience in a public university (it can be adapted to the Polish conditions);
- an experience is related to a European University (it is related to the development of the *European Research Area* and *the European Higher Education Area)*;
- an experience is related to a development strategy of a public university and employee development management;
- an experience can be generalised;
- an experience can be described (information is published and materials are available in English).

Nine European universities, fulfilling the aforementioned criteria, were selected for further analysis. All of them occupy high positions in various ranking lists and have well developed detailed human resource development strategies. This paper focuses on the presentation of one of these universities, i.e. Utrecht University. Utrecht University holds high positions in worldwide rankings of higher education institutions, e.g.:

- *The 2014 Academic Ranking of World Universities* conducted by Shanghai University ranks this university #13 in Europe and #57 in the world.
- *The National Taiwan University Ranking 2014* ranks it #34 in the world.
- *The World University Rankings 2014* conducted by the British magazine *Times Higher Education* ranks Utrecht University as #18 in Europe and #79 in the world.

Combining rich traditions, history, and values with the challenges of the 21st century and professionalism in management, it is one of the oldest and best research universities in Europe. The author has identified Utrecht University's specific strategy in the area of organisational development, which is connected with the school's general strategy. The case study has been conducted by way of analysing the content of relevant websites on the basis of the previously established research stages.

RESULT: Strategy of organisational development – a case study of Utrecht University

Founded in 1636, Utrecht University (http://www.uu.nl/en) skilfully combines its rich traditions, values, and modern management. This management is performed at the central level and at the level of the particular faculties. The highest governing body is the *Management Board* whose members are appointed by the *Supervisory Board*. The university consists of seven faculties which deal with teaching and research in the fields of the humanities, social sciences, law, economics, governance and organisation, geosciences, natural sciences, veterinary medicine and medicine as well as three so-called *Teaching institutes*. It is one of the largest research universities in Europe, with close to 30,000 students, 6000 employees, and an annual budget of 765 million euros (2014). Thanks to the efficient achievement of established objectives, the cultivation of traditions, and compliance with its principles and values, in 2014 the university was ranked number 47 in the Academic Ranking of World Universities.

The fundamental values determining the employees' and students' attitudes include the following: *inspiration, ambition, independence, and involvement*. Additionally, the university follows the regulations published in the document entitled *The Netherlands Code of Conduct for Academic Practice. Principles of Good Academic Teaching and Research*, which specifies the principles of academic conduct, including ethically responsible research. These principles comprise *honesty, scrupulousness, reliability, verifiability, impartiality, independence, and responsibility*. Utrecht University is also bound by two other documents focusing on ethical behaviour in the event of auxiliary activities (outside a contract with the university) as well as *The Code of Conduct on Inappropriate Behaviour*.

The objective of *The Strategic Plan of Utrecht University* (2012-2016) is to strengthen further the university's national and international position in the fields of education, research, and science. Utrecht University's vision presents it as an institution that is *curiosity-driven* and *relevant to society*, while according to its mission, it is a *large and multifaceted centre of knowledge offering education and research of international quality*. The university pursues also a social mission expressed as *Bright Minds, Better Future*. Clearly defined, Utrecht University's objectives include the following:
- to develop young people academically;
- to educate new generations of researchers;
- to educate academics who combine knowledge and professional skills;
- to conduct ground-breaking research;
- to contribute to solving issues in society.

The accomplishment of the established objectives and the maintenance of the leading position of one of Europe's best research universities is possible thanks to strong leadership which is cultivated and improved at each management level of the institution. The university's professional style of leadership is generally held in high regard because it strengthens its employees' trust and involvement, supports them in their professional development, and contributes to the building of a positive work atmosphere. Therefore, special attention is paid to ensuring that each manager is able to:
- develop a vision that others can adhere to;
- be open to feedback;
- offer confidence and scope for development;
- take decisions and make choices;
- discuss the professional skills and development, in conformity with the organisational objectives, of and with the members of staff;
- make optimum use of the qualities and talents of the staff members;
- provide support required for the staff members to achieve their goals.

The university emphasises the role of cooperation and knowledge sharing; hence an employee can receive support not only from her/his colleagues and direct superior, but also from the university's administration within the scope of the particular disciplines. Additionally, special motivational packages have been prepared for the employees.

In the achievement of its vision, mission, and objectives, the university relies on the motivated, involved, and professional employees responsible for their careers. They have the possibility of choosing from among the following development paths:

- specialisation; enhancing knowledge in a particular field;
- changing an academic discipline or field in connection with the broadening of horizons, e.g. undertaking new tasks, working temporarily in another place or within internal projects;
- changing the scope of duties, e.g. after reaching a new career level in connection with acquiring an academic degree, promotion, or transfer to another position.

The academics have the opportunity to participate in various development programmes leading to the acquisition of the *Basic Teaching Qualification* and subsequently the *Senior Teaching Qualification*. Each faculty has its own interpretation of the basic and required teaching qualifications. Subsequently, the academics can take advantage of the development programmes offered by the *Centre of Excellence in University Teaching*, e.g.: *Educational Leadership, a Master Class in University Teaching in English or a Master Class in Quality Assurance*. Academic managers, professors, and future leaders can also take part in the programme called *Leadership Academic*, while talented managers and employees have the additional opportunity to use individually tailored programmes aimed at developing leadership talents and skills necessary at various managerial and political positions (*talented management and support staff network-netwerk OBP-talent*).

Utrecht University aims at attracting and maintaining talented researchers from both the Netherlands and abroad. It encourages them to continuous professional development by way of implementing an effective personnel policy confirmed by the European Commission. For the purposes of the *Human Resource Strategy for Researchers* (HRS4R) programme, the university has conducted an internal audit and launched an action plan included in its strategic documents. For the results of these activities, the university has been awarded the logo of *HR* Excellence in Research.

Utrecht University is an example of an organisation which, combining its traditions, history, and values, has successfully managed to respond to the challenges of the 21st century. Taking advantage of strategic management and professional leadership, it has based the process of achieving its objectives on development management, personnel improvement, and organisational development.

DISCUSSION

The SHRM concept was criticised mainly because the issue of organisational change was becoming the domain of a specialist, separate problem or an expensive and time consuming process. In this concept, an important role was played by communication processes constituting the foundations for intended changes. In such context, the execution of an organisation's development strategy was a process of continual transformation characterised by the alternate occurrence of moderate changes and revolutionary changes. In the English speaking countries, the organisational development model was being developed for many years in response to the dynamic changes taking place in the business environment and society. Polish universities can learn from their Western European counterparts, taking into consideration both their good and bad experiences connected with the implementation of SHRM.

With respect to university management, there are some opinions that universities are frequently characterised by unclear and immeasurable objectives which are different at the level of particular organisational units (faculties) and whole universities. They frequently generate internal competition which prevents the achievement of strategic objectives, although they are important for universities' internal and external activities, in particular for the development of relationships with academic communities and other stakeholders. Furthermore, strategies tend to be very general documents including objectives and tasks which are difficult to achieve and incomprehensible for employees.

CONCLUSIONS

A clearly defined and consistently implemented SHRM strategy plays an important role in strengthening of a university's competitive advantage. This can be confirmed by the case of the organisational development strategy at Utrecht University, which effectively combines tradition and modernity in management. This case, however, is connected with the necessity to adopt a few guidelines which may appear difficult to follow in other conditions:

- managing a university consistently at the levels of the whole organisation, particular faculties, and other organisational units (without internal competition);
- managing a university on the basis of mutual relations and trust;
- treating employees as valuable assets, which results in benefits for an organisation (e.g. a higher position in world rankings) or for employees (e.g. deeper involvement);
- compliance with the adopted values, standards, and principles;
- open communication related also to the inclusion of employees in organisational problem solving processes and responsibility for decisions made;
- commissioning specialists to prepare a university's development strategies as well as specific strategies in the area of SHRM.

In the conditions of Polish universities, the practices described above can generate measurable results in human resource management, although they would require considerable modifications.

The presented research results do not exhaust the problem under analysis. Nevertheless, they constitute a good point of reference for the continuation of research in this area and a stimulus for a more dynamic discourse in a wider group of SHRM researchers.

References

Abdullah H. (2009). *Definitions of HRD: Key concepts from a national and international perspective.* "Journal of European Social Sciences", vol. 10, no. 4, pp. 486–495.

Armstrong M. (2011). *Zarządzanie zasobami ludzkimi.* Oficyna Wolters Kluwer business, Warszawa, pp. 43–58.

Armstrong M. (2010). *Strategiczne zarządzanie zasobami ludzkimi.* Oficyna Wolters Kluwer business, Warszawa.

Armstrong M., Baron A. (2002). *Strategic HRM: The Route to Improved Business Performance.* CIPID, London.

Beer M., Spector B., Lawrence P.R., Quinn Mills D., Walton R.E. (1984). *Managing human assets.* The FreePress, New York.

Czakon W. (2011). *Zastosowanie studiów przypadków w badaniach nauk o zarządzaniu* [in:] W. Czakon, (ed.), *Podstawy metodologii badań w naukach o zarządzaniu.* Oficyna Wolters Kluwer business, Warszawa, pp. 46–56.

Guest D.E. (1997). *Human resource management and performance: A review and research agenda.* "The International Journal of Human Resource Management", vol. 8, June.

Ehrenberg R.G., Smith R.S. (1994). *Modern Labor Economics.* Harper Collins, New York.

HRM. *Human Resource Management* (2013). From the editors, "Institute of Labor and Social Studies", vol. 6, no. 95(13), p. 7.

Human Resources Strategy for Researchers. http://ec.europa.eu/euraxess/index.cfm/rights/strategy4Researcher (access: 7.01.2015).

Kuc B.R., *Jak sformułować i rozwiązać problem badawczy?.* http://wydawnictwoptm.pl/content/8-artykuly-naukowe (access: 7.01.2015).

Listwan T. (1995). *Kształtowanie kadry menedżerskiej firmy.* Kadry, Wrocław.

Listwan T. (2010). *Rozwój badań nad zarządzaniem zasobami ludzkimi w Polsce* [in:] S. Lachiewicz, B. Nogalski (eds.), *Osiągnięcia i perspektywy nauk o zarządzaniu.* Oficyna Wolters Kluwer business, Warszawa, pp. 237–240.

Lundy O., Bowling A. (2001). *Strategiczne zarządzanie zasobami ludzkimi.* Dom Wydawniczy ABC – Oficyna Ekonomiczna, Kraków, p. 62.

McGuire D., Cseh M. (2006). *The development of the field of HRD: A Delphi study.* „Journal of European Industrial Training", vol. 30, no. 8, pp. 653–667.

McLean G.N., McLean L. (2001). *If we can't define HRD in one country, how can we define it in an international context?.* "Human Resource Development International", vol. 4, no. 3, p. 322.

Niemczyk J. (2011). *Metodologia nauk o zarządzaniu* [w:] W. Czakon (red.), *Podstawy metodologii badań w naukach o zarządzaniu.* Oficyna Wolters Kluwer business, Warszawa, p. 24.

Pocztowski A. (2007). *Zarządzanie zasobami ludzkimi. Strategie, procesy, metody.* PWE, Warszawa, pp. 273–274.

Relly P., Williams T. (2012). *Strategiczne zarządzanie zasobami ludzkimi.* Oficyna a Wolters Kluwer business, Warszawa, pp. 12–15.

Silverman D. (2008). *Prowadzenie badań jakościowych.* Wydawnictwo Naukowe PWN, Warszawa, pp. 171–175.

Steinmann H., Schreyögg G. (1995). *Zarządzanie. Podstawy kierowania przedsiębiorstwem. Koncepcje, funkcje, przykłady.* Oficyna Wydawnicza Politechniki Wrocławskiej, Wrocław, pp. 43–44.

Storey J. (1989). *Introduction: From personel management to human resource management* [w:] J. Storey (ed.), *New Perspectives on Human Resource Management.* Routledge, London.

Strużyna J. (2010). *Ewolucja strategicznego zarządzania zasobami ludzkimi.* „Zarzadzanie Zasobami Ludzkimi", vol. 3–4, pp. 12, 18–20.

Sułkowski Ł. (2011). *Struktura teorii naukowe w zarządzaniu* [w:] W. Czakon (ed.), *Podstawy metodologii badań w naukach o zarządzaniu.* Oficyna Wolters Kluwer business, Warszawa, pp. 169–175.

Tichy N.M., Fombrun C.J., Devanna M.A. (1982). *Strategic human resource management,* "Sloan Management Review", vol. 23, pp. 47–61.

Yin R.K. (2003). *Case Study Research. Design and Methods.* Sage Publications, Thousand Oaks – London – New Delhi, pp. 21–27.

Andrzej Pawluczuk
Bialystok University of Technology
e-mail: a.pawluczuk@pb.edu.pl

KNOWLEDGE MANAGEMENT IN PRIVATE AND PUBLIC ORGANISATIONS: COMPARISON AND RECOMMENDATIONS[1]

Abstract

Background. Public and private sectors have different characteristics, on the other hand, there is a tendency among citizens to expect the same quality of services in public administration organisations or in the wider public sector as in privates ones. Knowledge management can certainly improve the services of the public sector. History has shown that many of the original management concepts are implemented and refined in the private sector, and they are then transferred to the public sector. The ISO quality management system is a typical example. Case studies show that after a few years of ISO application, some municipalities do not certify it any longer. Knowledge management is not subject to certification as a quality system, but evaluation and continuous improvement of the quality system caused that the elements of knowledge management are included in the quality system.

Research aims. Knowledge management is present in scientific literature on both the private and public sectors. By comparing the approaches to knowledge management among employees at different levels and in different companies it will be possible to answer the question regarding the differences in knowledge management and how they extend.

Methodology. A questionnaire survey was conducted in 2014–2015 in private companies and different public organisations from various sectors located in Podlaskie Province.

Key findings. Perceptions of the degree of implementation of knowledge vary considerably between public and private organisations. The IT system plays significantly different roles in both types of organisations. The public organisations use mainly external databases and the Internet, while the companies use database management systems and superior customer support organisations and flow of knowledge. The

---

[1] The project was financed with the funds of the National Science Centre awarded pursuant to the decision no. DEC-2011/01/D/HS4/05663.

confidence levels also vary but the differences are not as significant as in other areas. Public sector workers also acknowledge significantly greater barriers in the implementation of knowledge management.

Keywords: knowledge management, public organisations, barriers of knowledge management.

INTRODUCTION

The mode of knowledge management was top in the 90s of the last century in western countries and then in the beginning of the new millennium in Poland. A wide diverse range of seminars and conferences for academics as well as practitioners was organised and we can read many scientific papers, books, or professional papers about knowledge management.[2] However, we hardly ever listen about knowledge management in the local media or local press, which causes a limited spillover effect in each type of organisation in a sense of conscious activities based on procedures. There are other facts that seem to be important to spread new methods of management like: type of organisation, level of innovation, leaders or/and managers, level of innovation, competence of staff, or access to information (Internet). Some concepts are more popular and could be easily implemented by consultant firms or by organisations. When we compare: organisational learning to knowledge management, we can observe that even the primary invented method could be covered by the next method. Each method could be implemented or operating in academic discussion or organisation practice at a different level.[3] For example the concept of learning organisation that was elaborated in a book entitled The fifth discipline: The art and practice of the learning organisation issued in Poland in 1990 has not gained so much input as knowledge management described in The Knowledge – Creating Company, 1995 by Nonake and Takeuchi. Of course in-depth literature study brings information, that Ch. Argyris and D.A. Schön wrote a book Organisational Learning: a Theory of Action Perspective, and even in Poland two papers were written by Bratnicki in the early 80s about learning organisation.[4] To reassume the introduction, there is no one right answer why one concept is more popular among academics and how or/and when the concept will be implemented in organisations and how aware workers are about the particular concept. In this paper the author focuses on knowledge management in public and private organisations.

---

[2] A. Błaszczuk, J. Brdulak, M. Guzik, A. Pawluczuk (2004). *Zarządzanie wiedzą w polskich przedsiębiorstwach*. Oficyna Wydawnicza SGH, Warszawa.

[3] L. Aggestam (2006). *Learning organization or knowledge management – which came first, the chicken or the egg?*. "Information Technology and Control", vol. 35, no. 3A, pp. 295–302.

[4] M. Bratnicki (1981). *Informacyjne przesłanki organizacyjnego uczenia się*. "Prakseologia", vol. 4; M. Bratnicki (1982). *Organizacyjne uczenie się w warunkach kryzysu*. "Problemy Postępu Technicznego", nr 6.

BACKGROUND

Knowledge is a key asset in individual or organisation level, what is obvious for many, but quite difficult to conduct in the light of the theory. We can find handbooks or other books, which are connected with knowledge management.[5] The inspiration of knowledge management comes from the private sector, like many others techniques: reengineering, reinvention, new technologies, citizen/consumer market analysis, differential pricing to influence patterns of demand.[6] So far in Poland many qualitative and quantitive research studies on knowledge management have been conducted in the last ten years.[7] The above-mentioned papers focus on public or on private organisations, discussing considerable advantages for companies. The concept of knowledge management is important that it can be implemented in many ways, therefore the author presented the arguments for doing research on that concept in public organisations.[8]

This research is unique, and fills the gap, because the author uses the same questionnaire to examine the public and private organisations. In the last decades public sector managerial reforms were conducted in many countries like the United Kingdom,

---

[5] A. Örtenblad (2014). *Handbook of Research on Knowledge Management. Adaptation and Context.* Edward Elgar Publishing, Cheltenham; K. Dalkir (2005). *Knowledge Management in Theory and Practice.* Elsevier/Butterworth Heinemann, London.

[6] L.R. Jones, F. Thompson (2007). *From Bureaucracy to Hyperarchy in Netcentric and Quick Learning Organizations.* Information Age Publishing, Charlotte.

[7] E.g. A. Błaszczuk, J. Brdulak, M. Guzik, A. Pawluczuk, *op.cit.*; J. Brdulak (2012). *Wiedza w zarządzaniu przedsiębiorstwem. Koncepcja, filary, dobre praktyki.* Szkoła Główna Handlowa w Warszawie – Oficyna Wydawnicza, Warszawa; B. Godziszewski, M. Haffer, M.J. Stankiewicz (eds.) (2005). *Wiedza jako czynnik międzynarodowej konkurencyjności w gospodarce.* Towarzystwo Naukowe Organizacji i Kierownictwa – Stowarzyszenie Wyższej Użyteczności „Dom Organizatora", Toruń; A. Glińska-Neweś (2007). *Kulturowe uwarunkowania zarządzania wiedzą w przedsiębiorstwie.* Towarzystwo Naukowe Organizacji i Kierownictwa, Toruń; J. Fazlagić (2009). *Zarządzanie wiedzą w polskiej oświacie. Diagnoza i perspektywy zmian.* Wydawnictwo Uniwersytetu Ekonomicznego w Poznaniu, Poznań; M. Strojny (2004). *Zarządzanie wiedzą w Polsce 2004.* Raport badawczy, KPMG; J. Ejdys (2011). *Model doskonalenia znormalizowanych systemów zarządzania oparty na wiedzy.* Oficyna Wydawnicza Politechniki Białostockiej, Białystok; S. Mazur, A. Płoszaj (eds.) (2013). *Zarządzanie wiedzą w organizacjach publicznych. Doświadczenia międzynarodowe.* Wydawnictwo Naukowe Scholar, Warszawa; K. Leja, P. Brozdowski, J. Dyrlico (2005). *Wybrane elementy zarządzania wiedzą w organizacji publicznej na przykładzie Urzędu Miasta Elbląga.* "E-Mentor", vol. 3, no. 2; T. Papaj (2012). *Zarządzanie publiczne – wybrane aspekty eksploracji wiedzy i jej aplikacji.* "Współczesne Zarządzanie", vol. 4, pp. 142–151; A. Pawluczuk (2005). *Zarządzanie wiedzą w jednostkach samorządu terytorialnego* [in:] J. Ejdys (eds.), *Wybrane aspekty zarządzania wiedzą w organizacji.* FUTURA, Poznań; K. Raczkowski (2010). *Zarządzanie wiedzą w administracji celnej w systemie bezpieczeństwa ekonomiczno-społecznego.* Difin, Warszawa; K. Raczkowski, A. Pawluczuk (2014). *Knowledge management in public organizations – status and perspective of development,* "Przedsiębiorczość i Zarządzanie", vol. XV, no. 6, cz. III, Wydawnictwo Społecznej Akademii Nauk, Łódź – Warszawa.

[8] T. Davenport, G. Probst (2000). *Knowledge Management Case Book.* MCD Verlag John Wiley & Sons, Munich; M. Ajmal, P. Helo, T. Kekale (2010). *Critical factors for knowledge management in project business.* "Journal of Knowledge Management", vol. 14, no. 1, pp. 156–168; F. Blackler (1993). *Knowledge and the theory of organizations: Organizations as activity systems and the reframing of management.* "Journal of Management Studies", vol. 30, no. 6, pp. 863–884; K. Dalkir, *op.cit.*; S. Kennedy-Reid, M. Ihrig (2013). *Strategic knowledge mapping at Boeing: An I-Space Pilot.* Boeing and I-Space Institute, Arlington.

Sweden, the Netherlands, Canada, Switzerland, Germany, Italy, Denmark, Finland, the United States of America, Argentina, Brazil, Singapore, China and Hong Kong, Mongolia, Thailand, Cambodia, Indonesia, New Zealand, and Australia. Reforming governments in the mentioned countries fostered the decentralization of authority, replacement of rules and regulations with incentives, development of budget based upon results, exposure of government operations to competition, search for the market rather than administrative solutions.[9] This reform requires change in management in public organisations and causes openness to new methods of management. Some countries, like Canada based the change on the concept of learning organisation.[10] However, knowledge management is return on well known too.[11] The concept of knowledge management should be also undertaken as more popular in Poland.

Table 1. Changes in private and public sector in the world

Private sector – period of change 1975–2007	Public sector – last decade
Trade liberalisation through the WTO causes opening of markets	Public services substituted partly by private organisations
The new countries from Asia as international competitors	Increased competition with private organisations in many sectors
Increasing political and economic stability and market orientation of many third world countries	Increase of inhabitants' awareness of the quality of public service
Technological change driven by the computer and Internet revolution	Different levels in using IT techniques by public organisations depending on the country
Related advance in information system technologies	Changing the government's role in the aspect of control
Increase of benefits of economic of scale by global firm	Increase of dates and procedures for daily work
Spreading the unification and certification procedures	Change of the law and regulations
Low cost of capital	Deal with various type of inhabitants regarding their knowledge, literacy, age, and religion
Global marketing and logistics allowed for small companies to operate in a global market	New range of services and techniques to use in daily work
Economic deregulation and privatization	
Increased efficiency and competitiveness in financial markets	Political influence and change in many public organisations
Better informed consumers	Various levels of efficiency and difficulties in measure
The quality revolution leading customers to expect quality goods and services as a standard.	Too slow reaction on changes in the private sector
	An increase in litigation by citizens

Source: private sector based on L.R. Jones, F. Thompson (2007). *From Bureaucracy to Hyperarchy in Netcentric and Quick Learning Organisations*. Information Age Publishing Charlotte. Public sector – own contribution.

---

[9] L.R. Jones, F. Thompson, *op.cit.*

[10] *A Public Service Learning Organization: From Cost to Coast to Coast* (2000). The Canadian Centre for Management Development, Policy, Strategy and Communications, Ottawa.

[11] J.M. Saussois (2003). *Knowledge management in government: An idea whose time has come.* "Journal of Budgeting", vol. 3, no. 3, OECD; E. Arora (2011). *Knowledge management in public sector.* "Researchers World – Journal of Arts Science & Commerce", vol. 2, no. 1, pp. 165–171; M. Massaro, J. Dumay, A. Garlatti (2015). *Public sector knowledge management: a structured literature review.* "Journal of Knowledge Management", vol. 19, no. 3, pp. 530–558; B. Moore, T. Ulrichsen, A. Hughes (2009). *The Evolution of the Infrastructure of the Knowledge Exchange System.* PACEC – Centre for Business Research, Cambridge – London.

RESEARCH METHODOLOGY

The procedures, attributes, and techniques were selected to constrain the questionnaire survey.[12] The questionnaire consists of such questions:
- opinion about the KM,
- degree of implementation,
- source of knowledge in the organisation,
- IT tools supporting KM,
- sharing knowledge,
- importance of leadership in the organisation,
- level of trust and co-operation,
- barriers in implementing KM.

The respondents are located in organisations in the Podlaskie region, which is not leading in a sense of economic level of development or international trade balance, or cooperation with international organisations. However, there are some well known and innovative firms or even institutions located there, such as the Provincial Labour Office (PLO). The PLO conducts many research studies together with academics and an innovative competition in the area of learning organisation to compare other domestic competitions conducted by public organisations. The Podlaskie Province is also located very close to the border with Belarus and Lithuania, countries which are not as demanding as Germany or Sweden.

The research was conducted in 2014 and completed in January 2015 among 423 respondents where 296 questionnaires came from the private sector (70%) and 127 from the public sector (30%). The sample characteristic was introduced in table 2. The population is not homogeneous, there are significant differences in age, education, years of seniority which cause some limits of the final conclusions in comparison of the public and private sector.

Table 2. Sample characteristic

Number	Feature	Public organisation	Enterprise
1.	Gender		
	female	65.4%	54.7%
	male	34.7%	45.3%
2.	Age		
	18–24	7.9%	34.2%
	25–34	39.7%	46.8%
	35–49	33.1%	13.9%
	50–64	19.7%	4.8%
	65 and more	0.0%	0.3%

---

[12] A. Błaszczuk, J. Brdulak, M. Guzik, A. Pawluczuk, *op.cit.*; K. Raczkowski, A. Pawluczuk, *op.cit*; M. Strojny, *op.cit.*

Number	Feature	Public organisation	Enterprise
3.	Education		
	junior high school and lower	0.0%	1.4%
	primary	14.2%	18.9%
	secondary, post-secondary	76.4%	79.7%
	higher	9.5%	0.0%
4.	Positions		
	managerial	7.9%	18.8%
	independent	67.7%	59.9%
	dependent	24.4%	21.2%
5.	Years of seniority in the organisation		
	for 2 years	19.8%	38.8%
	from 2 to 10 years	42.9%	47.5%
	from 11 to 20 years	15.9%	12.5%
	over 20 years	21.4%	1.3%

Source: own calculation.

The author wishes to thank many full-time and vocational students from the Faculty of Management, Białystok University of Technology, who take courses in Knowledge management, Learning organisation and Knowledge- based economy for gathering/ collecting the questionnaires. Approximately one third was filled by them and two thirds by the inhabitants from outside the university.

KNOWLEDGE MANAGEMENT IN PRIVATE AND PUBLIC ORGANISATIONS

At the beginning of the survey, the respondents were asked to share their opinions on knowledge management in organisations (figure1). The received answers indicated, that the concept of knowledge management in practice of administration functioning is in its initial stage of development (35.4% of total respondents), and 1/4 of respondents (28.3%) stated, that they had met such concept for the first time. Responders from private organisations declared that KM is in their initial level or they had met it for the first time by filling the survey (30.7% and 30.4% respectively). Confirmation that KM is a system, which works more often in firms instead of public organisations, was the third highest answer, 21.3% employees from companies declared this system in organisations compared to 15% of respondents from public organisations.

Respondents from both sectors indicated that the degree of implementation of knowledge management has still not reached the stadium of full development (figure 2), since less than one fifth of the respondents (18.4% for firms and 16.0% for public organisations) stated that there was a knowledge management system, which included accumulation, archiving, and sharing knowledge. The respondents from public organisations declared persons with knowledge duties in organisations almost

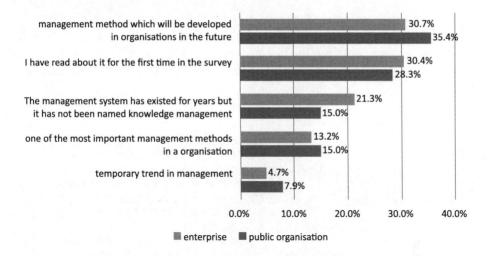

Figure 1. Opinion on knowledge management in organisations (Podlaskie Province)
Source: own work output on the basis of research findings.

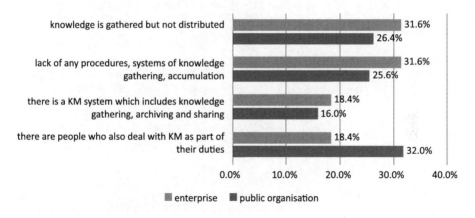

Figure 2. Degree of implementation of knowledge management in the organisation
Source: own work output on the basis of research findings.

two times more (32.0%) then in companies (18.4%). More than half of the respondents, with advantage in firms, responded that there was no KM system or their organisation did not care about knowledge at all.

According to Nonaka and Takeuchi[13] the process of creating knowledge, it turns outs that for workers in firms, tacit knowledge, also called non-codified plays an important role. In the socialisation process a very important source of knowledge are conversations with the superiors: 2.8 average (scale from 1 to 3), observing more

---

[13] I. Nonaka, H. Takeuchi (1995). *The Knowledge-Creating Company: How Japanese Companies Create the Dynamics of Innovation*. Oxford University Press, Oxford – New York.

experienced colleagues, and conversations with clients: both 2.7 average (figure 3). A slightly different answer was obtained among public sector employees, average 2.7 goes to conversation with the manager and training material. Among 19 items of different sources more critical were workers from the private sector, who gave a lower average.

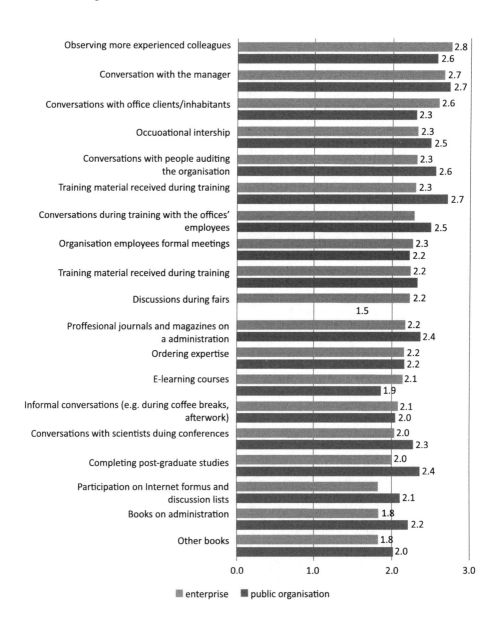

Figure 3. Source of knowledge in the organisation in %
Source: own work output on the basis of research findings.

IT tools in the time of information society play a significant role in knowledge management, which was also proven by research in both types of organisations (figure 4). According to respondents from the two types of organisations, the most important one was using the Internet: around 85%. The other sources differ respectively depending on the type of organisation: for the public sector: Lex database or other professional databases (68.3%), e-mails (52.6%), and document flow system (46.4%) and for the private sector: databases (57.1%) and team work system (40.2%). Private organisations use a wider and technologically sophisticated range of IT tools in comparison with the public sector, for example: tools for communication (Skype), e-learning platform, and management supporting systems. It is correlated with a low level of e-government in public organisations in Poland.

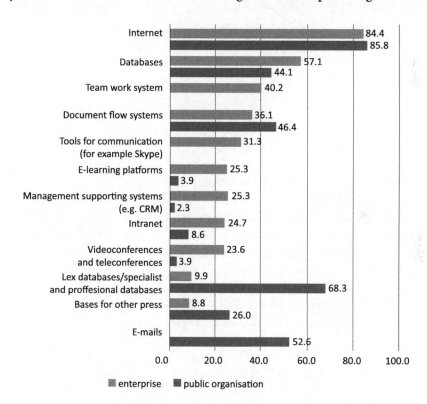

Figure 4. IT tools supporting knowledge management in the organisation in %
Source: own work output on the basis of research findings.

The motives for knowledge sharing differ slightly between the two analysed types of organisations. In public organisations two things are crucial: personal satisfaction (67.7%) and co-workers' sympathy (63.8%), figure 5. The same two motives are important for employees in private organisations, but a bit lower rates (61.8% and 61.5% respectively) were obtained. The private sector, which is more dynamic is less stable for workers, however the possibility of promotion gain was at 19.9% compared with 10.2% for the public sector and financial advantages were at 16.9% compared with 9.4% for public organisations.

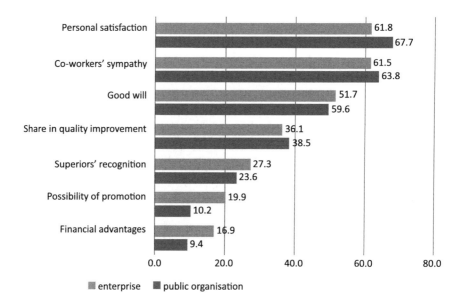

Figure 5. Sharing own knowledge and obtained experience with co-workers in %
Source: own work output on the basis of research findings.

An important role in public and private organisations should be played by leadership, which would create and support the knowledge management processes. All respondents gave the greatest value of this feature to trust (more than 71%). Further statements in public organisations regarding setting of clear norms and action frameworks received on average over 10% less and only 3% less regarding encouraging employees to share knowledge in the private sector. The other results are shown in table 3.

Table 3. Influence of leadership in the organisation on knowledge management in %

		\multicolumn{6}{c}{Influence of leadership in the organisation on knowledge management in %}					
		Lack of opinion		I do not agree		I agree	
No.	Category	public organisation	enterprise	public organisation	enterprise	public organisation	enterprise
1.	trusts me	17.6	18.0	11.2	10.2	71.2	71.9
2.	encourages employees to share knowledge	17.5	13.9	32.5	17.3	50.0	68.8
3.	sets clear norms and action frameworks	16.4	15.7	22.1	23.5	61.5	60.9
4.	provides challenges, which motivate me to work	19.4	16.7	25.0	22.8	55.7	60.5
5.	encourages me to be innovative and creative	19.8	14.6	24.6	25.8	55.6	59.7
6.	can constructively solve conflicts	16.1	19.4	30.7	24.8	53.2	55.8

		Influence of leadership in the organisation on knowledge management in %					
		Lack of opinion		I do not agree		I agree	
No.	Category	public organisation	enterprise	public organisation	enterprise	public organisation	enterprise
7.	facilitates and supports professional develop-ment	19.8	18.3	24.8	26.1	55.4	55.6
8.	values out-of-the-box solutions	33.6	21.4	21.6	25.4	44.8	53.2
9.	creates a comfortable learning environment	21.7	19.7	28.3	27.9	50.0	52.4

Source: own work output on the basis of research findings.

Among the factors supporting knowledge management there is also organisational culture, which in this research was not subjected to a detailed analysis, but was only one of the factors influencing knowledge sharing, which trust is. The respondents were asked to share their opinions on trust in the organisation at the level of an organisational unit and the whole organisation, and external trust towards superiors and auditing institutions, as well as trust to municipality customers/inhabitants or suppliers. The Likert scale measurement defined the level of trust subjectively. It turned out that the highest trust occurs in the private sector in own organisational units and the lowest towards inspections of public administration (figure 6). The public organisations gain slightly lower average in trust in comparison to firms and there was one exception: inspections of public administration ranked second.

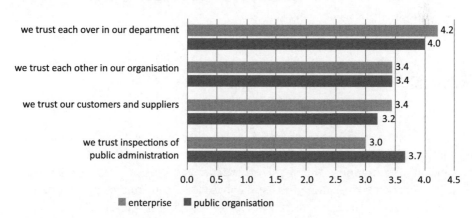

Figure 6. Level of trust and co-operation among employees in the organisation
Source: own work output on the basis of research findings.

The last question in the research part of the survey questionnaire regarded barriers, which occurred in the implementation or planned implementation of knowledge management. The respondents from both types of organisations indicated too high number of tasks realised by the organisation throughout the year (higher average assessments were in the public sector; 3.7 in contrast to 3.3 in companies on 1–5 Likert scale). Generally, higher average values were in public organisations, even the statement that they do not need such a system because of their good achievement: 3.4 in contrast to the private sector: the lowest average: 2.7 (figure 7).

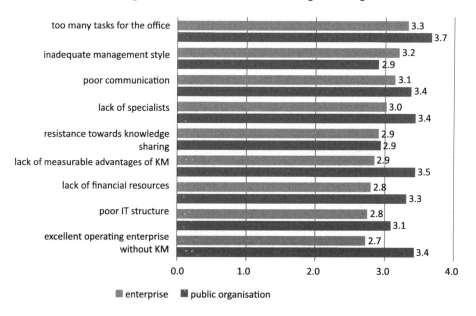

Figure 7. Barriers in implementing knowledge management in the organisation
Source: own work output on the basis of research findings.

CONCLUSION

Perceptions of the degree of implementation of knowledge vary considerably between public and private organisations. The IT system plays significantly different roles in both types of organisations. The public organisations use mainly external databases and the Internet, while the companies use database management systems and superior customer support organisations and flow of knowledge. The low level of e-government and still in progress infrastructure of the Internet, cause the low level of using new communications technologies by public organisations. The confidence levels also vary, but the differences are not as significant as in other areas. Public sector workers also acknowledge significantly greater barriers in the implementation of knowledge management and what was surprising is that many of them thought that they did not need the KM because of a good level of their organisation's efficiency.

Managers are flooded with a lot of information, so to catch the most important seems to be quite difficult. Workers also have no time to learn new models by themselves or without support by their organisations such as trainee programs. The results show that the transfer of knowledge from universities to practice meets barriers[14]. The delay is significant when the number of activities like seminars and training sessions are counted in their hundreds, the same like papers or short articles published in a wide range of journals. Ongoing work is not a relevant reason to be a barrier to the implementation of knowledge management or even learning about it, especially if we live in a knowledge-based economy, where the main asset is knowledge. The quality of the knowledge economy depends on the awareness and implemented techniques using knowledge by many kinds of organisations.

References

A Public Service Learning Organization: From Cost to Coast to Coast (2000). The Canadian Centre for Management Development, Policy, Strategy and Communications, Ottawa.

Aggestam L. (2006). Learning organization or knowledge management – which came first, the chicken or the egg? "Information Technology and Control", vol. 35, no. 3A, pp. 295–302.

Ajmal M., Helo P., Kekale T. (2010). Critical factors for knowledge management in project business. "Journal of Knowledge Management", vol. 14, no. 1, pp. 156–168.

Ajmal M.M., Kekale T., Takala J. (2009). Cultural impacts on knowledge management and learning in project-based firms. "VINE", vol. 39, no. 4, pp. 339–352.

Akbar H. (2003). Knowledge levels and their transformation: Towards the integration of knowledge creation and individual learning. "Journal of Management Studies", vol. 40, no. 8, pp. 1997–2021.

Andreeva T., Sergeeva A., Pavlov Y., Golubeva A. (2012). Knowledge Sharing in Public Sector Organizations: Evidence from Secondary Schools. OLKC 2012 International Conference on Organizational Learning, Knowledge and Capabilities, Valencia.

Argyris C., Schön D.A. (1978). Organizational Learning: A Theory of Action Perspective. Addison-Wesley, Reading, Mass.

Arora E. (2011). Knowledge management in public sector. "Researchers World – Journal of Arts Science & Commerce", vol. 2, no. 1, pp. 165–171.

Bhatt G.D. (2001). Knowledge management in organizations: Examining the Interaction between Technologies, Techniques, and People. "Journal of Knowledge Management", vol. 5, no. 1, pp. 68–75.

Binney D. (2001). The knowledge management spectrum – understanding the KM landscape. "Journal of Knowledge Management", vol. 5, no. 1, pp. 33–42.

Blackler F. (1993). Knowledge and the theory of organizations: Organizations as activity systems and the reframing of management. "Journal of Management Studies", vol. 30, no. 6, pp. 863–884.

Błaszczuk A., Brdulak J., Guzik M., Pawluczuk A. (2004). Zarządzanie wiedzą w polskich przedsiębiorstwach. Oficyna Wydawnicza SGH, Warszawa.

Bratnicki M. (1981). Informacyjne przesłanki organizacyjnego uczenia się, „Prakseologia", vol. 4.

Bratnicki M. (1982). Organizacyjne uczenie się w warunkach kryzysu, „Problemy Postępu Technicznego", vol. 6.

Brdulak J. (2012). Wiedza w zarządzaniu przedsiębiorstwem. Koncepcja, filary, dobre praktyki. Szkoła Główna Handlowa w Warszawie – Oficyna Wydawnicza, Warszawa.

Chunharas S. (2006). An interactive approach to translating knowledge and building a "learning organization" in health services management. "Bulletin of the World Health Organization", vol. 84, no. 8, pp. 652–657.

Cuel R., Manfredi F. (2006). Toward a project learning organization: A multifaceted view. "Journal of Univesal Knowledge Management", vol. 1, no. 3, pp. 255–270.

---

[14] J.N. Lavis, J.M. Woodside, C.B. McLeod, J. Abelson, Knowledge Transfer Study Group (2003). How can research organizations more effectively transfer research knowledge to decision makers?. "The Milbank Quarterly", vol. 81, no. 2, pp. 221–248.

Dalkir K. (2005). *Knowledge Management in Theory and Practice*. Elsevier/Butterworth Heinemann, London.

Davenport T., Probst G. (2000). *Knowledge Management Case Book*. MCD Verlag John Wiley & Sons, Munich.

Ejdys J. (2011). *Model doskonalenia znormalizowanych systemów zarządzania oparty na wiedzy*. Oficyna Wydawnicza Politechniki Białostockiej, Białystok.

Fazlagić J. (2009). *Zarządzanie wiedzą w polskiej oświacie. Diagnoza i perspektywy zmian*. Wydawnictwo Uniwersytetu Ekonomicznego w Poznaniu, Poznań.

Godziszewski B., Haffer M., Stankiewicz M.J. (eds.) (2005). *Wiedza jako czynnik międzynarodowej konkurencyjności w gospodarce*. Towarzystwo Naukowe Organizacji i Kierownictwa – Stowarzyszenie Wyższej Użyteczności „Dom Organizatora, Toruń.

Glińska-Neweś A. (2007). *Kulturowe uwarunkowania zarządzania wiedzą w przedsiębiorstwie*. Towarzystwo Naukowe Organizacji i Kierownictwa, Toruń.

Jones L.R., Thompson F. (2007). *From Bureaucracy to Hyperarchy in Netcentric and Quick Learning Organizations*. Information Age Publishing, Charlotte.

Kennedy-Reid S., Ihrig M. (2013). *Strategic Knowledge Mapping at Boeing: An I-Space Pilot*. Boeing and I-Space Institute, Arlington.

Lavis J.N., Woodside J.M., McLeod C.B., Abelson J., The Knowledge Transfer Study Group (2003). *How can research organizations more effectively transfer research knowledge to decision makers?*. "The Milbank Quarterly", vol. 81, no. 2, pp. 221–248.

Lee J.N. (2001). *The impact of knowledge sharing, organizational capability and partnership quality on IS outsourcing success*. "Information & Management", vol. 38, no. 5, pp. 323–335.

Leja K., Brozdowski P., Dyrlico J. (2005). *Wybrane elementy zarządzania wiedzą w organizacji publicznej na przykładzie Urzędu Miasta Elbląga*. "E-Mentor", vol. 3, no. 2.

Markus M.L. (2001). *Toward a theory of knowledge reuse: Types of knowledge reuse situations and factors in reuse success*. "Journal of Management Information Systems", vol. 18, no. 1, pp. 57–93.

Massaro M., Dumay J., Garlatti A. (2015). *Public sector knowledge management: A structured literature review*. "Journal of Knowledge Management", vol. 19, no. 3, pp. 530–558.

Mazur S., Płoszaj A. (eds.) (2013). *Zarządzanie wiedzą w organizacjach publicznych. Doświadczenia międzynarodowe*. Wydawnictwo Naukowe Scholar, Warszawa.

Moore B., Ulrichsen T., Hughes A. (2009). *The Evolution of the Infrastructure of the Knowledge Exchange System*. PACEC – Centre for Business Research, Cambridge – London.

Nonaka I., Takeuchi H. (1995). *The Knowledge-Creating Company: How Japanese Companies Create the Dynamics of Innovation*. Oxford University Press. Oxford – New York.

Örtenblad A. (2014). *Handbook of Research on Knowledge Management. Adaptation and Context*. Edward Elgar Publishing, Cheltenham.

Papaj T. (2012). *Zarządzanie publiczne – wybrane aspekty eksploracji wiedzy i jej aplikacji*. "Współczesne Zarządzanie", vol. 4, pp. 142–151.

Pawluczuk A. (2005). *Zarządzanie wiedzą w jednostkach samorządu terytorialnego* [in:] J. Ejdys (ed.), *Wybrane aspekty zarządzania wiedzą w organizacji*. Futura, Poznań.

Perechuda K. (2010). *Knowledge Diffusion Methods in a Networking Company Knowledge Business Models*. Publishing House of Wrocław University of Economics, Wrocław.

Perechuda K., Sobicińska M. (eds.) (2008). *Scenariusze, dialogi i procesy zarządzania wiedzą*. Difin, Warszawa.

Piech K., Skrzypek E. (eds.) (2007). *Wiedza w gospodarce, społeczeństwie i przedsiębiorstwach: pomiary, charakterystyka, zarządzanie*. Instytut Wiedzy i Innowacji, Warszawa.

Raczkowski K., Pawluczuk A. (2014). *Knowledge management in public organizations – status and perspective of development*. "Przedsiębiorczość i Zarządzanie", vol. XV, no. 6, cz. III, Wydawnictwo Społecznej Akademii Nauk, Łódź – Warszawa.

Raczkowski K. (2010). *Zarządzanie wiedzą w administracji celnej w systemie bezpieczeństwa ekonomiczno-społecznego*. Difin, Warszawa.

Saussois J.M. (2003). *Knowledge management in government: An idea whose time has come*. "Journal of Budgeting", vol. 3, no. 3, OECD.

Strojny M. (2004). *Zarządzanie wiedzą w Polsce 2004*. Raport badawczy, KPMG.

BIBLIOGRAPHY

A Public Service Learning Organization: From Cost to Coast to Coast (2000). The Canadian Centre for Management Development, Policy, Strategy and Communications, Ottawa.

Abdullah H. (2009). *Definitions of HRD: Key concepts from a national and international perspective.* "Journal of European Social Sciences", vol. 10, no. 4, pp. 486–495.

Abrams D., Hogg M.A., Hinkle S., Otten S. (2005). *The Social Identity Perspective on Small Groups. Theories of Small Groups – Interdisciplinary Perspectives.* Sage Publications Inc., Thousand Oaks, London – New Delhi.

Adams B.D., Sartori J. (2006). *Validating the Trust in Teams and Trust in Leaders Scales.* DRDC No. CR-2006-008, Defence Research & Development, Toronto.

Adler P.S. (2001). *Market, hierarchy, and trust: The knowledge economy and the future of capitalism.* "Organization Science", vol. 1, no. 2.

Aggestam L. (2006), *Learning organization or knowledge management – which came first, the chicken or the egg?.* "Information Technology and Control", vol. 35, no. 3A, pp. 295–302.

Agle B.R., Caldwell C.B. (1999). *Understanding research on values in business.* "Business and Society", vol. 38, no. 3, pp. 326–387.

Aguilera R., Williams C., Conley J.M., Rupp D.E. (2006). *Corporate governance and social responsibility: a comparative analysis of the UK and the US.* "Corporate Governance: An International Review", vol. 14, no. 3, pp. 147–158.

Ajmal M., Helo P., Kekale T. (2010). *Critical factors for knowledge management in project business.* "Journal of Knowledge Management", vol. 14, no. 1, pp. 156–168.

Ajmal M.M., Kekale T., Takala J. (2009). *Cultural impacts on knowledge management and learning in project-based firms.* "VINE", vol. 39, no. 4, pp. 339–352.

Akbar H. (2003). *Knowledge levels and their transformation: Towards the integration of knowledge creation and individual learning.* "Journal of Management Studies", vol. 40, no. 8, pp. 1997–2021.

Aladwani A.M. (2001). *Change management strategies for successful ERP implementation*, interaktyvus. "Business Process Management Journal", vol. 7, no. 3, pp. 266–275.

Amidon D. (2003). *The Innovation Highway.* Butterworth-Heinemann, Boston.

Andersson T., Appelquist J., Serger S. (2004). *Public Research and Innovation Policy for the good of society: How to assess the way forward?* Background Paper at joint IKED/INNOVA seminar. November 8. Berns, Salonger, Stockholm.

Andreeva T., Sergeeva A., Pavlov Y., Golubeva A. (2012). *Knowledge Sharing in Public Sector Organizations: Evidence from Secondary Schools.* OLKC 2012 International Conference on Organizational Learning, Knowledge and Capabilities. Valencia.

Angyal Á. (2009). *Vállalatok társadalmi felelőssége. Műhelytanulmány* (working paper). Vállalatgazdaságtan Intézet, Budapest.

Arah O.A., Westert G.P., Hurst J., Klazinga N.S. (2006). *A conceptual framework for the OECD Health Care Quality Indicators Project.* "International Journal for Quality in Health Care", September, pp. 5–13.

Aramavičiūtė V., (2005a). *Auklėjimas ir dvasinė asmenybės branda.* Gimtasis žodis, Vilnius.

Aramavičiūtė V. (2005b). *Vertybės kaip gyvenimo prasmės pamatas.* "Acta Paedagogica Vilnensia", vol. 14, pp. 18–26.

Argyris C., Schön D.A. (1978). *Organizational Learning: A Theory of Action Perspective.* Addison-Wesley, Reading, Mass.

Armstrong M. (2010). *Strategiczne zarządzanie zasobami ludzkimi.* Oficyna Wolters Kluwer business, Warszawa.

Armstrong M. (2011). *Zarządzanie zasobami ludzkimi.* Oficyna Wolters Kluwer business, Warszawa.

Armstrong M., Baron A. (2002). *Strategic HRM: The Route to Improved Business Performance.* CIPID, London.

Arnold R. (2004). *Evaluating research and innovation policy: A system world needs systems evaluation.* "Research Evaluation", vol. 13, no 1, pp. 3–17.

Arora E. (2011). *Knowledge management in public sector.* "Researchers World – Journal of Arts Science & Commerce", vol. 2, no. 1, pp. 165–171.

Badaracco J.L. (1991). *The Knowledge Link: How Firms Compete Through Strategic Alliances.* Harvard Business School Press, Boston, MA.

Baily M.N., Garber A.M. (1997). *Health care productivity.* "Brookings Papers on Economic Activity: Microeconomics", pp. 143–215. http://nrs.harvard.edu/urn-3:HUL.InstRepos:11595722 (access: 28.08.2015).

Baron R.M., Kenny D.A. (1986). *The moderator-mediator variable distinction in social psychological research: Conceptual, strategic and statistical considerations.* "Journal of Personality and Social Psychology", vol. 51, pp. 1173–1182.

Bartlett C., Ghoshal S. (2002). *Building competitive advantage through People Magazine: Winter 2002.* "Research Feature", January 15.

Bathelt H., Munro A.K., Spigel B. (2011). *Social foundations of regional innovation and the role of university spin-offs.* "Industry and Innovation", vol. 18, no. 5, pp. 461–486.

Beer M., Spector B., Lawrence P.R., Quinn Mills D., Walton R.E. (1984). *Managing Human Assets.* The FreePress, New York.

Bennett J.L. (1996). *Building relationships for technology transfer.* "Communications of the ACM", vol. 39, no. 9, pp. 35–36.

Bergek A., Jacobssen S., Carlsson B., Lindmarki S., Rickne A. (2008). *Analysing the functional dynamics of technological innovation systems.* "Research Policy", vol. 37, pp. 407–429.

Berger I.E., Kanetkar V. (1995). *Increasing environmental sensitivity via workplace experiences.* "Journal of Public Policy and Marketing", vol. 14, no. 2, pp. 205–215.

Berna-Martinez J., Macia-Perez F. (2012). *Overcoming resistance to change in business innovation processes*, interaktyvus. "International Journal Of Engineering & Technology", vol. 4, no. 3, pp. 148–161.

Berson Y., Oreg S., Dvir T. (2005). *Organizational Culture as A Mediator of Ceo Values And Organizational Performance.* Academy of Management Proceedings, New York.

Bhatt G.D. (2001). *Knowledge management in organizations: Examining the interaction between technologies, techniques, and people.* "Journal of Knowledge Management", vol. 5, no. 1, pp. 68–75.

Bibb S., Kourdi J. (2004). *Trust matters for organizational and personal success.* Palgrave Macmillan, New York, pp. 161–167.

Binney D. (2001). *The knowledge management spectrum – understanding the KM landscape.* "Journal of Knowledge Management", vol. 5, no. 1, pp. 33–42.

Bjornberg A. (2015). *Euro health consumer index 2014 report.* "Health Consumer Powerhouse", 2015.01.27. http://www.healthpowerhouse.com/files/EHCI_2014/EHCI_2014_report.pdf (access: 14.09.2015).

Blackler F. (1993). *Knowledge and the theory of organizations: Organizations as activity systems and the reframing of management.* "Journal of Management Studies", vol. 30, no. 6, pp. 863–884.

Blomqvist K., Stahle P. (2000). *Building Organizational Trust.* 16th Annual IMP Conference, Bath, UK.

Blomqvist K. (1997). *The many faces of trust.* "Scandinavian Journal of Management", vol. 13, no. 3, pp. 271–286.

Błaszczuk A., Brdulak J., Guzik M., Pawluczuk A. (2004). *Zarządzanie wiedzą w polskich w przedsiębiorstwach.* Oficyna Wydawnicza SGH, Warszawa.

Bounfour A. (2013), *The Management of Intangibles: The Organisation's Most Valuable Assets.* Routledge, London – New York.

Bratnicki M. (1981). *Informacyjne przesłanki organizacyjnego uczenia się.* „Prakseologia", no. 4.

Bratnicki M. (1982). *Organizacyjne uczenie się w warunkach kryzysu.* „Problemy Postępu Technicznego", no. 6.

Brdulak J. (2012). *Wiedza w zarządzaniu przedsiębiorstwem. Koncepcja, filary, dobre praktyki.* Szkoła Główna Handlowa w Warszawie – Oficyna Wydawnicza, Warszawa.

Bronstein L.R. (2003). *Model for interdisciplinary collaboration.* "Social Work", vol. 48, no. 3, pp. 297–306.

Bugdol M. (2010). *Zaufanie jako element systemu wartości organizacyjnych.* „Współczesne Zarządzanie", no. 2, pp. 11–25.

Cameron K.S., Quinn R.E. (1999). *Diagnosing and changing organizational culture: Based on the competing values framework*. Addison-Wesley, Reading, MA.

Campbell S., Braspenning J., Hutchinson A., Marshall M. (2002). *Research methods used in developing and applying quality indicators in primary care*. "Quality and Safety in Health Care", vol. 11, pp. 358–364.

Carroll A.B. (1999). *Corporate social responsibility: Evolution of a definitional construct*. "Business and Society", vol. 38, no. 3, pp. 268–295.

Charmaz K. (2009), *Shifting the grounds: Constructivist grounded theory methods for the twenty-first century* [in:] J.M. Morse, P.N. Stern, J.M. Corbin, B. Bowers, K. Charmaz, A.E. Clarke (eds.), *Developing Grounded Theory: The Second Generation*, University of Arizona Press, Left Coast Press, Walnut Creek, CA.

Chikán A. (2008). *Vállalati versenyképesség és társadalmi felelősség*. "Harvard Business Manager", vol. 11, pp. 6–13.

Chunharas S. (2006). *An interactive approach to translating knowledge and building a "learning organization" in health services management*. "Bulletin of the World Health Organization", vol. 84, no. 8, pp. 652–657.

Čiuladienė G. (2006). *Paauglių vertybinis aspektas ir raiškos tendencijos*. "Acta Paedagogica Vilnensia", vol. 16, pp. 106–117.

Council of Canadian Academies (2013). *Innovation Impacts: Measurement and Assessment. The Expert Panel on the Socioeconomic Impacts of Innovation Investments*. Council of Canadian Academies.

Covey S.M. (2009). *How the Best Leaders Build Trust*. Leadership Now. http://www.leadershipnow.com/CoveyOnTrust.html (access: 22.11.2015).

Creed W., Miles R. (1996). *Trust in organizations: A conceptual framework linking organizational forms, managerial philosophies, and the opportunity costs of controls* [in:] R.M. Kramer, T.M. Tyler (eds.), *Trust in Organizations: Frontiers of Theory and Research*. SAGE Publications, Thousand Oaks, CA, pp. 16–39.

Cruysen A. van, Hollanders H. (2008). *Are Specific Policies Needed to Stimulate Innovation in Services?*. INNO Metrics 2007 Report. European Commission, DG Enterprise, Brussels.

Cuel R., Manfredi F. (2006). *Toward a project learning organization: a multifaceted view*. "Journal of Univesal Knowledge Management", vol. 1, no. 3, pp. 255–270.

Cummings L.L., Bromiley P. (1996). *The Organizational trust inventory (OTI): Development and Validation* [in:] R.M. Kramer, T.R. Tyler (eds.), *Trust in Organisations: Frontiers of Theory and Research*. Sage, Thousand Oaks, CA, pp. 302–331.

Czakon W. (2009). *Przedsiębiorstwo oparte na wiedzy w kontekście międzyorganizacyjnym* [in:] R. Krupski (ed.), *Zarządzanie strategiczne. Problemy kierunki badań*. Prace Naukowe Wyższej Szkoły Zarządzania i Przedsiębiorczości. Wydawnictwo Wałbrzyskiej Wyższej Szkoły Zarządzania i Przedsiębiorczości, Wałbrzych.

Czakon W. (2011). *Zastosowanie studiów przypadków w badaniach nauk o zarządzaniu* [in:] W. Czakon (ed.), *Podstawy metodologii badań w naukach o zarządzaniu*. Oficyna Wolters Kluwer business, Warszawa.

Daily B., Bishop J.W., Govindarajulu N. (2008). *A conceptual model for organizational citizenship behavior*. "Directed toward the Environment. Business & Society", vol. 48, no. 2, pp. 243–256.

Dalkir K. (2005). *Knowledge Management in Theory and Practice*. Elsevier/Butterworth Heinemann, London.

Daniel C., Wilde-Ramsing J., Genovese K., Sandjojo V. (2015). *Remedy Remains Rare*. An analysis of 15 years of NCP cases and their contribution to improve access to remedy for victims of corporate misconduct, OECD Watch, Amsterdam.

Davenport T., Probst G. (2000). *Knowledge Management Case Book*. MCD Verlag John Wiley & Sons, Munich.

Davis K. (1960). *Can business afford to ignore social responsibilities?*. "California Management Review", vol. 2, pp. 70–76.

De Furia G.L. (1997). *Facilitators Guide to the Interpersonal Trust Surveys*. Pfeiffer & Co, London.

De Prins P. (2011). *Duurzaam HRM: Synthetische academische introductie*. I. Rompa, explorative research on Sustainable Human Resource Management. http://www.innovatiefinwerk.nl/sites/.../sustainable_hrm.pdf (access: 2.09.2015).

Dicken P. (2003). *Global Shift Reshaping the Global Economic Map in the 21st Century*. Sage Publication, London.

Donabedian A. (1966). *Evaluating the Quality of Medical Care*. "Milbank Memorial Fund Quarterly", vol. 44, no. 3, pp. 166–206.

Dudin A.S. (2007). *Korporativnaja kul'tura*. "Professija Direktor", no. 6, pp. 96–100.

Dunning T. (2012). *Natural Experiments in the Social Sciences: A Design-Based Approach (Strategies for Social Inquiry)*, Cambridge University Press, Cambridge.

Dylus A. (2005). *Globalizacja, refleksje etyczne*. Zakład Narodowy im. Ossolińskich, Wrocław.

Early P.C. (1986). *Trust, perceived importance of praise and criticism, and work performance: An examination of feedback in the United States and England*. "Journal of Management", no. 12.

Ecko K., Globa H. (2012). *Tipologija organizacionnyh kul'tur municipal'nyh bol'nic respubliki Moldova* [in:] *Military and Political Sciences in the Context of Social Progress, Problems and Ways of Modern Public Health Development*, materials digest of the XV and XVI International Scientific and Practical Conferences.

Edwards J., Cable D.A. (2009). *The Value of Value Congruence*. "Journal of Applied Psychology", vol. 94, no. 3, pp. 654–677.

Edwards J., Rothbard N. (2000). *Mechanisms linking work and family: Clarifying the relationship between work and family constructs*. "Academy of Management Review", vol. 25, no. 1, pp. 178–199.

Ehnert I., Harry W. (2012). *Recent developments and future prospects an sustainable human resource management: Introduction to the special issue*. "Management Review", vol. 23, no. 3, pp. 221–238.

Ehnert I. (2009). *Sustainable HRM*. Physica Verlag, Heidelberg.

Ehnert I. (2006). *Sustainability Issues in Human in Human Resource Management: Linkages, Theoretical, Approaches, and Outlines for an Emerging Field*, paper prepared for 21st EIASM SHRM Workshop, Aston, Birmingham, March 28th–29th. http://www.sfb637.uni-bremen.de/.../SFB637-A2-06-004-I (access: 2.09.2015).

Ehrenberg R.G., Smith R.S. (1994). *Modern Labor Economics*. New York, Harper Collins.

Ejdys J. (2011). *Model doskonalenia znormalizowanych systemów zarządzania oparty na wiedzy*. Oficyna Wydawnicza Politechniki Białostockiej, Białystok.

Elloy D.F., Smith C.R. (2003). *Patterns of stress, work-family conflict, role conflict, role ambiguity and overload among dual career couples: An Australian study*. "Cross Cultural Management", vol. 10, no. 1, pp. 55–66.

Enderwick P. (2005). *Attracting "desirable" FDI: Theory and evidence*. "Transnational Corporations", vol. 14, no. 2, pp. 93–119.

Engels Y., *et al.* (2005). *Developing a framework of, and quality indicators for, general practice management in Europe*. "Oxford Journal, Family Practice", vol. 22, no. 2, pp. 215–222.

European Commission (2014). *Communication from the Commission: Framework for State Aid for Research, Development and Innovation* (2014/C 198/01).

European Commission (2011). *Renewed EU strategy 2011–2014 for Corporate Social Responsibility*. Brussels.

EY, *EY's Attractiveness Survey Europe 2014. Back in the Game*. http://www.ey.com/GL/en/Issues/Business-environment/european-attractiveness-survey (access: 10.05.2015).

Fazlagić J. (2009). *Zarządzanie wiedzą w polskiej oświacie. Diagnoza i perspektywy zmian*. Wydawnictwo Uniwersytetu Ekonomicznego w Poznaniu, Poznań.

Fernandez E., Junquera B., Ordiz M. (2003). *Organizational culture and human resources in the environmental issue: A review of the literature*. "The International Journal of HRM", vol. 14, no. 4, pp. 634–656.

Fitzpatrick R., *et al.* (2000). *Framework for Design and Evaluation of Complex Interventions to Improve Health*. http://www.ncbi.nlm.nih.gov/pmc/articles/PMC1118564/ (access: 3.09.2015).

Flor M.L., Oltra M.J. (2004). *Identification of innovating firms through technological innovation indicators: An application to the Spanish ceramic tile industry*. "Research Policy", vol. 33, pp. 323–336.

Friedman M. (1970). *The social responsibility of business is to increase its profits*. "New York Times Magazine", no. 9.

Furman J.L., Porter M.E., Stern S. (2002). *The determinants of national innovative capacity*. "Research Policy", vol. 31, no. 6, pp. 899–933.

Garalis A. (2004). *Besimokanti organizacija: mokymo (si) metodai ir jų taikymo galimybės // Ekonomika ir vadyba: aktualijos ir perspektyvos 2004*. Ernesto Galvanausko mokslinė konferencija. Šiauliai: Šiaulių universiteto leidykla, no. 4, pp. 81–87.

Gay L.R. (1992). *Educational Research*, 4th edition, Merrill, New York.

Gillespie N., Dietz G. (2009). *Trust repair after an organization-level failure.* "Academy of Management Review", vol. 34, no. 1, pp. 127–145.

Glińska-Neweś A. (2007). *Kulturowe uwarunkowania zarządzania wiedzą w przedsiębiorstwie.* Towarzystwo Naukowe Organizacji i Kierowania, Toruń.

Godziszewski B., Haffer M., Stankiewicz M.J. (eds.) (2005). *Wiedza jako czynnik międzynarodowej konkurencyjności w gospodarce.* Towarzystwo Naukowe Organizacji i Kierownictwa – Stowarzyszenie Wyższej Użyteczności Dom Organizatora, Toruń.

Goodpaster K.E., Matthews J.B. (1982). *Can a corporation have a conscience?.* "Harvard Business Review", vol. 60, no. 1, pp. 132–141.

Górniak J., Mazur S. (2012). *Zarządzanie strategiczne rozwojem.* Ministerstwo Rozwoju Regionalnego, Warszawa.

Gronskienė I. (2008). *Žemės ūkio organizacijų deklaruojamų vertybių modelis.* "Vadybos mokslas ir studijos – kaimo verslų ir jų infrastruktūros plėtrai", vol. 13, no. 2, pp. 54–61.

Grudzewski W., Hajduk I.K., Sankowska A., Wańtuchowicz M. (2009). *Zarządzanie zaufaniem w przedsiębiorstwie.* Wolters Kluwer, Kraków.

Grudzewski W., Hejduk I.K., Sankowska A., Wańtuchowicz M. (2007). *Zarządzanie zaufaniem w organizacji wirtualnej.* Difin, Warszawa.

Guest D.E. (2002). *Perspectives on the study of work-life balance.* "Social Science Information", vol. 41, no. 2, pp. 255–279.

Guest D.E. (1997). *Human resource management and performance: A review and research agenda.* „The International Journal of Human Resource Management", no. 8, June.

Gurkov I. (1998). *Mil'ner B.Z. "Theory of Organizations".* "Voprosy Economiki", vol. 11.

GUS (2014). *Oświata i wychowanie w roku szkolnym 2013/2014.* Warszawa.

Gustafsson R., Autio E. (2006). *Grounding for Innovation Policy: The Market, System and Social Cognitive Failure Rationales, Innovation Pressure – Rethinking Competitiveness. Policy and the Society in a Globalised Economy* – International ProACT Conference, Tampere, Finland, March 15–17, 2006.

Hacker S.K., Willard M.L. (2002). *The Trust Imperative: Performance Improvement through Productive Relationship.* American Society for Quality, Milwaukee, Wisconsin.

Hamel G. (1991). *Competition for competence and inter-partner learning within international strategic alliances.* "Strategic Management Journal", no. 12.

Handfield R.B., Bechtel C. (2004). *Trust, power, dependence, and economics: can SCM research borrow paradigms?.* "International Journal of Integrated Supply Management", vol. 1, no. 1, pp. 3–32.

Handy C. (1995). *Trust and the virtual organization.* "Harvard Business Review", vol. 73, no. 3.

Hardin R. (2006). *Trust.* Polity Press, Cambridge.

Hardy C., Phillips N., Lawrence T. (1998). *Distinguishing trust and power in interorganizational relations: Forms and facades of trust in trust within and between organizations* [in:] Ch. Lane, R. Bachman (eds.), *Conceptual Issues and Empirical Applications.* Oxford University Press, Oxford.

Hatch M.J. (2002). *Teoria organizacji.* Wydawnictwo Naukowe PWN, Warszawa.

Haugh H., McKee L. (2004). *The cultural paradigm of the smaller firm.* "Journal of Small Business Management", vol. 42, no. 4, pp. 377–394.

Hekkert M.P., Suurus R.A.A., Negro S.O., Kuhlmann S., Smits R.E.H.M. (2007). *Functions of innovation systems: A new approach for analysing technological change.* "Technological Forecasting & Social Change", vol. 74, pp. 413–432.

Hellriegel D., Slocum J.W., Woodman R.W. (1998). *Organizational Behavior*, light edition. South Western College Publishing, Ohio.

Hemingway C.A. (2002). *An Exploratory Analysis of Corporate Social Responsibility: Definitions, Motives and Values.* Research Memorandum 34, Centre for Management and Organisational Learning Hull University Business School, Hull, UK, pp. 1–25.

Holland W. (1991). *An Community Atlas of "Avoidable Death"*. Oxford University Press, Oxford. HRM. Human Resource Management (2013). *From the editors.* "Institute of Labor and Social Studies", vol. 6, no. 95/13.

http://ec.europa.eu/euraxess/index.cfm/rights/strategy4Researcher (access: 7.01.2015).

http://idc.com; http://www.gartner.com; http://www.computerworld.pl (access: 3.06.2015).

http://standishgroup.com; http://www.versionone.com (access: 3.06.2015).

Huizinga J. (1985). *Homo ludens. Zabawa jako źródło kultury.* Wydawnictwo „Czytelnik", Warszawa.

Iezzoni L.I. (ed.) (2012). *Risk adjustment for measuring health care outcomes.* 4th edition, Health Administration Press, Chicago, Illinois.

Inglehart R. (1997). *Modernization and postmodernization – cultural and political change in 43 societies.* "New Jersey Journal", vol. 10, no. 1. Princeton University Press, pp. 53–68.

Ireland P. (2010). *Limited liability, shareholders rights and problem of corporate irresponsibility.* "Cambridge Journal of Economics", vol. 34.

Irfan S.M., Hussain T., Yousaf I. (2009). *Organizational culture: Impact on female employees' job performance.* "Journal of Quality and Technology Management", vol. V, no. I1, pp. 1–16.

Jager P. (2001). *Resistance to change: A new view of an old problem,* interaktyvus. "The Futurist", vol. 35, no. 3, pp. 24–27.

Jokubaitis A., (2012). *Vertybių tironija ir politika.* Vilniaus universiteto leidykla, Vilnius.

Jones G.R., George J.M. (1998). *The Experience and Evolution of Trust: Implications for Cooperation and Teamwork.* "Academy of Management Review", vol. 23, no. 3, pp. 531–546.

Jones L.R., Thompson F. (2007). *From Bureaucracy to Hyperarchy in Netcentric and Quick Learning Organizations.* USA, Information Age Publishing.

Josang A., Presti S.L. (2004). *Analysing the relationship between risk and trust* [in:] *Proceedings of the Second International Conference on Trust Management.* Springer-Verlag, Berlin–Heidelberg, pp. 135–145.

Jovaiša L. (2007). *Enciklopedinis edukologijos žodynas.* Gimtasis žodis, Vilnius.

Jucevičienė P., Poškienė A., Kudirkaitė L., Damanskas N. (2000). *Universiteto kultūra ir jos tyrimas.* Technologija, Kaunas.

Juchnowicz M. (2007). *Zaufanie organizacyjne.* "Kwartalnik Nauk o Przedsiębiorstwie", vol. 2, no. 3.

Kanter R.M. (1977). *Work and Family in the United States: A Critical Review and Agenda for Research and Policy.* Russell Sage Foundation, New York.

Kardelis K. (2007). *Mokslinių tyrimų metodologija ir metodai* [Research Methodology and Techniques]. Lucilijus, Šiauliai.

Kaziliūnas A. (2004). *Visuomenei teikiamų paslaugų kokybės ir organizacinės kultūros sąveika.* "Viešoji politika ir administravimas", no. 9, p. 71–78.

Kemp R. (1994). *Technology and the transition to environmental sustainability – the problem of technological regime shifts.* "Futures", vol. 26, no. 10, pp. 1023–1046.

Kennedy-Reid S., Ihrig M. (2013). *Strategic knowledge mapping at Boeing: An I-Space Pilot.* Boeing and I-Space Institute, Arlington.

Kline S. (1985). *Innovation is not a Linear process.* "Research Management", vol. 28, no. 4, pp. 36–45.

Koivula N. (2008). *Basic Human Values in the Workplace,* vol. 17. University of Helsinki, Helsinki, pp. 1–141.

Kossek E.E., Lambert S. (2005). *Work and Life Integration: Organizational, Cultural, and Individual Perspectives.* Lawrence Erlbaum Associates. Mahawa, New Jersey.

Kostera M. (2003). *Antropologia organizacji. Metodologia badań terenowych.* Wydawnictwo Naukowe PWN, Warszawa.

Kostera M. (1996). *Postmodernizm w zarządzaniu.* Polskie Wydawnictwo Ekonomiczne, Warszawa.

Kotter J., Schlesinger L.A. (1979). *Choosing strategines for change,* interaktyvus. "Harvard Business Review", vol. 57, no. 2, pp. 106–114.

Kouzes J.M., Posner B.Z. (2003). *Iššūkis vadybai.* Smaltija, Kaunas.

Kożuch B. (2014). *Organizacyjna perspektywa zaufania publicznego. Zarys koncepcji* [in:] Ł. Sułkowski, A. Woźniak (ed.), *Przedsiębiorczość i zarządzanie.* "Zarządzanie Humanistyczne", vol. XV, no. 11, part III, pp. 41–51.

Kożuch B., Dobrowolski Z. (2014). *Creating Public Trust. An Organisational Perspective*. Peter Lang GmbH, Frankfurt am Main.

Kożuch B., Kożuch A. (2015). *Zarządzanie partycypacyjne* [in:] B. Kożuch, Ł. Sułkowski (eds.), *Instrumentarium zarządzania publicznego*. Difin, Warszawa.

Kożuch B., Sienkiewicz-Małyjurek K. (2015). *Dimensions of Intra-organisational Trust in Local Public Administration*. Proceedings of International Research Society For Public Management Conference, Birmingham.

Kożuch B., Sienkiewicz-Małyjurek K. (2014). *New requirements for managers of public safety systems*. „Procedia – Social and Behavioral Sciences", no. 149.

Kożuch B., Zaremba W. (2005). *Czynniki sukcesu organizacji publicznych*. „Prace i Materiały Wydziału Zarządzania Uniwersytetu Gdańskiego", no. 4, pp. 125–135.

Kramer R.M., Tyler T.R. (1996). *Trust in Organizations: Frontiers of Theory and Research*. Sage Publications, California.

Kuc B.R., *Jak sformułować i rozwiązać problem badawczy?*. http://wydawnictwoptm.pl/content/8-artykuly-naukowe (access: 7.01.2015).

Kvedaravičius J. (2006). *Organizacijų vystimosi vadyba*. Vytauto Didžiojo Universitetas, Kaunas.

Kvedaravičius J., Lodienė D. (2002). *Pokyčiai ir organizacijų sėkmė*. "Organizacijų vadyba: sisteminai tyrimai", pp. 114–124.

Lavis J.N., Woodside J.M., McLeod C.B., Abelson J., Knowledge Transfer Study Group (2003). *How can research organizations more effectively transfer research knowledge to decision makers?*. "The Milbank Quarterly", vol. 81. no. 2, pp. 221–248.

Lee J.N. (2001). *The impact of knowledge sharing, organizational capability and partnership quality on IS outsourcing success*. "Information & Management", vol. 38, no. 5, pp. 323–335.

Leja K., Brozdowski P., Dyrlico J. (2005). *Wybrane elementy zarządzania wiedzą w organizacji publicznej na przykładzie Urzędu Miasta Elbląga*. "E-Mentor", vol. 3, no. 2.

Lenart R. (2014). *Zarządzanie wiedzą w tworzeniu konkurencyjności szkoły*. Wolters Kluwer, Warszawa.

Listwan T. (2010). *Rozwój badań nad zarządzaniem zasobami ludzkimi w Polsce* [in:] S. Lachiewicz, B. Nogalski (eds.), *Osiągnięcia i perspektywy nauk o zarządzaniu*. Oficyna Wolters Kluwer business, Warszawa.

Listwan T. (1995). *Kształtowanie kadry menedżerskiej firmy*. Kadry, Wrocław.

Loeb J.M. (2004). *The current state of performance measurement in health care*. "International Journal for Quality in Health Care", vol. 16, suppl. 1, pp. i5–i9.

Luhmann N. (1995). *Social Systems*. Stanford University Press, Stanford, CA.

Lundy O., Bowling A. (2001). *Strategiczne zarządzanie zasobami ludzkimi*. Dom Wydawniczy ABC – Oficyna Ekonomiczna, Kraków.

Maccoby M. (2003). *To build trust, ethics are not enough*. "Research Technology Management", vol. 46, no. 5.

Malerba F. (2005). *Sectoral systems: How and why innovation differs across sectors* [in:] J. Fagerberg, D. Movery, E. Nelson, *The Oxford Handbook of Innovation*, Oxford University Press, Oxford.

Maniukaitė G. (2003). *Akademinio jaunimo vertybinės orientacijos: autoritetų ir idealų krizė. Jaunimo vertybinės orientacijos*, red. A. Vosyliūtė. Socialinių tyrimų institutas, Vilnius, pp. 22–28.

Mansor M., Mat N., Abu N., Johari A. (2013). *Factors influencing intention resistance to change: A study of service organization in Malaysia*, interaktyvus. "Journal Of Applied Sciences Research", vol. 9, no. 4, pp. 2620–2630.

Marginson P. (2006). *Europeanisation and regime competition*, "Industrielle Beziehungen", vol. 13, no. 2, pp. 98–113.

Markus M.L. (2001). *Toward a theory of knowledge reuse: Types of knowledge reuse situations and factors in reuse success*. "Journal of Management Information Systems", vol. 18, no. 1, pp. 57–93.

Martišauskienė E. (2004). *Paaugliu dvasingumas, kaip pedagoginis reiškinys: monografija*. VPU, Vilnius.

Massaro M., Dumay J., Garlatti A. (2015). *Public sector knowledge management: a structured literature review*. "Journal of Knowledge Management", vol. 19, no. 3, pp. 530–558.

Matsumoto D. (2002). *Methodological requirements to test a possible ingroup advantage in judging emotions across cultures: Comments on Elfenbein and Ambady and evidence.* "Psychological Bulletin", no. 128, pp. 236–242.

Maxwell J.A (2005). *Qualitative Research Design: An Interactive Approach.* Sage, Thousand Oaks, CA.

Mayer R.C., Davis J.H. (1999). *The effect of the performance appraisal system on trust for management: A field quasi-experiment.* "Journal of Applied Psychology", no. 84, pp. 123–136.

Mayer R.C., Davis J.H., Schoorman F.D. (1995). *An integrative model of organizational trust.* "Academy of Management Review", no. 20, pp. 709–734.

Mazur B. (2013). *Linking diversity management and corporate social responsibility.* "Journal of Intercultural Management", vol. 5, no. 3, pp. 39–47.

Mazur S., Płoszaj A. (eds.) (2013). *Zarządzanie wiedzą w organizacjach publicznych. Doświadczenia międzynarodowe.* Wydawnictwo Naukowe Scholar, Warszawa.

McGonigal J. (2011). *Reality is Broken: Why Games Make Us Better and How They Can Change The World.* Penguin Press HC, London.

McGuire D., Cseh M. (2006). *The development of the field of HRD: A Delphi study.* „Journal of European Industrial Training", vol. 30, no. 8, pp. 653–667.

McLean G.N., McLean L. (2001). *If we can't define HRD in one country, how can we define it in an international context?.* "Human Resource Development International", vol. 4, no. 3.

Meeran R. (1999). *Liability of Multinational Corporations: A Critical Stage.* http://www.labournet.net/images/cape/campanal.htm (access: 20.02.2015).

Metcalfe J.S. (2005). *Systems failure and the case for innovation policy* [in:] P. Llerena, M. Matt (eds.), *Innovation Policy in a Knowledge Based Economy.* Springer, Berlin.

Miedziński M. (2008). *Wybrane zagadnienia ewaluacji polityki innowacyjnej* [in:] K. Olejniczak, M. Kozak, B. Ledzion (eds.), *Teoria i praktyka ewaluacji interwencji publicznych, Podręcznik akademicki.* Wydawnictwa Akademickie i Profesjonalne, Warsaw, pp. 480–498.

Miłosz E., Miłosz M. (1995). *Symulatory systemów gospodarczych w kształceniu menedżerów.* "Komputer w Edukacji", vol. 3–4, Wydawnictwo Leopoldinum Fundacji dla Uniwersytetu Wrocławskiego, Wrocław.

Ministry of Economy (2015). *Nowe przepisy UE dotyczące ujawniania danych pozafinansowych.* http://www.mg.gov.pl/node/22566 (access: 21.01.2015).

Mishra A.K. (1996). *Organizational responses to crisis: The centrality of trust* [in:] R.M. Kramer, T.R. Tyler (eds.), *Trust in Organizations: Frontiers of Theory and Research.* Sage, Thousand Oaks, CA.

Mittal S. (2012). *Managing employee resistance to change a comparative study of indianan organizations and MNCSIin Delh–NCR region,* interaktyvus. "Researchers World: Journal Of Arts, Science & Commerce", vol. 3, no. 4, pp. 64–71.

Molina-Azorín J.F., Claver-Cortés E., López-Gamero M.D., Tarí J.J. (2009). *Green management and financial performance: A literature review.* "Management Decision", vol. 47, no. 7, pp. 1080–1100.

Moore B., Ulrichsen T., Hughes A. (2009). *The Evolution of the Infrastructure of the Knowledge Exchange System.* PACEC and the Centre for Business Research, Cambridge – London.

Moore D., McCabe D. (1993). *Introduction to the Practice of Statistics.* Freeman, New York.

Morgan G. (2008). *Obrazy organizacji.* Wydawnictwo Naukowe PWN, Warszawa.

Morgan R.M., Hunt S.D. (1994). *The commitment-trust theory of relationship marketing.* "Journal of Marketing", vol. 58, no. 3, July, pp. 24–38.

Muster V. (2011). *Companies promoting sustainable consumption of employees.* "Journal of Consumer Policy", vol. 34, no. 1, pp. 161–174.

Muster V., Schrader U. (2011). *Green work-life balance: A new perspective for green HRM.* "German Journal of Research in Human Resource Management", vol. 25, no. 2, pp. 140–156.

Nazelskis E. (2010). *Profesinio orientavimo ir konsultavimo priemonių taikymas darbuotojų kaitai mažinti. Profesinis rengimas.* "Tyrimai ir realijos", vol. 19.

Nerenz D.R., Neil, N. (2001). *Performance Measures for Health Care Systems.* Michigan State University, Virginia Mason Medical Centre. Commissioned Paper for the Center for Health Management Research. http://www.hret.org/chmr/resources/cp19b.pdf (access: 2.08.2015).

Ng'ang'a M.J., Nyongesa W.J. (2012). *The Impact of Organisational Culture on Performance of Educational Institutions*. "International Journal of Business & Social Science", vol. 3, no. 8, p. 217.

Niemczyk J. (2011). *Metodologia nauk o zarządzaniu* [in:] W. Czakon (ed.), *Podstawy metodologii badań w naukach o zarządzaniu*. Oficyna Wolters Kluwer business, Warszawa.

Nolte E., McKee M. (2004). *Does Healthcare Save Lives? Avoidable Mortality Revisited*. The Nuffield Trust, London.

Nonaka I., Takeuchi H. (1995). *The Knowledge-Creating Company: How Japanese Companies Create the Dynamics of Innovation*. Oxford University Press, Oxford.

O'Brien R.C. (1995). *Employee involvement in performance improvement: a consideration of tacit knowledge, commitment and trust*. "Employee Relations", vol. 17, no. 3.

OECD and Eurostat (2005). *Oslo Manual. Guidelines for Collecting and Interpreting Innovation Data*, 3rd edition.

OECD and Eurostat (2005). *The Measurement of Scientific and Technological Activities. Proposed Guidelines for Collecting and Interpreting Technological Innovation Data*. A joint publication of OECD and Eurostat, Oslo Manual.

OECD (2012). *2011 Update of OECD Guidelines for Multinational Enterprises*. Comparative Table of Changes to the 2000 Texts. https://mneguidelines.oecd.org/text/ (access: 10.05.2015).

OECD (2011). *OECD Guidelines for Multinational Enterprises*, OECD Publishing. http://dx.doi.org/10.1787/9789264115415-en (access: 10.05.2015).

OECD (2007). *Annual Report on the OECD Guidelines for Multinational Enterprises 2007*. Corporate responsibility in the financial sector. http://www.oecdbookshop.org/en/browse/title-detail/Annual-Report-on-the-OECD-Guidelines-for-Multinational-Enterprises-2007/?K=5L4JHXPQN8XS (access: 10.05.2015).

Örtenblad A. (2014). *Handbook of Research on Knowledge Management. Adaptation and Context*. Cheltenham Glos, Edward Elgar Publishing.

Pabian A. (1998). *Uwarunkowania sukcesu przedsiębiorstwa na rynku. Zarys problematyki*. Wydawnictwo Politechniki Częstochowskiej, Częstochowa.

Pacevičius J., Janulytė E. (2009). *Mobingas kaip organizacinio gyvenimo problema: priežasčių, raiškos ir pasekmių įvertinimas ir analizė*. "Ekonomika ir vadyba: aktualijos ir perspektyvos", vol. 1, no. 14, pp. 187–196.

Palidauskaitė J. (2001). *Viešojo administravimo etika*. Technologija, Kaunas.

Paliszkiewicz J. (2013). *Zaufanie w zarządzaniu*. Wydawnictwo Naukowe PWN, Warszawa.

Papaj T. (2012). *Zarządzanie publiczne – wybrane aspekty eksploracji wiedzy i jej aplikacji*. "Współczesne Zarządzanie", vol. 4, pp. 142–151.

Patapas A., Labenskytė G. (2011). *Organizacinės kultūros ir vertybių tyrimas N apskrities valstybinėje mokesčių inspekcijoje*. "Viešoji politika ir administravimas", vol. 4, pp. 589–603.

Paužuolienė J., Trakšelys K. (2009). *Komunikacijos reikšmė organizacinėje kultūroje*. "Vadyba", vol. 14, no. 2, pp. 157–162.

Pavitt K. (1988). *Uses and abuses of patent statistics* [in:] A.F.J. van Raan (ed.), *Handbook of Quantitative Studies of Science and Technology*. Elsevier Science Publishers, Amsterdam, from: B. Hall (2013). *Using Patent Data as Indicators*. http://eml.berkeley.edu/~bhhall/papers/BHH13_using_patent_data.pdf (access: 11.12.2015).

Pawluczuk A. (2005). *Zarządzanie wiedzą w jednostkach samorządu terytorialnego* [in:] J. Ejdys (ed.), *Wybrane aspekty zarządzania wiedzą w organizacji*. Futura, Poznań.

Perechuda K. (2010). *Knowledge Diffusion Methods in a Networking Company Knowledge Business Models*. Publishing House of Wrocław University of Economics, Wrocław.

Perechuda K. (2008). *Scenariusze, dialogi i procesy zarządzania wiedzą*. Difin, Warszawa.

Perechuda K., Sobicińska M. (eds.) (2008). *Scenariusze, dialogi i procesy zarządzania wiedzą*. Difin, Warszawa.

Piech K., Skrzypek E. (eds.) (2007). *Wiedza w gospodarce, społeczeństwie i przedsiębiorstwach: pomiary, charakterystyka, zarządzanie*. Instytut Wiedzy i Innowacji, Warszawa.

Pikčiūnas A. (2002). *Organizacijos ryšių sistema*. Vytauto Didžiojo universiteto leidykla, Kaunas.

Pikturnaitė I., Paužuolienė J. (2013). *Organizacinės kultūros Institucionalizavimas*. "Tiltai", vol. 4, pp. 93–108.

Pirson M. (2008). *Facing the Trust Gap Measuring and Managing Stakeholder Trust*. SVH, Saarbrucken.

Pocztowski A. (2007). *Zarządzanie zasobami ludzkimi. Strategie, procesy, metody*. PWE, Warszawa.

Pogosian S., Dzemyda I. (2012). *Inovacijos versle ir jas lemiantys veiksniai teoriniu ir politiniu aspektu.* "Ekonomika ir vadyba: aktualijos ir perspektyvos", vol. 1, no. 25, pp. 63–76.

Quazi A.M., O'Brien D. (2000). *An Empirical Test of a Cross-national Model of Corporate Social Responsibility*. "Journal of Business Ethics", vol. 25, no. 1, pp. 33–51.

Raczkowski K., Pawluczuk A. (2014). *Knowledge management in public organizations – status and perspective of development*. "Przedsiębiorczość i Zarządzanie", vol. XV, no. 6, cz. III. Wydawnictwo Społecznej Akademii Nauk, Łódź–Warszawa, pp. 31–44.

Raczkowski K. (2010). *Zarządzanie wiedzą w administracji celnej w systemie bezpieczeństwa ekonomiczno- -społecznego*. Difin, Warszawa.

Ramus C.A. (2002). *Encouraging innovative environmental actions: What companies and managers must do*. "Journal of World Business", vol. 37, pp. 151–164.

Rancova G. (2004). *Dėmesio – kolektyve naujokas. Naujų darbuotojų adaptacijos organizacijoje sistema.* "Biuro administravimas", vol. 11, pp. 3–6.

Rashid M., Sohail M., Aslam M. (2011). *Impact of employee adaptability to change towards organizational competitive advantage*, interaktyvus. "Global Journal of Management and Business Research", vol. 11, no. 7, pp. 9–15.

Rashid N.R., Wahid N.A., Saad N.M. (2006). *Employees Involvement in EMS, ISO 14001 and its Spillover Effects in Consumer Environmentally Responsible Behaviour*. International Conference on Environment Proceedings (ICENV 2006), 13th–15th November, Penang, Malaysia.

Relly P., Williams T. (2012). *Strategiczne zarządzanie zasobami ludzkimi*. Oficyna Wolters Kluwer business, Warszawa.

Rokita J. (2005). *Zarządzanie strategiczne. Tworzenie i utrzymywanie przewagi konkurencyjnej*. PWE, Warszawa.

Rosinaitė V., Bernotas D., Biveinytė S., Blažienė I., Česnuitytė V., Gražulis V., Gruževskis B., Misiūnas A., Pocius A., Stancikas E., Šileika A., Šlekienė K., Zabarauskaitė R. (2007). *Magistrantų integracijos į darbo rinką monitoringo sistemos sukūrimas*. Darbo ir socialinių tyrimų institutas. http://www.dsti.lt/ tyrimai.html (access: 22.11.2013).

Rothbard N., Phillips K., Dumas T. (2005). *Managing multiple roles: Work-family policies and individuals' desires for segmentation*. "Organization Science", vol. 16, no. 3, pp. 243–258.

Ryan A.M., Kossek E.E. (2008). *Work-life policy implementation: Breaking down or creating barriers to inclusiveness?*. "Human Resource Management Journal", vol. 47, no. 2, pp. 295–310.

Salen K., Zimmerman E. (2003). *Rules of Play: Game Design Fundamentals*. The MIT Press, Boston.

Sander M., Weywara B. (2006). *Markenvertrauen im Rahmen des Markenmanagements, Konsumentenvertauen: Konzepte und Andwendungen für ein nachhaltiges Kundenbindungsmanagement*. Vahlen Franz Gmbh, München.

Sankowska A. (2013). *Further understanding of links between interorganisational trust and enterprise innovativeness – from a perspective of an enterprise*. "International Journal of Innovation and Learning", vol. 13, no. 3.

Sankowska A. (2011). *Wpływ zaufania na zarządzanie przedsiębiorstwem. Perspektywa wewnątrzorganizacyjna*. Difin, Warszawa.

Saussois J.M. (2003). *Knowledge management in government: An idea whose time has come*. "Journal of Budgeting". OECD, vol. 3, no. 3.

Savanevičienė A., Šilingienė V. (2005). *Darbas grupėse*. Technologija, Kaunas.

Schell J. (2008). *The Art of Games Design a Book of Lenses*. Morgan Kaufmann, Burlington.

Schrodt P. (2002*). The relationship between organizational identification and organizational culture: Employee perceptions of culture and identification in a retail sales organization*. "Communication Studies", vol. 53, no. 2, pp. 189–202.

Schwartz S.H. (2003). *A Proposal for Measuring Value Orientations across Nations* [in:] *Questionnaire Development report of the European Social Survey*, chap. 7. http://naticent02.uuhost.uk.uu.net/questionnaire/chapter_07.doc (access: 20.05.2013).

Schwartz S.H. (2006). *Value orientations: Measurement, antecedents and consequences across nations* [in:] R. Jowell, C. Roberts, R. Fitzgerald, G. Eva (eds.), *Measuring Attitudes Cross-nationally – Lessons from the European Social Survey*. Sage, London.

Seilius A. (2004). *Aplinkos poveikio ir sėkmingo vadovavimo organizacijoms prielaidos. Iš Valdymo problemos: teorija ir tendencija. Kolektyvinė monografija*. KU leidykla, Klaipėda.

Shahzad F., Luqman R.A., Khan A.R., Shabbir L. (2012). *Impact of organizational culture on organizational performance: An overview*. "Interdisciplinary Journal of Contemporary Research in Business", vol. 3, no. 9, pp. 975–985.

Sharfman M.P., Fernando C.S. (2008). *Environmental risk management and the cost of capital*. "Management Journal", vol. 29, no. 6, pp. 569–592.

Shaw R.B. (1997). *Trust in the Balance: Building Successful Organizations on Results, Integrity, and Concern*. Jossey-Bass, San Francisco.

Siebert W.S., Zubanov N. (2009). *Searching for the optimal level of employee turnover: A study of a large U.K. retail organization*. "Academy of Management Journal", vol. 52, pp. 294–313.

Siegall M., McDonald T. (2004). *Person-organization value congruence, burnout and diversion of resources*. "Personnel Review", vol. 33, no. 3, pp. 291–301.

Silverman D. (2008). *Prowadzenie badań jakościowych*. Wydawnictwo Naukowe PWN, Warszawa.

Šimanskienė L., Seilius A. (2009). *Komandos: Samprata, Kūrimas, Vadovavimas. Team: Concept, Development, Leadership*. KU leidykla, Klaipėda.

Šimanskienė L. (2008). *Organizacinės kultūros poveikis organizacijų valdymui*. "Management Theory and Studies for Rural Business and Infrastructure Development", vol. 15, no. 4, pp. 175–180.

Šimanskienė L. (2008). *Organizacinės kultūros diagnozavimo metodika*. KU leidykla, Klaipėda.

Sinha S., Singh A., Gupta N., Dutt R. (2010). *Impact of work culture on motivation and performance level of employees in private sector companies*. "Acta Oeconomica Pragensia", vol. 6, pp. 49–67.

Sitkin S.B., Roth N.L. (1993). *Explaining the limited effectiveness of legalistic remedies for trust/distrust*. "Organization Science", vol. 4.

Smith P.C., Mossialos E., Papanicolas I., Leatherman S. (2010). *Performance Measurement for Health System Improvement: Experiences, Challenges and Prospects*. Cambridge University Press, Cambridge.

Söderholm P. (2010). *Environmental Policy and Household Behaviour: Sustainability and Everyday Life*. Earthscan, London.

Spitzer D.R. (2007). *Transforming Performance Measurement: Rethinking the Way we Measure and Drive The Organizational Success*. Amacon, New York.

Ståhle P. (1998). *Supporting a System's Capacity for Self-Renewal, A Doctoral Dissertation*. Research Reports 190, University of Helsinki, Dodgson.

Stankevičienė A., Liučvaitienė A., Šimelytė A. (2010). *Personalo kaitos stabilizavimo galimybės Lietuvos statybos sektoriuje*. "Verslas: teorija ir praktika", vol. 11, no. 2, pp. 151–158.

Stankeviciute Z., Savaneviciene A. (2013). *Sustainability as a concept for Human Resource Management*. "Economics and Management", vol. 18, no. 4, pp. 838–846.

Stankuvienė A. (2013). *Autoritarizmo veiksniai ir diagnostiniai instrumentai*. "Socialinių mokslų studijos", vol. 5, no. 1, pp. 57–73.

Steinmann H., Schreyögg G. (1995). *Zarządzanie. Podstawy kierowania przedsiębiorstwem. Koncepcje, funkcje, przykłady*. Oficyna Wydawnicza Politechniki Wrocławskiej, Wrocław.

Steklova O.E. (2007). *Organizacionnaja kuļątura*. UlGTU, Uľjanovsk.

Robbins S.P. (2003). *Organizacinės elgsenos pagrindai*. Poligrafija ir informatika, UAB.

Stern E. (2005). *What do we know about the utilization of evaluation?*, I Evaluation conference Towards the development of standards in emergency management training and education. "Disaster Prevention and Management", vol. 12, no. 2, pp. 113–123.

Storey J. (1989). *Introduction: From personel management to human resource management* [in:] J. Storey (ed.), *New Perspectives on Human Resource Management*. Routledge, London, pp. 1–18.

Storz C. (2008). *Dynamics in innovation system: Evidence from Japan's game software industry*. "Research Policy", vol. 37, no. 37, pp. 1480–1491.

Strautmanis J. (2008). *Employees' values orientation in the context of corporate social responsibility.* "Baltic Journal of Management", vol. 3, no. 3, pp. 346–358.

Street A., Hakkinen U. (2010). *Health system* [in:] P.C. Smith, *et al.* (eds.), *Performance Measurement for Health System Improvement: Experiences, Challenges and Prospects.* Cambridge University Press, Cambridge.

Strojny M. (2004). *Zarządzanie wiedzą w Polsce 2004.* Raport badawczy, KPMG.

Strużyna J. (2010). *Ewolucja strategicznego zarządzania zasobami ludzkimi.* „Zarzadzanie Zasobami Ludzkimi", vol. 3–4.

Šukytė R., Rudnickienė L. (2010). *Viešosios organizacijos darbuotojų atranka ir adaptacija. Vadyba.* "Socialiniai mokslai", vol. 1, no. 17, pp. 167–180.

Sułkowski Ł. (2012). *Metodologie emic i etic w badaniach kultury w zarządzaniu.* "Management and Business Administration. Central Europe", vol. 1, no. 114, pp. 64–71.

Sułkowski Ł. (2011). *Struktura teorii naukowej w zarządzaniu* [in:] W. Czakon (ed.), *Podstawy metodologii badań w naukach o zarządzaniu,* Oficyna Wolters Kluwer business, Warszawa.

Sydow J. (1998). *Understanding the constitution of interorganizational trust in trust within and between organizations* [in:] Ch. Lane, R. Bachman (eds.), *Conceptual Issues and Empirical Applications.* Oxford University Press, Oxford.

Szabó-Benedek A. (2014). *A CSR-gyakorlat vizsgálata a vállalatvezetői értékek és attitűdök tükrében.* PhD értekezés Szent István Egyetem, Gazdálkodás és Szervezéstudományok Doktori Iskola.

Sztompka P. (2002). *Socjologia. Analiza społeczeństwa.* Znak, Kraków.

Szymański M.J. (1998). *Młodzież wobec wartości.* Wydawnictwo Instytutu Badań Edukacyjnych, Warszawa.

Tan H., Lim A. (2009). *Trust in co-workers and trust in organizations.* "The Journal of Psychology", vol. 143, no. 1, pp. 45–66.

Thulcinkij G.L. (2000). *PR firmy: tehnologija i jeffektivnosť.* Aletejja, Sankt-Peterburgskij gosudarstvennyj universitet kuľtury i iskusstv, Sankt-Peterburg.

Tichy N.M., Fombrun C.J., Devanna M.A. (1982). *Strategic human resource management.* "Sloan Management Review", vol. 23, pp. 47–61.

Tidikis R. (2003). *Socialinių Mokslų Tyrimų Metodologija. Social Science Research Methodology.* Lietuvos teisės universiteto Leidybos centras, Vilnius.

Tkaczyk P. (2012). *Grywalizacja.* One Press, Helion, Gliwice.

Trzciński R. (2009). *Wykorzystanie techniki propensity score matching w badaniach ewaluacyjnych.* Polska Agencja Rozwoju Przedsiębiorczości, Warszawa.

United Nations (2011). *Guiding Principles on Business and Human Rights.* New York – Geneva.

Unterschutz J. (2009). *Prawo pracy. Zarys instytucji.* WSAiB, Gdynia.

Uzdila J.V. (2008). *Šeimotyros kaip dalyko poveikis studentų matrimonialinėms nuostatoms.* "Pedagogika", vol. 89, pp. 151–160.

Vaitkevičius R., Saudargienė A. (2006). *Statistika Su Spss Psichologiniuose Tyrimuose.* SPSS Statistics psychological research. VDU, Kaunas.

Van Dick R. (2009). *Navigating organizational change: Change leaders, employee resistance and work-based identities, interaktyvus.* "Journal of Change Management", vol. 9, no. 2, pp. 143–163.

Vanagas P. (2004). *Visuotinės kokybės vadyba.* Technologija, Kaunas.

Vasiliauskas R. (2005). *Vertybių ugdymo teoriniai ir praktiniai aspektai.* "Acta Paedagogica Vilnensia", vol. 14, pp. 8–17.

Verplanken B. (2004). *Value congruence and job satisfaction among urses: A human relations perspective.* "International Journal of Nursing Studies", vol. 41, no. 6, pp. 599–605.

Vveinhardt J. (2009). *Mobingo kaip diskriminacijos darbuotojų santykiuose poveikis organizacijos klimatui.* "Verslas: teorija ir praktika-Business: Theory and Practice", vol. 10, no. 4, pp. 285–297.

Werbach K., Hunter D. (2012). *For the Win: How Game Thinking Can Revolutionize Your Business.* Wharton Digital Press, Boston.

The World Health Organization (2000). *World Health Report 2000: Health Systems: Improving Performance.* http://www.ctc-health.org.cn/file/whr00_en.pdf (access: 15.08.2015).

Wójcik-Karpacz A. (2014). *Zaufanie w relacjach międzyorganizacyjnych: substytucja i komplementarność.* Prace Naukowe Uniwersytetu Ekonomicznego we Wrocławiu, no. 366.

Yin R.K. (2003). *Case Study Research. Design and Methods.* Sage Publications, Thousand Oaks, London – New Delhi, pp. 21–27.

Young L., Albaum G. (2003). *Measurement of trust in salesperson-customer relationships in direct selling.* "Journal of Personal Selling and Sales Management", vol. 24, no 3, pp. 253–269.

Zaheer A., McEvily B., Perrone V. (1998). *Does trust matter? Exploring the effects of interorganizational and interpersonal trust on performance.* "Organization Science", vol. 9.

Zakarevičius P. (2003). *Pokyčiai organizacijose: priežastys, valdymas, pasekmės. Monografija.* VDU, Kaunas.

Zakarevičius P., Kvedaravičius J., Augustauskas T. (2004). *Organizacijų vystymosi paradigma.* VDU, Kaunas.

Zichermann G., Cunningham C. (2011). *Gamification by Design: Implementing Game Mechanics in Web and Mobile Apps,* 1st edition, O'Reilly Media, Sebastopol – California.

Zichermann G., Linder J. (2013). *The Gamification Revolution: How Leaders Leverage Game Mechanics to Crush the Competition.* McGraw-Hill, New York.

Zucker L.G. (1986). *Production of trust: Institutional sources of economic structure.* "Organizational Behavior", vol. 8.

Žukauskaitė I. (2008). *Naujų darbuotojų kaita: ryšys su organizacine socializacija.* "Organizacijų vadyba: sisteminiai tyrimai", vol. 48, pp. 153–169.

Zwick T. (2002). *Employee resistance against innovations,* interaktyvus. "International Journal Of Manpower", vol. 23, no. 6, pp. 542–552.

TECHNICAL EDITOR
Agnieszka Stęplewska

PROOFREADER
Gabriela Niemiec

TYPESETTER
Tomasz Pasteczka

Jagiellonian University Press
Editorial Offices: ul. Michałowskiego 9/2, 31-126 Kraków
Phone: +48 12-663-01-97, Fax: +48 12-631-01-98